THE PLACES OF
MODERNITY IN EARLY
MEXICAN AMERICAN
LITERATURE,
1848–1948

Postwestern Horizons

GENERAL EDITOR
William R. Handley
University of Southern California

SERIES EDITORS
José Aranda
Rice University

Melody Graulich
Utah State University

Thomas King
University of Guelph

Rachel Lee
University of California, Los Angeles

Nathaniel Lewis
Saint Michael's College

Stephen Tatum
University of Utah

THE PLACES OF MODERNITY IN EARLY MEXICAN AMERICAN LITERATURE, 1848–1948

JOSÉ F. ARANDA JR.

University of Nebraska Press   Lincoln

© 2022 by the Board of Regents of
the University of Nebraska

Acknowledgments for the use of copyrighted
material appear on pages xii–xiii, which
constitute an extension of the copyright page.

All rights reserved. ∞

The University of Nebraska Press is part of a land-grant institution with campuses and programs on the past, present, and future homelands of the Pawnee, Ponca, Otoe-Missouria, Omaha, Dakota, Lakota, Kaw, Cheyenne, and Arapaho Peoples, as well as those of the relocated Ho-Chunk, Sac and Fox, and Iowa Peoples.

Publication of this volume was assisted by
the School of Humanities and the Office
of Research at Rice University.

Library of Congress Cataloging-in-Publication Data
Names: Aranda, José F., 1961– author.
Title: The places of modernity in early Mexican American literature, 1848–1948 / José F. Aranda Jr.
Description: Lincoln : University of Nebraska Press, [2022] | Series: Postwestern horizons | Includes bibliographical references and index.
Identifiers: LCCN 2021013953
ISBN 9781496224132 (hardback)
ISBN 9781496229106 (paperback)
ISBN 9781496229892 (epub)
ISBN 9781496229908 (pdf)
Subjects: LCSH: American literature—Mexican American authors—History and criticism. | American literature—19th century—History and criticism. | American literature—20th century—History and criticism. | Modernism (Literature) | Mexican Americans—Intellectual life. | BISAC: LITERARY CRITICISM / American / Hispanic & Latino | LCGFT: Literary criticism.
Classification: LCC PS153.M4 A727 2022 | DDC 810.9/86872—dc23
lc record available at https://lccn.loc.gov/2021013953

Set in Arno Pro by Laura Buis.
Designed by L. Auten.

Para Benito y Jesse
Always in my heart

CONTENTS

Acknowledgments ix

Introduction: Recovering Modernity in Early Mexican American Literature 1

1. Modernity Deferred: "There Never Was a More Peaceful or Happy People" 29

2. Californio Settler History: Nostalgia as Patrimony 67

3. Game of Modernities: Coloniality and Racial Loyalty in the U.S. West 107

4. Me Llaman Mexicana: Gender and Choice under Coloniality 149

5. Barrio Modernity: Speaking Pocho, Being Chicana/o 185

Afterword 227

Notes 237

Bibliography 243

Index 257

ACKNOWLEDGMENTS

In 1997 I was invited by Nicolás Kanellos to join the board of advisors to Recovering the U.S. Hispanic Literary Heritage. Because of Kanellos's leadership and mentorship, and because of all my colleagues on the board, including now countless Recovery conferences over the last three decades, I owe the genesis of this project to all of them, as well as the opportunity to live out the archive of the Recovery Project in real time. To me, the Recovery archive is not an abstract, academic exercise but living, engaged research, networked with scholars throughout the United States and throughout the world. It has been an amazing partnership to work with Recovery leaders like Carolina Villarroel and Gabriela Ventura.

As a worlding project, the Recovery Project has shaped my research, teaching, university service, and service to the Hispanic communities of Houston. It was through the literatures, discourses, and histories of Recovery that I directed my first graduate students. The earliest iterations of this project began with former students such as Shannon Leonard, Andrea Tinnemeyer, Priscilla Ybarra, Lourdes Alberto, and John Escobedo. Over time, this project evolved with Amanda Ellis, Lorena Gauthereau, Brittany Henry, Elena Valdez, Scott Pett, Samuel F. Stoeltje, Sólveig Ásta Sigurðardóttir, Sonia Del Hierro, and Sophia Martinez-Abbud. I am grateful to all of them for challenging me to be a better teacher and researcher, and for producing scholarship that has inspired me over the years.

Sustaining me throughout the length of this project, and also a significant influence in my teaching and mentoring of graduate students, are all my colleagues in the Western Literature Association. As much as this book owes it critical genealogies to the Recovery Project and Chicanx studies, it is a project that recognizes the value of place. WLA has been instrumental in reminding me of the critical importance of place in literary analysis and critical race theory. For their scholarship and their support of my own place-based studies, I want to thank Stephen Tatum, Melody Graulich, Bill Handley, Neil Campbell, Susan Kollin, Chad Allen, Karen Ramirez, Nicolas Witschi, Nancy Cook, Richard Hutson, Susan Bernardin, Victoria Lamont, David Fenimore, Florence Amamoto, Robert Thacker, Emily Lutenski, Michael Johnson, Tom Lynch, Alex Hunt, Audrey Goodman, Sylvan Goldberg, Will Lombardi, Stefano Rosso, Kirby Brown, Cathryn Halverson, Christine Bold, and Johannes Fehrle.

This project also owes a debt to the many participants of the Rice University–University of North Texas summer workshop Avanzamos: El Taller Chicana/o/x, which Priscilla Ybarra and I began in 2011. At some point or another, most of this project was presented at Taller. Besides many of the above-named people who have participated in Taller, I'm also grateful for the generous comments and advice from Taller cofounder Melina Vizcaíno-Alemán, and participants John Morán González, Raúl Coronado, Jaime Javier Rodríguez, Díana Noreen Rivera, Erin Murrah-Mandril, Elizabeth Martínez, and many others. A significant consideration of this project was how to think about a Latinx nineteenth century. Here I drew inspiration from the ongoing archival and theoretical work of Kirsten Silva Gruesz, Jesse Alemán, Rodrigo Lazo, and John Morán González. In particular, Jesse and Rodrigo's shepherding of the collection of essays, *The Latino Nineteenth Century* (2016), was a watershed moment not only for the Recovery Project but also for U.S. nineteenth-century studies. My participation in that collection drove home for me what was at stake in this project. Plus, it enhanced my own thinking of the nineteenth century through the exciting scholarship of Marissa K. López, John Alba Cutter, Alberto Varon, and Carmen E. Lamas. Similarly, my participation in the collection *Keywords for Latina/o Studies* (2017), with the editorial guidance of Deborah R. Vargas, Nancy Raquel Maribal, and Lawrence La Fountain-Stokes (gracias), provoked the necessity to deal thoroughly with my keyword, modernity, and its implications for the field as a whole.

Support for archival research comes in many forms. I say this in gratitude for the support of the Feminist Reading Group at Rice University that funded a whole afternoon workshop seminar on my Jovita González chapter, which included bringing María Cotera to read, discuss, and advise me. That was an extraordinary moment with María, and I got to share her expertise with several of my Rice colleagues who were also generous with their time and comments, including Rosemary Hennessy, Helena Michie, Susan Lurie, and Lora Wildenthal. A good theoretical portion of this project stems from the body of work from Latin America known as philosophy of liberation. My colleagues in the former department of Spanish, Portuguese and Latin American Studies were the best interlocutors one could wish for on this topic. I am forever grateful to Beatriz González-Stephan, Luis Duno-Gottberg, Gisela Heffes, Rafael Salaberry, and Nicolas Shumway for the countless hours of discussion about these theories and philosophies, as well as for their support as chair of this department for many years. My work with these colleagues led to a critical evolution of my teaching at Rice. In 2015 I began an undergraduate translation initiative focused on translating fiction written in Spanish and published in the Spanish-language press of the United States before 1960. Because of the work of dozens of Rice students, we have translated novels and short fiction, including novels by Jorge Ainslie. Our work together as translators shadows significantly what I was able to accomplish in chapter 5.

Many staff and archivists facilitated the research for this project. I am grateful to them and their institutions: Fondren Library, Rice University; the Bancroft Library, University of California, Berkeley; the Benson Latin American Collection, University of Texas, Austin; the Lily Library, Indiana University, Bloomington; Sterling Memorial Library, Yale University.

This project has always been part of my family life. Besides our sons who I have dedicated this book to is my partner in life and colleague in scholarship and teaching, Krista Comer. Her countless hours listening to me, reading my material, and my reading her scholarship are woven into this project. Here too are my wonderful in-laws, Jean Comer, Corrine Comer, and Mike Griffing whose home in Alameda was my refuge after long days at the Bancroft. My own siblings—Jorge, Carlos, and Laura—are here too, as this project stands with them and we with our parents, José F. Aranda Sr. and Edelmira Aranda Castro, who immigrated from Monterrey, Nuevo León, Mexico. Researching for this project and writing it brought me closer to them and to my grandparents, who were children when the Mexican Revolution finally ended. This book project has also crossed the border several times because of my colleagues and friends at the Tecnológico de Monterrey, especially Donna M. Kabalen Vanek, Blanca Guadalupe López Morales, and María Teresa Mijares Cervantes. Through the auspices of the Jornada Internacional de Fronteras/Borderlands, I, a pocho and Chicano from Houston, brought my research to the faculty and students of el Tec. Beyond words, I am grateful for their support in helping me to develop my project, and also in bringing me closer to my family in Monterrey. That phrase, *ni aquí ni allá*, "neither here nor there," dogs me just a little less these days.

In the following pages, prior published material will be found significantly revised and reframed for the purposes of this project. Portions of the introduction draw from "When Archives Collide: Recovering Modernity in Early Mexican American Literature," published in *The Latino Nineteenth Century*, edited by Rodrigo Lazo and Jesse Alemán (New York: New York University Press, 2016). Chapter 3 has an expanded and revised version of material found in "The Recovery Project and the Role of History in Chicana/o Literary Studies," published in *A History of Western American Literature*, edited by Susan Kollin (New York: Cambridge University Press, 2015). A portion of chapter 4 is drawn from "Mexican" in "Keywords: On the Occasion of the 50th Anniversary of the Western Literature Association," edited by Krista Comer and Susan Bernardin, special issue, *Western American Literature* 53, no. 1 (Spring 2018). In chapter 5, biographic material for Mexican writer Jorge Ainslie and portions of a close reading of Ainslie's novel, *Los pochos*, are drawn from "Critical Translation: The Politics and Writings of Jorge Ainslie," in the twenty-fifth anniversary volume of *Recov-*

ering the U.S. Hispanic Literary Heritage, edited by Antonia Castañeda and Clara Lomas (Houston: Arte Público Press, 2020).

A special thanks to Sabine Barcatta, director of operations at Western Literature Association, for editing the manuscript and sharing her many talents to make this a better book.

My sincere gratitude for the support and care that the University of Nebraska Press bestowed on this project. My thanks to Bridget Barry, Heather Stauffer, Erika Rippeteau, Haley Mendlik, and Andrea Shahan, including a deep thanks to the readers of my manuscript for their expert guidance. Finally my thanks to Sarah C. Smith of Arbuckle Editorial for helping me to close the covers on this book.

THE PLACES OF MODERNITY IN EARLY MEXICAN AMERICAN LITERATURE, 1848–1948

Introduction

Recovering Modernity in Early Mexican American Literature

This book examines the first one hundred years of Mexican American literary and print production, from 1848 to 1948. It is a period of production when neither its writers nor its texts, and especially not its print culture, were considered productive for the nation-state of either the United States or Mexico. Through the lens of liberation philosophy from Latin America and in concert with nineteenth-century Latinx literary criticism, settler-colonial criticism, and critical regionalism, this project examines how the burdens of modernity—the darker side of modernity, as Walter Mignolo describes—become the dominant discursive logic for understanding why people of Mexican descent nonetheless wrote and invested in print culture without any guarantee of its social, cultural, or political efficacy.

Specifically, I argue that before the civil rights movement in general and the Chicana/o Movement in particular, cultural and literary production by people of Mexican descent in the United States unfolded within a geographic, cultural, and political terrain in which the more typical markers of the nation-state did not operate. And because these productions were politically, and later linguistically, alienated from the evolving nation-state apparatus of Mexico, these cultural and literary artifacts did not cohere under the auspices of the Republic of Mexico. Despite the absence of an official state sponsorship, this period nonetheless witnessed tremendous production by writers, artists, and publishers of Mexican descent. Caught between a hostile Anglo-American culture on the one hand and an indifferent country of origin (Mexico) on the other, Mexican Americans strove to make a case for themselves and their communities through literature and print culture, thereby invoking a myriad of strategies to deal with their collective political condition as racialized, second-class citizens of the United States.

Within this context, the burdens of modernity reveal themselves as former Mexican citizens transition from one settler-colonial history and set of power structures to another settler-colonial matrix. This transition requires their submission to an Anglo-American hierarchy of racial formation and political economies. Over time, the alternative modernities that emerge from the collision of these distinct settler colonialisms are forced to dialogue, and at times merge, with those modernities that migrated over the border from Mexico, especially during the Mexican Revolution. Altogether, modernity becomes the broad discursive canvas whereupon writers of Mexican descent can find a logic for their material existence and an outlet for their cultural productions. In these productions, I argue, one finds versions of Walter Mignolo's "colonial difference," the space where those who are the targets of colonialism create strategies to diagnosis and resist their own subjugation. Their local histories over time reveal the global designs of modernity itself. But these versions of colonial difference are de-linked from the nation-state and thus perennially untethered in ways that nonetheless make visible what I call "modernities of subtraction," a peculiar mode of modernity whose darker side, coloniality, operates at a greater distance from the rationalizations and promises of Enlightenment ideology.

The writers and texts examined here acknowledge their relationship to modernity, but modernity's high costs and depleting consequences force ever-deepening critiques of the United States, as well as a growing resolve to remain committed to the politics of place-making and regional identities. In the absence of a viable nation-state apparatus, and despite the subtractive elements of the modernities they experience after 1848, these writers, publishers, and editors work to create a print culture that anticipates without assurances the civil rights paradigm beginning to take literary shape by 1948. The writers included here range from members of the Vallejo family in California to Apache leader Geronimo to South Texas folklorist Jovita González. The texts under consideration also range in kind and genre—from published magazine articles and unpublished materials to a serialized novel and radio transcripts. Critical biography also plays a major role. Overall, this study follows the geographic contours of early twentieth-century notions of the Southwest and West where most people of Mexican descent were understood to live.

With this book, I seek a more complete knowledge project of Mexican America. Through it, I explore what recently recovered Mexican American authors, texts, and histories have to say about modernity. My goal is to produce a nuanced rendering of a set of little-understood processes with Mexican Americans at the center. I hope to promote and make accessible a growing historical literary archive for future scholarship but also to bolster the argument that people of Mexican descent, despite their forced marginality, have always led vital, purposeful lives in the United States. Overall, I theorize and demonstrate how history, culture, and geography might come together in a study of modernity and early Mexican American literature.

Recovering Modernity, Recovering Coloniality

Walter Mignolo offers the following: "Modernity" is a European narrative that hides its darker side, "coloniality." "Coloniality, in other words, is constitutive of modernity—there is no modernity without coloniality.... De-colonial thinking and doing emerged, from the sixteenth century on, as responses to the oppressive and imperial bent of modern European ideals projected to, and enacted in, the non-European world" (40).[1]

I begin through Argentine theorist Mignolo to remind us of what is at stake when dealing with any consequence of European colonialism, which includes Mexican American literature. For the outcomes of modernity are the outcomes of coloniality. Only after we contend with the darker sides of modernity can we interrogate the recovery of early Mexican American literature as evidence of "de-colonial thinking and doing" (40). To study modernity in early Mexican American literature is to recover the various strategies and philosophies for survival, accommodation, resistance, and adaptation that developed in the long period after the Mexican-American

War but before the emergence of a civil rights movement—the focus of this book.

While there is, in the archive that evolved after 1848, no absence of hardship, broken dreams, anger, and pathos, there is also a solace and inspiration to be derived from those of Mexican descent who chose to stay north of the border after the war. These people chose not to emigrate south according to the terms of the Treaty of Guadalupe Hidalgo. Later this archive evolves and absorbs the stories of those who fled the devastations set in motion by the Mexican Revolution. In fleeing, they made "el México de afuera," that "other" Mexico in the United States, despite all its complications, their new home. From 1848 on, folklore, letters, print culture, and literary production show growing apprehension about the new Anglo-American political imaginary that revises and realigns centuries-old discourses on race, gender, class, family, religion, citizenship, power, and sovereignty. For Mexican Americans, modernity will be less about particular angst over imperial designs or dread about cultures of capitalism, as it was for some Anglo-Americans. It will center instead on the anxiety and frustration of becoming and being an unrecognized underclass Other for two nation-building projects: the United States as it emerges in the nineteenth century as an imperial world power and Mexico as it stages a hemispheric socialist response to the imperial incursions of the West in the twentieth century.

Recovering modernity, therefore, means recovering coloniality and in doing so chronicling the localized responses to both. Coloniality, as Aníbal Quijano has coined it, identifies the lingering powerful structures begat by European colonialism that morphed into the current mode of globalization. "Coloniality," he observes in "Coloniality and Modernity/Rationality," "is still the most general form of domination in the world today, once colonialism as an explicit political order was destroyed" (170). If coloniality persists as a global experience, then how should we understand modernity for communities of Latinidad in the United States? Quijano provokes us to consider how a new world order arose first through the conquest of societies and cultures today called Latin America and then expanded throughout the planet (168). Living, working, and producing histories in the United States, Mexican Americans, and Latinas/os more broadly, are part of that world order, which in its current mode includes globalization. Latina/o histories are replete with examples of this coloniality of power: its instruments, institutions, and ideologies of domination developed by European colonialism, including capitalism, to manage and control populations constructed as racial others for the benefit of Europe and their settler communities in the Américas.

For Quijano, "coloniality of power was conceived together with America and Western Europe, and with the social category of 'race' as the key element of the social classification of colonized and colonizers" (171). We should therefore understand the histories of Latinas/os in the United States as "raced" through multiple layers of colonial actors of Eurocentric origin in specific regions since 1492. Because of the vagaries of race and the multiplicity of Eurocentric colonizers, however, the divide between colonized and colonizer became increasingly subject to interpretation. When "European culture was made seductive" as a culture of centering power, it came to embody the promise of "access to power" (169). Because of these seductive but also contradictory structures of power, hybridity in many forms emerges and comes to underwrite Latinidad in the United States. Settler hybridity—the fusion, collapsing, and reconstitution of colonizer and colonized identities at specific times and places—becomes a central feature of what we find when we unveil the burden of modernity in early Mexican American literature.

As is made abundantly clear by Recovering the U.S. Hispanic Literary Heritage, a recovery project that began in 1991 and now enters its third decade, the archive of Hispanic America is very deep and resists singular coherence.[2] What survives in the record is as diverse as the individuals and individual circumstances that have produced that record. For people of Mexican descent in the United States, the anarchy of this archive lies in its intersections with the emergent national narratives of both Mexico and the United States. Notwithstanding this crucial fact, these intersections are rarely acknowledged in their own times and never claimed by national or regional imaginaries of either country.

Consider, for example, the biography of Juan Nepomuceno Seguín of Texas, a nineteenth-century landowner, soldier, and politician. His biography clearly reflects a contorted set of identities. Is Seguín to be remembered as one of the surviving heroic defenders of the Alamo? Is he better remembered as the mayor of San Antonio, falsely accused of aiding Santa Anna's failed 1842 attempt to retake Texas? Should Seguín be lauded for his eventual political maturity when he fought on the Mexican side of the Mexican-American War of 1846? Further, how should an individual of Mexican descent who is both hero and sellout to three countries—Mexico, the Republic of Texas, and the United States—and still later memorialized by a Chicana/o Movement be understood now? Seguín's memoirs as historical and literary texts engage all these identities, as well as the national and regional imaginaries that constitute the foundations of his writings.[3] In his lifetime, Seguín comes to embody a settler hybridity he could not have anticipated. In this regard, while settler hybrids like Seguín are present in the Recovery archive, other forms of settler hybridity are just as likely to be found.

I invoke the term *settler hybrid* here to underscore an evolving hybridity of identities found in communities of Mexican descent in the United States after 1848. First, I deploy hybridity in the manner Avril Bell does in framing the colonial discourses that constructed authenticity as the linchpin for the conveyance of settler and indigenous identities that would further the goals of modernity and maintain the power of coloniality. For Bell, modernity's projection of authenticity onto settler and indigenous communities alike insured the constructed superiority of the colonials and their settler descendants over all indigenous communities, including when mixed-raced indigenous are targeted through settler assimilationist policies. Rather than undermining the logics of settler coloniality, the in-betweenness of mixed-raced indigenous people was used to reinforce modernity's supposed relationship to the ontological and epistemological dimensions of authenticity.[4]

Second, I used this term, *settler hybrid*, to highlight the double historical role people of Mexican descent in the United States have come to represent as both colonizer and colonized. In this double role, I argue hybridity also characterizes a historic community whose members were agents of modernity, as well as targets of coloniality. This doubleness signals a different variation of the conundrum that authenticity posed for the evolving relationships of all those who resided in a settler nation, including indigenous, settlers, arrivants, immigrants, and settler hybrids. Importantly, the latter acknowledges a historical shift that occurred in the settler status of Spanish-indigenous-Mexican communities in the wake of Mexican American War. While this shift would come to inaugurate a new set of identities, the former settler identities did not simply disappear. Instead, these former identities, because of their connection to settler power, would come to shadow this community's uneven accommodation and resistance to coloniality, especially with regard to settler land claims and their accompanying material and affective intrastructures for belonging to a place. Authenticity with regards to twice colonized places—the settler logics for tying identity with structures of feelings for a place and any subsequent construction of spatial belonging—comes to locate the settler hybrid as much as it also displaces.

This book understands such contorted, settler hybrid identities and their contradictory relation to place, and any instances of nationalisms as measures of the meaning and effect of modernity found in early Mexican American literature. Modernity for Mexican Americans should not solely be understood in terms of an invasion of proto-industrialized capital to regions like the Southwest or the West or the border with Mexico. While modernity's negative alteration of local economies, politics, cultures, and languages are undeniable, the spectrum of its effects and the diversity of actors continue to be underestimated and undervalued as a topic worthy of analysis.

For this reason, I focus on the places of modernity as a way to mark and to think through the influence of the evolving border between the United States and Mexico on identity formation after 1848. This concept of place is helpful when analyzing the broad influence of indigenous peoples in the Southwest and the West on Mexican American communities, as well as holding these same communities accountable for dispossessing indigenous peoples of their lands. The places of modernity also name the regional differences that become visible from Texas to California over the latter half of the nineteenth century, especially as settler identities take root because of westward expansion. By the early twentieth century, one finds in print culture alone all of the following possible identity locations: Mexican,

Mexican expatriate, Mexican rebel, Mexican exile, Mexican American, Californio, Tejano, Spanish American, Latin American, Chicana/o, pachuca/o, chola/o, pocha/o. Navigating the differences each social location entails is in the end a useful way to recover the histories of ethnic formation otherwise marginalized or, worse, forgotten. But each term in itself has the capacity to reveal a deeper anarchy to which all archives are beholden in their meanings over time.

Such formations of identities after 1848 are symptomatic of the broader effects of modernity on the conquered territories. Drawing from Latin Americanists who have contributed to liberation philosophy, such as Enrique Dussel, Aníbal Quijano, and Walter Mignolo, I read this archive for its articulation of modernity in texts made available by the Recovery Project.[5] This book is beholden to their collective work to unpack the relationship of modernity to colonialism in the Américas. Together, they developed theories of liberation with terms such as *coloniality* and *coloniality of power* to better understand how the Enlightenment and liberal concepts, such as the rights of man and social change mechanisms like revolutions, were deeply compromised by their roots in territorial conquest and the rise of capitalism. Mapping the effects of this modernity on communities of Mexican descent who made their lives on indigenous lands conquered and settled by Spanish, Mexican, and U.S. colonialisms is key to understanding the first one hundred years of Mexican American literature.

Mapping Mexican American Modernity

Among the many twists and turns in any discussion of modernity and Mexican American communities post-1848 but pre–Chicano Movement lies the difficulty of understanding the role of literature for a people caught so precariously betwixt and between the nation-state. Most literary studies today take for granted that literature was a primary mechanism for establishing the foundational narratives of the nation-state in Europe and in its former settler colonies. By contrast, and for decades after the Mexican-American War, Mexican American communities existed outside the state narratives of nation-building. "Mexican" by language, culture, and religious habits, these people had nevertheless no binding influence on the republic of the

Estados Unidos Mexicanos. Their status as "American," as negotiated by the 1848 Treaty of Guadalupe Hidalgo, only occasionally entitled them access to the rights and privileges of U.S. citizenship. Despite completely debilitating circumstances, people wrote in most of the popular genres of the time, including the press, producing narratives of belonging outside the realm of the nation-state and without literary benefit of foremothers or forefathers.

Recorded in these literary and print productions are the pressures and reactions to living under the peculiar weight of a modernity that had settled on places and communities between the United States and Mexico. Early Mexican American literature thus provides historical and cultural frames from which to evaluate the consequences of a modernity fueled by a coloniality of power that serviced the imaginaries of a globalized Europe but, in practice, issued from geographies at some distance from it. These cultural productions evidence a variety of regional rationales for their existence as separate from but not ignorant of the nation-states of the United States and Mexico. The coloniality of power and the places of modernity that reside in them are often double-edged, fighting off an Anglo-American colonial presence only to hide, naturalize, or complicate older Spanish Mexican colonial narratives.

Through a thick description of a territory that underwent a profound reconstitution, my goal in this book is to render visible what Eurocentric modernity would otherwise keep invisible. Only by rendering modernity truly legible can one perceive the local and historical dimensions of what Mignolo calls "colonial difference." This legibility paves the way to name the modernity that was visited on a territory conquered by war and words in the mid-nineteenth century of North America. While this territory after 1848 will undoubtedly evidence its evolving consolidation under the nation-state of the United States, that consolidation and its benefits will rest on biased racialized terms. So too will the promises of the Enlightenment, with such terms as *freedom*, *liberty*, and *democracy*, reflect the biased foundation of a settler-colonial imaginary.

On the relationship between modernity, the nation-state, and the promise of Enlightenment in las Américas, Quijano understands modernity's first task, the subjugation of the barbaric other, as always part of the growth and consolidation of labor under capitalism. In "Coloniality of Power, Eurocentrism, and Latin America," he identifies modernity's proffering of "something new and different" and its proliferation of "changes in the material dimensions of social life" to those communities it subjugated as requiring constant guarding and redirecting by elites who sought to control and profit from the labor of the subjugated (546, 547). Quijano explains, "For those exploited by capital, and in general those dominated by the model of power, modernity generates a horizon of liberation for people of every relation, structure, or institution linked to domination and exploitation, but also the social conditions in order to advance toward the direction of that horizon. Modernity is, then also a question of conflicting social interests. One of the interests is the continued democratization of social existence. In this sense, every concept of modernity is necessarily ambiguous and contradictory" (548). In short, the success of coloniality and modernity rested on the promises offered by the Enlightenment, what Quijano calls "a horizon of liberation." Over time a new elite class would emerge, and this elite class would mete out those promises of liberation selectively among members of the more deserving barbaric other.

Mignolo's work on modernity and coloniality mirrors Quijano's assessment of modernity and its construction of the "social," but always with an emphasis on the processes of exchange, transaction, accommodation, and refutation. Mignolo understands colonialism as a dynamic, multivalent, multisituated force that invokes and engages a disparate range of actors. He foregrounds modernity's dynamism in order to make concrete by contrast the agency of those barbaric others who did not submit: "The history of the ways of life adopted by those who were there before the expansion occurred . . . [as well as the history] of those 'in-between': the natives or immigrants who had to deal with colonial situations and the postcolonial intellectuals who had to negotiate a cognitive space between the fragments of the European legacy and the forces of Amerindian ruins" ("Afterword," 180). Altogether this body of liberation philosophy represented by the likes of Quijano, Mignolo, and others agrees on the range and extent of forces brought to bear to convert, correct, and manage a New World in the self-aggrandizing image of Europe. Just as important, this body of work foregrounds the archives produced by those in-between who confronted their colonial situation with new thinking spaces. Of course, those in-between, like their colonial situation, will come to vary geographically, as well as temporally, across the many landscapes of the New World.

What also will vary is the character and structure of modernity in the New World. Dussel names this phenomenon "transmodernity," where *trans* refers to those things, processes, and inventions that are related to but external, hence considered extraneous and unimportant, to the maintenance of a Eurocentric modernity.[6] While modernity is linked to an analysis that posits not just its rise with capitalism and racism but as an invention that arose from Europe's colonization of the Américas, Dussel's transmodernity would remind us that there exist modernities whose articulations service their place of origin in the New World. This distinction plays a major role in understanding how the settler state and coloniality come to reinforce one another over time as separate from coloniality's role in Europe.

Although liberation philosophy is mainly concerned with modernity in relation to Latin America, these theories begin to shed light on the status of modernity in those territories eventually lost by Mexico and gained by the United States, especially how to take up more concretely those caught in between layers of different colonial enterprises. One can and should claim that up to that moment of the signing of the Treaty of Guadalupe Hidalgo in 1848, Mexico had been on the road to its own definition of modernity and nationalism. This started the moment Padre Miguel Hidalgo launched a war of independence in 1810. Securing independence from Spain in 1821, it was not until 1824 that the Mexican political process codified its first constitution as a republic. It was the Constitution of 1824 and its liberal policies that drew American and European settlers to Mexico's northern territories like Texas.[7]

In this relatively secure period, Mexico began to develop and deepen the instruments of its national identity. For example, Raymond Craib writes, "Mexico's first geographic society—Instituto Nacional de Geografía Estadística (later to become Sociedad Mexicana de Geografía y Estadística)—had been created in 1833 by Valentín Gómez Farías, a president who believed that the accumulation of a production of geographic and statistical knowledge of the nation's territory was critical for national development."⁸ In the context of the perceived "horizon of liberation," such documents of modernity offered and imagined, it is no wonder the repeal of the 1824 Constitution by President Antonio López de Santa Anna later, in 1833, ushered in a series of secessionist movements in Mexico, including the successful Texas War of Independence in 1836.

Ten years later the various regional nationalist agendas that were set in motion in 1776 and 1810 respectively came to a head during the Mexican-American War. Using Texas as a fulcrum, the United States consolidated and expanded its territorial claims on the continent, thereby superimposing its own narratives of nation-building (Manifest Destiny) over lands and peoples that up to that point had also proceeded under the sign of modernity, but a modernity that was only weakly supported by a nationalist superstructure called Mexico. Nevertheless, the signs and artifacts of the previous Spanish Mexican colonialisms and modernities were many and deep, from language to religion, from land use practices to land grant documents, from racial practices according to a castas system to architecture, the arts, and print culture.⁹ The residual presence of things Spanish, Mexican, indio, and mestizo could not be Americanized overnight.

Yet, despite of the dizzying multitude of examples of this residual past from Texas to California, February 2, 1848, marks the official narrative of separation from the nation and modernity that continues under the sign of Mexico. For those people, communities, and cultures that remained and survived after 1848, another colonialism and a different iteration of modernity becomes their burden to negotiate, to witness the slow erosion, the fading of their residual shared cultural past. And perhaps these twin burdens could have been borne under the logic of U.S. democracy and citizenship. But the "horizon of liberation" that Quijano speaks about as constitutive of modernity was obstructed by Anglo-American ideologies of racial superiority and by the industrial and agricultural economies of the United States and its desire for cheap, available labor. As they were for other ethnic and immigrant groups, institutions were set up to require former Mexican nationals to assimilate into a nationalist set of American identities but also to discipline and alienate those deemed beyond civic incorporation.[10] This alienation from the modernity of America was never completely totalizing. During moments of crisis, like war, men of Mexican descent were deemed appropriate for the military. A political willingness to send Mexican bodies into American wars has been shown since the Civil War. During other moments of crisis, though, such as the Great Depression of 1930s, Mexicans and Mexican Americans were rounded up like criminals and without due process deported to Mexico. Institutions such as courts, schools, banks, and voting rights were notoriously steeped in the racism of their day.[11]

Had these been the only adverse conditions under Anglo-American modernity, the Mexican American community would have certainly weathered them and risen to the challenges. But the economic and political instability of the waning years of Porfirio Díaz's dictatorship in early 1900s, followed by the Mexican Revolution, introduced successive waves of Mexican refugees that had the effect of destabilizing local strategies to Americanize the population of Mexican descent in the United States, as well as redefining local strategies to resist that Americanization. Many of these refugees quickly evolved into immigrants. Ironically, these massive influxes of immigrants re-Mexicanized large areas of the Southwest and West. It is important to notice that this Mexican immigration imported the competing modernities of Mexico itself, and over time the sustained movement of people, goods, technologies, and ideas created uneven palpable circuits between the conditions of modernity effecting Mexican Americans and those effecting Mexican nationals.

Places of Modernity

Without a doubt, the competing and conflicted circuits I outline here are a regional expression of the "alternative modernities" first explored by Dilip Parameshwar Gaonkar in the late 1990s, but with one sharp difference.[12] The status of the nation-state does not cohere in any normal, sustained manner. To be more precise, whereas state functions and institutions, like laws, courts, and taxes, abound both north of the border and south of it, even during a civil war, the concept of the nation, la nación, exists only very faintly for most, as something to move toward. For many, as Raúl Coronado has explored, the nation conjures memories of a dream never quite realized.[13] In contrast to Anglo-Americans or Mexicanos who come to inherit the Mexican Revolution, national belonging for Mexican Americans is continually questioned and questionable on either side of the border. As a result, regional identities become all the more important to communities of Mexican descent, all the more diverse along the two-thousand-plus-mile border shared with Mexico.

In Texas, Mexican American life over time has become symbolically and politically organized around the Texas Revolution (1836). "Remembering" the Alamo colors everything about being Mexican in the state. In New Mexico, members of a centuries-old, aristocratic landed gentry survive the Anglo-American invasion by transforming themselves into Spanish Americans. In California, extreme demographic shifts, first introduced by the gold rush in 1849, succeed in minoritizing the once combined majority of Californios and Native Americans to such a degree that by the early twentieth century, Spanish California, with its deteriorating missions and fake folklore, like Helen Hunt Jackson's *Ramona* (1884), becomes a commodity. Tourists, land speculators, and Easterners looking for a new life seek it in California through romanticized links to a genteel Spanish past. In such environments, where "Mexican" is a pejorative, there was no national imaginary on either side of the border that offered something better.

To think through the difficulty of this in-between place of modernity, we must historicize and map the whole territory, not just the border or borderlines or borderlands ceded to the United States after the Mexican-American War. A mapping of this kind must also be open to and in dialogue with the evolving nation-states of both Mexico and the United States. Once mapped, the places of modernity for Mexican Americans evidence clearly what Mignolo means by "colonial difference" and why cultural production within this complex, identified space carries so much import. He writes:

> The colonial difference is the space where the coloniality of power is enacted. It is also the space where the restitution of subaltern knowledge is taking place and where border thinking is emerging.

The colonial difference is the space where local histories inventing and implementing global designs meet local histories, the space in which global designs have to be adapted, adopted, rejected, integrated, or ignored. The colonial difference is, finally, the physical as well as imaginary location where the coloniality of power is at work in the confrontation of two kinds of local histories displayed in different spaces and times across the planet. ("Preface," ix)

All cultural production within this space is embedded in relationships to modernity and coloniality of power. In this regard, the cultural production of people of Mexican descent in the United States is no different. The Mexican American archive resonates with cultural productions that seek to name its own historical conditions before 1948. Where these cultural productions do differ is precisely how they are de-linked from any nation-building project. Thus, these cultural productions that sought to name their own historical conditions were invariably frustrated by a logic of modernity and coloniality that favored the nation-state. All the same, given the heterogeneity of their communities and the political and economic contingencies these communities had to deal with, their attempts to name their historical conditions, however forestalled, became a signature feature of their combined efforts to write themselves into history.

Because of their accumulated attempts to chronicle, philosophize, strategize, and imagine, it is now possible to recover the histories and literatures of early Mexican Americans. Further, it is now possible to name their modernity and deepen the analysis that the relationship of modernity to coloniality, and vice versa, would otherwise keep opaque. Quijano writes: "And since 'modernity' is about processes that were initiated with the emergence of America, of a new model of global power (the first world system), and of the integration of all the peoples of the globe in that process, it is also essential to admit that is about an entire historical period. In other words, starting with America, a new space/time was constituted materially and subjectively: this is what the concept of modernity names" ("Coloniality of Power," 547). I take up Quijano's insight that modernity names "a new space/time" as an especially fruitful method for conceptualizing early Mexican American literature and the territories the United States won by war. Equally important, I take up Quijano's optimism that these more shadowy, darker, and troublesome modernities of the periphery can be named, and that the naming itself is essential to any critique. Within a contact zone of evolving and competing modernities associated with those lands reterritorized by the United States, people of Mexican descent experienced and negotiated a modernity better understood as one of subtraction. While this modernity of subtraction has its origins in the territorial designs of colonialism beginning in 1492, this particular iteration of modernity has everything to do with the traumatic turn for these lands and peoples in 1848.

Subtractive Modernities

I borrow and modify this idea of subtraction from a sociological study of one the most enduring and harmful instruments of Americanization affecting children of Mexican descent: education. Angela Valenzuela concludes that American schools function through principles of "subtractive education." Her work is focused in areas where the high school dropout rates are highest among Mexican immigrant and Mexican American populations. Her conceptual model holds true for any period after 1848 and in many social arenas beyond education. Valenzuela understands the process of subtractive education in this manner: "School subtracts resources from youth in two major ways. First, it dismisses their definition of education which is not only thoroughly grounded in Mexican culture, but also approximates the optimal definition of education advanced by Noddings (1984) and other caring theorists. Second, subtractive schooling encompasses subtractively assimilationist policies and practices that are designed to divest Mexican students of their culture and language" (20). Grounded in Mexican culture, argues Valenzuela, is these students' expectation that their schools and teachers care for them. When schools only privilege the care that students demonstrate about their own individual education, these schools miss an opportunity to recognize pedagogically the legitimacy of their communal cultural values. Then, when these same schools implement practices that are intended to "de-Mexicanize" students, the end result is a culture that reduces their overall social capital. Valenzuela finds most schools are set up to denigrate and demean the Mexican and Mexican American cultural norms that already bind students, families, and communities to care for each other's educational progress. Valenzuela observes that friendship groups are "of special consequence to regular-track, U.S.-born Mexican youth, who often lack a well-defined and effective achievement orientation" (123). By insisting on de-Mexicanizing students in favor of a global Americanness, schools invariably "subtract," nullifying the social capital that would otherwise be of great potential for these students.

The coloniality of power that explicitly works through schools as a disciplining vehicle of the nation-state is not lost on Christine Sleeter. In her foreword to Valenzuela's book, Sleeter identifies the colonialist origins of such schooling: "Schools are an instrument of the maintenance of colonial relationships in that they constitute an arm of the state through which belief systems and cultural relationships are taught. Public school curricula proclaim the 'triumph of democracy' to the virtual exclusion of any serious analysis of the U.S. conquest" (xvii–xviii). While Sleeter's observations relate specifically to public school policy since the 1980s, it is easy to perceive a broader set of disciplinary mechanisms designed to insure the domination of the Southwest and West since 1848. Valenzuela helps us to understand the pervasive effects of processes of de-Mexicanization and assaults on Mexican social capital. This analysis also aptly describes social life before the civil rights period. The Chicana/o Movement will come to intervene significantly upon decades-long burdens of a U.S. modernity, precisely through naming and promoting a reconstitution of social capital based on pride and respect for communal identity.

Valenzuela's "subtractive schooling" speaks loudly to the darker side of modernity for Mexican Americans as stemming north of the border. What about south of the border? If a modernity of subtraction begins to name the experience of Americans of Mexican descent, it also articulates the subtraction, the loss, the nullification that hails from south of the border. De-Mexicanization, coming from Mexico and aimed at "Mexicanos del otro lado," or Mexican Americans, is well documented in literature, history, and in border theory. Américo Paredes's formulation of the "Greater Mexico" thesis—that Mexico also resides in memory and in those immigrants separated from the Mexican nation—was his attempt to grapple with this devaluation of the Mexican American. Octavio Paz's denigration of the figure of the pachuco in *Labyrinth of Solitude* (1950) is an infamous example in point. Like its northern version, this southern subtraction carries its own emptying of social capital.[14]

All the same, this modernity of subtraction, this emptying of social capital—past, present, and future—could not survive its own logic without some mechanism of counterbalance. In other words, were this modernity of subtraction totalizing, there would be no Mexican Americans—no Mexican American history. And yet the figure of the "Mexican" in U.S. culture is clearly a needed commodity, as is the figure of the "Mexican" in the United States from the vantage point of Mexico. For such "Mexicans," there exists a social mechanism that perpetuates colonial conditions while also providing a cultural space from which to launch a variety of social, political, and cultural reactions, including critique, toward a promised "horizon of liberation." Like Homi Bhabha's observation that the "discourse of post-Enlightenment English colonialism often speaks in a tongue that is forked, not false," this counter-balancing mechanism takes the form of colonial mimicry. According to Bhabha, colonial mimicry "emerges as one of the most elusive and effective strategies of colonial power and knowledge" (85). This mimicry begins to suggest why an archive of early Mexican American writing exists at all, and simultaneously why the archive is so uniquely ambiguous, conflicted, and compromised. Its ambiguities stand apart from those in the conflicted and compromised archive that emerges during and after the Chicana/o Movement. Only in the last thirty years with the Recovery Project has this older archive become accessible.

Reading Modernity Geographically

How might we apply a sense of place to analyzing histories and interpreting texts that are themselves imbued by their communities and their writers with a differential awareness of recolonized terrains? It is within this differential awareness that a modernity of subtraction for Mexican Americans becomes visible. Through an appreciation for place, we can notice in the available primary and secondary sources by and about Mexicans and Mexican Americans several broad trends of historical and cultural value in this early period. Foremost among these is that despite the hegemonic pull to see all historical matters as a confirmation and validation of the United States, North America is the site of not one or two but multiple European-inspired colonial enterprises, from 1492 to 1898. And further, these colonial enterprises often conspired against each other for New World domination. This observation should guide how archives deemed central to Mexican Americans are identified. The United States and Mexico engaged in a prolonged colonizing contest over territories, now regarded as the Southwest and West, beginning in 1821 and culminating in 1848. Despite U.S. nationalist conditioning since 1848, these disputed territories were never "tierras incógnitas." On the contrary, numerous indigenous people on these lands had been under colonial scrutiny and pressure since the Ponce de León and Coronado expeditions. These territories were already colonized and "civilized" to various degrees before the Mexican-American War began in 1846.[15]

In contrast to those archives that regularly represent U.S. history, it is highly critical to keep center stage that the Mexican-American War was not over empty, unpopulated spaces or underutilized land. The war was precisely about peopled lands, deep harbors with towns long accustomed to exporting and importing to a global market, whether on the Gulf of Mexico or the Pacific in San Diego or San Francisco. The war was over natural and mineral resources. And it was fought most over markets and the expansion thereof, as Stephanie LeMenager shows in detail.[16] In short, the war was predicated on what already existed in the coveted territories west and south of the Mississippi River. The Anglo-American territorial impulse represented a political unconscious that coveted what Spanish and Mexican colonialisms had achieved over three centuries of effort. What the United States gained came at the expense of what Mexican America came to lose. Over time those who remained and those who joined them as immigrants would come to experience the subtracting effects of modernity precisely by existing at the periphery of the nation-states of Mexico and the United States.

While the remnants of these prior colonial domains now enter national critical discussions about historical narrative, the historical treatment of archives, and settler colonialism, these discussions rarely escape the ghost of marginality. Seldom are these analyses attuned to the structures of feelings and materiality of the particular places and times of settler Hispanic experience as central to U.S. history. In the absence of a thoroughly shaped knowledge project related to Mexican Americans, postmodern, poststructuralist, and postcolonial theories have been very useful, giving us means to comprehend the social and political conditions of a minority community in the era of late capitalism. But the very contemporary origin of these theories has given us only a limited, historical comprehension of the order of things.

Like Raymond Williams's sense of the importance of "residual" histories and traces, early Mexican American literature is full of deep remnants—prior moments of another world that was already full, fully present in its own cultural and political underpinnings.[17] That other world was always already evolving into future states of a colonial ideology that was Mexico's own political discourse in 1846. What we find in early Mexican American literature are important glimpses into a state of collective being that was "anterior," "antes," before the new reality that began in 1848 with the signing of the peace treaty. As one of the many casualties of war, however, this anterior state becomes fragmented, demoted in social value, and displaced to the peripheral of the newly arrived official history of the United States. For the newly constructed class of U.S. citizens of Mexican descent, el tiempo anterior, the time before, which had been everything, suddenly becomes an irretrievable past. It is not just the basis for nostalgia of a golden age but a past whose recalling cannot help but create a bifurcated sense of well-being. At the center of that split, between the before and after, is the issue of lost lands.

The loss of land erodes a sense of place—one that was understood as timeless, if far from perfect, under a Spanish Mexican cosmology. Loss, erosion, and dislocation anchor a modernity of subtraction for Mexican Americans. Within this particular rendering of colonial difference, these anterior moments we find in early Mexican American literature cannot help but do war against an Anglo-Puritan world order. The anterior of early Mexican American literature here opposes (yes), resists (yes), and even proposes itself as an alternative to many a drifting son or daughter of latter-day Congregationalists. But never do these "anteriors" achieve confidence in themselves. Because the future for Mexican Americans, despite the U.S. Constitution and the Treaty of Guadalupe Hidalgo, is not about belonging to the conquering nation. Instead, for more than one hundred years, the conquering nation has treated its citizens of Mexican descent as barely tolerated foreigners. Because this modernity of subtraction is so tied to territorial loss, the cultural work at play representing anterior states and geographies is very freighted indeed.

While territorial loss underwrites a modernity of subtraction for post-1848 communities of Mexican descent, including those who immigrate, this loss alone does not explain how one settler nation comes to burden one broad community as part of its victory over another settler nation. And since the darker side of modernity always seeks to make itself invisible, hence impervious to critique and intervention, how does this same community ever express and expose the burden of modernity? This question returns us to the archive where the flows, and in particular the excesses, of modernity and coloniality are recorded and preserved. Significantly, they often contest and conflict with the logics of their own formation. Like water poured into a cup, one can perceive the work of modernity and coloniality. It flows and fills a space previously empty of its influence, but because this flow is never satisfied, very often this space is filled to excess. This excess then flows layers upon layers of modernity and coloniality over the same space of colonial domination. Because these overflows happen in specific spaces at specific times, the matrix of modernity and coloniality is always most visible at the point of excess, especially when the point of excess is the space of overlapping and competing colonialisms. It is here in the space of excess and overlap that one often finds the burdens of modernity more clearly marked.

In a space that had already been territorialized, cultured, racialized, and gendered once by Spain and then again by an independent Mexico, the post-1848 writer of Mexican descent in the United States appears as both colonizer and colonized, as beneficiary and victim of settler colonialism, as white and nonwhite, and as gendered in accordance with a European patriarchal system. Excess is what symbolically, figuratively, and rhetorically characterizes the writings of such individuals—to the extent that these individuals behave as settler hybrids. From María Amparo Ruiz de Burton to Sandra Cisneros, Mexican American literature offers us a surplus of representations of excess, be it of violence, poverty, sadness, irrationality, silence, or death. The excess of one time/space continuum often reveals a history of excesses. In this sense, to remember the Alamo vis-à-vis Juan Seguín can never just be about Anglo Texas in 1836 but must include the mission system that constructed it in the first place and the indigenous peoples the Catholic church subjugated, converted, or eliminated. The transformation of a Spanish/Mexican colonial space into the Manifest Destiny of Anglo America created an anarchy of excess, a process of contradictory collisions, some of which were captured in the archives that followed.

What a Modernity of Subtraction Makes Visible

What should critics do with glimpses of bygone colonialisms captured in archives? What methodologies will help us to approach indigenous genocide and displacement, miscegenation, the promotion and establishment of Catholicism in the New World, including the importation of feudal serf-based labor systems? How do we in Chicanx studies understand oppositionality and resistance when so much of early Mexican American writings is steeped in settler colonialism and coloniality of power? Further, what do these glimpses tell us about a modernity of subtraction? The answers to these questions and others lie in what has enabled us to have this critical inquiry in the first place: the Recovery Project and its reconstruction of a Mexican American archive.

Clearly, like the publication of *The Latino Nineteenth Century* (2016), one major consequence of the Recovery Project has been the culmination of more than thirty years of scholarship on topics ranging from colonialism in the Américas, struggles for independence, immigration to the Spanish-language press, and a diverse literary record.[18] The field of Chicana/o literary criticism now straddles at least three distinctive periods: the Chicana/o Movement–inspired literatures, dating roughly from 1960 to 1990; the pre-movement writers of the colonial period up to 1960; and the post-movement writers since 1990. Although there is plenty of gray and overlap between all of these periods, it is essential for the future of

Chicanx literary studies that these periods structure our understanding of the archive as a whole and help develop anew our critical definitions of Mexican American literature.

One recent development in Recovery scholarship lies in serious attempts to grapple with the inherent regionalism of Mexican American writers since 1848. Regionalism has been noted often enough in passing. But its significance has been given short shrift because mainstream "regionalism" as a field has been less immediately relevant to spatial analyses in critical race theory and border studies. Hispanic scholars, like their counterparts in African American and Asian American studies, have invested critical attention on other ways to think geographically. Recently, Chicana literary scholar Melina Vizcaíno-Alemán has advocated the need to take a "critical approach to regionalism" (5). She analyzes the still-underexamined nationalist origins of Chicanx studies and locates her analyses in an aesthetics of place that does not adhere to nationalist, transnationalist, or postnational literary histories. In doing so, she begins to renovate regionalism to make its local and global dimensions more apparent.

Vizcaíno-Alemán's sense of critical regionalism squares with that of Krista Comer, who uses the concept to make the local more global, and to globalize more effectively any so-called local's relationship to worlds beyond it.[19] Critical regionalism has evolved as a method of analysis to describe the inroads of late capitalism between the local and global, to further transnational analyses, and to grasp the significance of post-9/11 states of exceptions. Along with political questions, Comer argues that critical regionalism "marks a willingness to reckon with such philosophical questions" about place itself and being in place.[20] For Comer, critical regionalism is an important tool in the de-centering of U.S. exceptionalism. Writing about the significance of place in an age of global citizenship, she insists "that deconstructed placeness still matters and that different constituencies come at these questions from different stakes in discussions of space, power, the state, language, aesthetics, and knowledge" (162). This latter point is particularly significant for Chicanx studies, given how the U.S. West is historically and contemporaneously home to most people of Mexican descent in the United States.

Similar to Comer, for José Limón critical regionalism is the retention and appreciation of the local to evidence deep and varied relationships to the global; it enhances the comparison of discrete regions vis-à-vis the historical record while also grappling with the nation-state.[21] Following the work of Heinz Ickstadt, Cheryl Herr, and Douglass Powell, Limón embraces critical regionalism for its "abiding and fulsome respect for and rendering of the complexity of local cultures in comparison to others in the world, while recognizing that all are in constant but critical interaction with the global" (168). In other words, comparisons or contrasts are only as good as the historical record and the thick cultural description they stand on. In the end, Limón's preference for critical regionalism over global studies has to do with a worry of how critics, already inclined toward the global, might under-read the local historical record. While a critical regional analysis benefits all three major periods of Mexican American literature, because of 1848, this method of analysis is keenly important for regions under extreme colonial refashioning.

The critical regionalism of this study thinks geographically to theorize prior notions of the local/global as it relates to colonialism, coloniality of power, and the entrenchment of Europe's modernity. Critical regionalism, paired with what I call modernity of subtraction, helps to visualize and illustrate better Hispanic writing properly in its own historical moment and with its particular regional character. Thus, what is often understood as the transnational character of Mexican American literature has to do more precisely with a transmodernity that reflects the processes of transition, transitoriness, and transparency imposed by coloniality. More specifically, the *trans* has to do with the transitions that occurred when one colonial matrix gave way to yet a more powerful one in 1848; it has to do with the transitory promises of a modernity that accompanied the Anglo-American colonial matrix but also the sense of betrayal and confusion that the prior Spanish Mexican order, also a product of modernity, was so vulnerable and could be defeated; and finally, it has to do more with the transparency of the raw, naked power of the nation-state when you are the subject of its settler colonialism as its perpetual other.

In the case of Recovery literature, geography is, of course, hemispheric. But it is also transatlantic. In settler countries such as the United States, Canada, and Australia—countries in which the colonial masters have been reinscribed as the natural natives of the colonized land—it has been extremely difficult to apprehend the evolution of colonialism. Consequently, it has been difficult to assess the colonial status of the indigenous people who themselves have become incorporated into the nationalist imaginaries of settler states. As will become apparent, the renderings of geography are a stunning means of theorizing Hispanic writers' appreciation for the specific brand of colonialism that erupted after 1848, both in the United States and throughout Latin America. To invoke early Mexican American writing requires attention to the regional dimensions of literature and modernity itself. Recovering the effects of modernity demonstrates how authors dialogued with coloniality through their apprehension of the local and how that modernity reflects Mexican Americans' marginal status in the United States.

Recovery literature provides one opportunity after another to read geographically for modernity. Early Mexican American literature self-consciously situates itself in place and region. Its situation is one where the global is never far from the local. At stake here is our ability to recognize and appreciate the worldly attributes of Mexican Americans, because to see the worldly is to see the historic figure of the Mexican American as occupying a much larger role in human history. Such situatedness reveals modernity for early Mexican American literature as a political unconscious that is trying to narrate the uneven erosions and fusions of two historically competing colonialisms, as well as a narrative that advances a sense of an in-between community existing between Mexico and the United States.

In order to best frame and execute an analysis of coloniality in early Mexican American literature, I structure the ensuing chapters by calling attention to discrete responses to modernity after 1848. Chapter 1, "Modernity Deferred: 'There Never Was a More Peaceful or Happy People,'" takes up that long period of transition from a Spanish Mexican settler culture to a culture dominated by an Anglo-American settler state. It begins by comparing and contrasting how differing notions of self and land reveal the coloniality of power that conditioned the initial subtractive responses to the aftermath of the Mexican-American War. While this transition varied from region to region, the Anglo-Californio tensions produced in this period are particularly noteworthy and well documented in print culture, especially by the extended Vallejo family. Who and whose community gets to narrate a Californio society that is quickly receding into the realm of archives and artifacts is the driving question for a modernity deferred. Chapter 2, "Californio Settler History: Nostalgia as Patrimony," continues to focus on place, property, race, and memory about Californios. But it is now the early twentieth century, and the promises of partaking in an American progressive experience are all but shattered in the wake of many disappointments. The earlier contests over land grants, political representation, and economic opportunity have shifted into the discursive realms of culture, high society, and patronage. In the hands of Californio descendants such as Francisca Vallejo, nostalgia becomes an alternative terrain from which to launch critiques of Anglo America while celebrating the accomplishments of a Californio settler society. All the same, as a dwindling Californio elite struggles to be heard and validated for their past family connections, the state of California prospers from the labor of more recent arrivals of Mexican immigrants. Alternating from moments of identification to denial because of the increased presence of Mexican immigrants, Californio nostalgia plays a vital, if at times contradictory, role in shaping and securing a homeland for Californios, even as it attempts to keep at bay the state's second-class treatment of all people of Mexican descent.

Chapter 3, "Game of Modernities: Coloniality and Racial Loyalty in the U.S. West," describes a new world order predicated on survival, change, and compromise. Inherent in this new world order is a range of dislocations from a previous colonial structure, one that leads to a bewilderment of shifting identities under a new imperial regime. Movement, immigration (internal and external), labor, and new technologies are all part of the social processes remapping traditional notions of place and belonging. Of chief interest here is the development of new racial and social categories alongside increasingly rigid disciplining instruments of surveillance and punishment. Anchoring the analysis is Apache war chief Geronimo's autobiography in 1906, which details his warrior life extensively in the Arizona, New Mexico, and Sonora homelands of his tribe. Geronimo's often-repeated hatred for the Spanish and Mexican colonialists in his autobiography dovetails with the complex racial narratives found in Miguel Antonio Otero Jr.'s memoir, *The Real Billy the Kid* (1936). Although ostensibly about rendering to history the "real" Billy the Kid, and not just the outlaw as killed by Pat Garrett, Otero offers instead a kind of territorial biography where Nuevo Mexicanos increasingly experience life as settler hybrids. In the decades following the Civil War, both texts reveal how racialized loyalties in the West underwrote the tenuous relation of Mexican Americans to civic life during a period of sustained military presence.

Chapter 4, "Me Llaman Mexicana: Gender and Choice under Coloniality" builds from the history of conflicts and violence that were incited on the borderlands between the United States and Mexico because of land, race, and politics. This chapter explores how Jovita González embraces her Mexicanness despite its social and political shortcomings as an identity in Texas. Though she laments and resists the limits that a Mexican heritage places on women, her writings and her presence as a public figure work against the cultural logic of the melting pot theory of Americanization. González frames the burdens of coloniality and modernity for Mexican American women as a gendered dilemma that forces a false choice between the modern and la raza. This choice is negotiated through regional markers and regional identification, creating a critical regionalism that forwards Mexicanness, not as nostalgia for the past, but as heritage for the future, a future that includes Anglo Texans. As a scholar, writer, teacher, and public intellectual, González envisions a bicultural future for Mexican American women in Texas.

Chapter 5, "Barrio Modernity: Speaking Pocho, Being Chicana/o," takes up the issue of language, immigration, deportations, migrant labor, and the formation of immigrant Mexican communities by way of fiction and journalism. The focus here on a diasporic Mexico is also meant figuratively, since tales of immigrants often take note of locations that segregate them from mainstream society and its citizens, U.S. and Mexican alike. A chief concern is the development of the figure of the pocho, the Mexican who has forgotten his origins and family language. This figure is analyzed in the 1934–35 serialized novel *Los pochos* by Mexican expatriate writer Jorge Ainslie, published in the major Spanish-language newspaper of that period, *La Prensa* of San Antonio, Texas. Both the novel and *La Prensa* are examples of how print culture at the time attempted to theorize Mexican immigrant life in the United States. This chapter concludes with how the Spanish-language press was ultimately instrumental in validating the figure of el pocho for its readers. While this same press would come to articulate a social grammar that would make sense of the pocho for its readers, that same grammar had to evolve further to validate the figure of the chicano and chicana, especially as these figures came to shoulder the civil rights movement for Mexican Americans after 1948.

Lastly, although the vast majority of quoted archival or published material is in English, occasionally when no extant translation exists, some materials will be quoted from their Spanish sources and without translation. For more than thirty years now, scholars of Recovering the U.S. Hispanic Heritage have been publishing scholarship that reflects the Spanish dominance of its archives. This scholarship reflects the bilingual ability of its critics, but it also represents a critical prioritizing of a bilingual/multilingual approach to its research commitments. So the editorial decision here is not unusual. All the same, there has been every attempt to follow up quotes in Spanish with a thick paraphrase to provide content for the non-Spanish reader. Having said that, this author hopes that this small gesture to disrupt the English-language dominance of U.S. literary studies goes some way to acknowledge those other archives that exist in languages other than English or Spanish and to demonstrate solidarity with the scholars of those archives and languages. To be certain, a multilingual approach to U.S. literary studies is long overdue.

1 Modernity Deferred

"There Never Was
a More Peaceful or
Happy People"

> It was a picturesque life, with more sentiment and gayety in it, more also that was truly dramatic, more romance, than will ever be seen again on those sunny shores. The aroma of it all lingers there still; industries and inventions have not yet slain it; it will last out its century,—in fact, it can never be quite lost, so long as there is left standing one such house as the Senora Moreno's.
> —Helen Hunt Jackson, *Ramona: A Story*, 1884

In the December 1889 issue of the *Overland Monthly*, Ninetta Eames, a periodicals writer whose first two husbands worked for the *Overland Monthly*, published a curious travel narrative of her tour of Southern California with her friend Margaret and the Judge, their male escort.[1] Far from simple, in "Autumn Days in Ventura," Eames blends regional boosterism and what we would now call ethnography with a survey of old Californio agricultural practices versus industrialized methods that included pumping water out of wells to irrigated fields.[2] Eames even gets to marvel at the production values of an early oil field in Santa Paula. But she begins her narrative by stopping at Rancho Camulos, part of the Californio Del Valle family land grant, which by then had earned the reputation of being the supposed inspiration for Rancho Moreno in Helen Hunt Jackson's *Ramona* (1884). According to Dydia DeLyser, given the highly romanticized portrayal of Ramona and Alessandro and the allure of Spanish Californio culture, tourists began to arrive at Rancho Camulos in search of the "real" Ramona shortly after the novel was published (x–xii). In 1887 the Southern Pacific Railroad opened a rail line that would stop at the Del Valle land grant to take advantage of this touristic phenomenon. By the time Eames and her friends arrive at Rancho Camulos, unannounced visitors had become all too common for the Del Valle family (DeLyser, 75).

Soon after departing the train from this very same spot, Eames and company spy the figure of myth made flesh:

> On a wide veranda a beautiful girl was swinging in a hammock, the gauze-like folds of her summery gown sweeping the floor. Above her head ripe clusters of Mission grapes hung pendent in their grayish green leaves, out of which a ruddy-breasted linnet chirruped to us invitingly.
>
> "A veritable Ramona!" Margaret exclaimed under her breath.
>
> Our shadows fell across the fierce patch of light on the sun-baked earth directly before the porch, and the young lady dropped her book with a gesture of impatience as she turned toward us haughtily, the rich color deepening in her eyes and cheeks.
>
> The Judge hurried forward with outstretched hand: "We are *bona fide* visitors, Miss Belle, and have no intention of invading the premises without permission."
>
> The Señorita was on her feet in an instant, laughing infectiously while she greeted us with the incomparable grace and warmth of a true *Castellano*.
>
> "You must forgive me for mistaking you for more of those dreaded tourists, who insist upon seeing everything from the bed rooms to the sheep corral," she said apologetically; then went on to explain in her perfect English how much they had been annoyed by people coming at all times and hours to visit the home of the far-famed Ramona.
>
> "Nothing will convince them that our mother is not that atrocious Señora Moreno, or that Ramona is not to be found in either my sister or myself. The fact is, we were all in Los Angeles when Mrs. Jackson called, and consequently have never met the lady." (562)

To what degree this is a factual representation of her group's encounter with Miss Belle, we may never know or be satisfied as critics. Nonetheless, Eames's description has the air of truth behind it, especially as she feels obliged to defend Jackson against the slightest hint of criticism that Ramona might have been overly fictionalized:

> Certainly the author of "Ramona" has given her readers an accurate description of this best preserved of all the old Mexican homes in California. Here are the great stone jars of which she writes, which were made generations ago by the patient hands of the San Luis Obispo Indians; and here the fountain yet drips murmuringly into the deep pool of its basin, the orange groves hold out their waxy blossom and yellowing balls, the grape vines on the long arbor drop through the lattice their heavy bunches purpling with wine, while the honeysuckles still twist themselves around the pillars and eves of the *casa*, and fling their flowering mantels over the cracking wall of the garden. (562)

In fact, Eames seems to protest too much with her defense of Jackson. Perhaps with an eye toward retaining her readership who might prefer fantasy, Eames writes indulgently in a drawn-out lyricism that's reminiscent of Jackson's style in *Ramona*. So Eames's response to Miss Belle's deconstruction of the myth of Ramona is to indulge her readers with even more "romancing" of those facts and artifacts that are present at Rancho Camulos.

Here romancing is both the disguise that means to veil the coloniality of power that centers Miss Belle as Ramona and not Ramona and the means by which Eames, and Jackson by extension, assert their authority and legitimacy over the mildest of protests by the ethnic other, who must remain charming and picturesque while simultaneously approachable as a "perfect" English speaker. Here too the semiotic exchange cannot help but expose flattery as yet another means of subjugation. The Judge's promise not to invade without permission is ironic but odd, since who or what "invades" with permission is never actually established. Instead, Eames controls the light banter of gentility only to declare hers the authoritative voice. All the same, one fact remains: Eames and company invaded Miss

Belle's space just like every other tourist before them, and so too Eames's readers. In the face of such resounding persistence to override the voice of the speaking Californio or Californiana, with more "romancing," where would someone like a Miss Belle get a hearing?

As Helen Hunt Jackson's observation, "so long as there is left standing one such house as the Senora Moreno's," makes clear, the viability or authenticity of any Californio story was contingent on Californios' all-too-literal survival. Once gone, it was not clear there would be anyone left to tell their story faithfully. As it is, DeLyser notes that the Del Valle would come to sell Rancho Camulos to a "Swiss immigrant" who saw the property's potential for oil extraction. Thus, caring for the famed adobe home and ranch buildings, and their histories, would pass on to non-Californio owners (DeLyser, 82–83). Decades later the property would be granted National Historic Landmark status, "upon which much potential funding for the future museum relied, hinged on the *fictional* role of the house as the Home of Ramona" (DeLyser, 83).

This chapter delves into the literal and symbolic forms of declension endured by Californios and Californianas in the last forty-some-odd years of the nineteenth century. The initial enthusiasm for the Anglo-American presence in 1848, expressed by such Californio elites as Mariano Guadalupe Vallejo or recent transplants like María Amparo Ruiz de Burton, had all but faded at the turn of the century. In light of the drastic demographic shift occasioned by the gold rush, the dispossession of land grants through the infamous Land Commission, and the conversion to large-scale farming practices brought to California no less than under the auspices of the railroad magnates, Californio life was all but disappearing.[3] But even as it was disappearing, there began a movement to preserve for posterity the early history of California, and especially the stories of its "finest" families, as Hubert Howe Bancroft often pursued. But how or who would get to tell this history and these stories became as contested as everything else in post-1848 California. Why the narrating of California had become a contest had everything to do with the much broader suturing of narratives under the umbrella of Manifest Destiny that were being woven that very same moment to consolidate a national history with distinct chapters like California's. But California's colonial past posed a problem too.

As evidenced by an anecdote that pits a fictional Ramona against a living Californiana, there was evidently something at stake culturally—something big enough to persuade the Southern Pacific Railroad to capitalize on eager tourists seeking the real Ramona, and yet incredulous and ready to reject when a veritable model of such a figure departed from the novel's representation. DeLyser writes, "Amid a flurry of regional promotion, and in a responding rush of incoming upper- and middle-class white tourists and homeseekers, the region was transformed into a seat of Anglo population and power" (xi). Further, writes Alberto Varon, "The romantic invention of California's physical and imaginative landscape as a result of the Ramona boom extended far beyond the novel's immediate fame, lasting decades and generations" (66). Thus, the collision of the fictional with the real produced a moment of excess between overlapping and competing colonialisms in one confined and identifiable local. In this space of excess, we, the belated reader, can see Eames both eager "to represent" but also eager to frame the "real" as disappointing, something less than what Jackson imagined. For all her initial eagerness to represent Rancho Camulos, Eames's journey through Ventura County, taking specific and detailed notice of the agricultural and industrial gains of the county's new residents, steadily distances her reader from Rancho Camulos.

By the end of her travel essay, Eames participates in what was already a fairly well-known trope, California as paradise:

> On these semi-trophic shores the hour immediately after the disappearance of the sun is, of all the twenty-four, most sacred and soothing. Then all Nature is devotional, and the soul becomes conscious of an ineffable awakening of diviner instincts. . . . Through the supernal glare the mountains rose, rank above rank, crown above crown, until old Topatopa's striped front upreared sublimely over all the rest—a mighty shrine on which the fires of heaven were kindled. Before the revelations of such a sunset sky, one waits in vague expectancy of some

new vision—some colossal glory yet to be revealed, whose rush of splendor shall flood a trembling universe. (579–80)

Eames ends her journey more like a naturalist, painting a sublime picture of a natural world existing side by side profound examples of Anglo-American Christianity, husbandry, and engineering. Whatever was noted as charming or exotic about the residents of Rancho Camulos has been firmly displaced now, all but forgotten, because of a natural world waiting to be guided by a "new vision" that Californios evidently lacked. In short, they lacked the right modernity. Narrating that story—a story of declension, a story of modernity deferred—and the reasons for that deferral, seems to have become a necessary event to chronicle for the ultimate subjugation of a previously colonized space. As if to leave no doubt, the discursive subjugation of all things Californio was meant to leave a lasting impression not just on the subjugated but on the ruling class that succeeded them. The displacement of a Californio past, especially the failure and decline of the Californios, evidently had to be coordinated. After all, the narrative of that decline had regional and national consequences for the transference of settler wealth and futures alike.

And yet, within this same discursive landscape, Californios and Californianas evidenced a remarkable tenacity and resistance to go quietly into the dark. They refused the terms of colonization being offered. While their refusals relied on privileges brokered by colonialism itself, their collective retorts nonetheless record the price that the promises of modernity extolled on even colonizers. Their experience of a modernity of subtraction is most visible when, as in the Eames anecdote, the space and place of authenticity, of belonging, is disrupted not by guests but interlopers seeking to displace. The grounds of Eames's displacement, industry and innovation, are all the more ironic given the "progressive" changes introduced to Rancho Camulos by the Del Valle brothers, Reginaldo and Ulpiano (DeLyser, 67). Whenever possible, like these brothers, others would remind their Anglo-American neighbors of their fitness for modernity. They would devise rhetoric strategies, when formal politics failed, to distance themselves from any identification with those other Mexicans who were already beginning to present themselves as settler hybrids. For as long as possible, they insisted that their modernity was equal to and aligned with Anglo America. In what follows, I focus on the rhetorical strategies they devised to resist their colonization. Featured here are the writings about Old California by Californios and Californianas that appeared in prominent English-language magazine publications in the 1890s, as well as poetry, public speech, memoir, and biography.

"The Gold Hunters of California"

Although they had done so periodically before and will do so afterward, it is not clear from the pages of the *Century Magazine* of New York why its editors chose in late 1890 to launch a series of more than forty articles on California. Spread over fifteen volumes, from November 1890 to February 1892, the *Century Magazine* made a concerted effort to depict, at times melodramatically, the meteoric rise of the material and cultural significance of California to the nation. The editors solicited some of the most respected commentators on California, such as General John Bidwell, Charles Howard Shinn, John Charles Frémont, and General William Tecumseh Sherman. They made a spectacular effort to commission by then well-known Western artists, including Frederick Remington, Mary Hallock Foote, and Charles Nahl, to provide a range of visual representations of California. The editors were even able to surpass their predecessors at competing magazines and journals by soliciting materials from actual Californios. In all five cases, they were women, Californianas, all well connected to a recent Spanish Mexican Californio past.[4] In this context, the *Century Magazine* had succeeded in printing what had by then become the most elusive and vanishing voice in all California historiography.

Given the difficulty of securing Californio-told tales, their inclusion must have been celebrated as a journalistic coup. If so, the celebration was a quiet affair, like most instances of a Californio past. Instead, the editors of the *Century Magazine* are audibly self-congratulatory about making a substantial contribution to an ever-growing historiography of California. In an article entitled "Topics of the Time: Gold Hunters of California, the Making of California," the editors rehearse a well-traveled narrative of Anglo-American exceptionalism, an exceptionalism focused now on

California. Without too much difficulty, one can easily hear the undertones of a Jacksonian cultural politic that equates individualism with material acquisition, the latter more often than not the result of territorial expansionism and universal white male suffrage. In explaining why the *Century Magazine* decided to devote a series on California, the editors depend on what is racially perceived to be a self-evident truth: "*The Century Magazine* begins a systematic record of some of the chief features of the Anglo-Saxon movement to California, a part of the national life which has no parallel either in our own country or in that of any country. We say a part of the national life, for though the immediate scene of the search for gold and of the foundation of one of our greatest commonwealth, was a narrow strip of Pacific coast, the line of sympathy and interest at that day reached to every quarter of the country, if not to every quarter of the globe."[5] Citing the uniqueness of the Anglo-Saxon movement, rather than migration, which might have provoked unwelcomed comparisons with immigrants from Eastern and Southern Europe, the *Century Magazine* editors draw attention to the gold rush and its global impact. Even though in the executed series the gold rush era is only one of many illustrated historical moments, the editors nonetheless choose to preface its articles under the overall rubric of the "Gold Hunters of California." The gold rush era, not the particulars of the Mexican-American War, nor President Polk's initial designs for exploiting the maritime potential of California's harbors that faced Asian markets, brokers what is deemed relevant to report about California in 1890.

California was, of course, especially after the gold rush of 1849, a national and international topic for print culture. But even before the gold rush and even before the Mexican-American War (1846–48), California was clearly of interest to U.S. readers of both political reviews and popular magazines. In 1840 Henry Richard Dana's travel narrative *Two Years before the Mast* was not only published in book form by Harper and Brothers but copiously quoted, for example, in the *United States Magazine and Democratic Review* (October 1840). Here an anonymous reviewer accentuates Dana's own biased and ambivalent attraction of what he finds among the inhabitants in California. To Dana's description of Californio race politics, the aristocratic manners of the ruling elite, and the exotic appearances of señoritas and the sensuous lilt of their voices, the reviewer adds: "The people of California are suspicious of foreigners, and none are allowed to settle in the city but those who become united to the Catholic church" (325). By not so subtly resurrecting La Leyenda Negra (the Black Legend), a centuries-old mythology that demonized anything Spanish in origin—especially its brand of Catholicism—the reviewer goes on to raise his own suspicions: "Yet the trade of Monterey is mostly in the hands of English and Americans who have married Californians, and brought their children up Catholic and Spaniards, without teaching them the English language" (325). No doubt speaking for his class, the reviewer effectively disguises his contempt by asserting that the Anglo-Saxon in California concedes only to reassert himself: "In this way they secure popularity and often rise to be persons of consequence. The chief Alcaldes in Monterrey and Santa Barbara are Yankees by birth" (325). As personal stories and anecdotes about California found their way into print, these eyewitness accounts fueled curiosity and desire about "unsettled" lands and exotic cultures. Jacksonian politics of the 1820s and 1830s had created by then an Anglo-American society ready to read "opportunity" anywhere land was perceived to be managed improperly.

Thus, the above reviewer firmly locates what would become a standard opinion about California in future decades, that California is a land of opportunity only lacking the sturdy masculine hand of Anglo-Americans who can turn potential into prosperity: "Monterey is pleasantly situated, with one of the best harbors in the world, in a productive region enjoying one of the finest climates in the world, but the people are lazy and thriftless almost beyond conception" (324). In six short years, in the pages of the *American Review*, this racialized opinion would emerge as the bedrock of a foreign policy that would acquire California for the Union: "While California remains in possession of its present inhabitants, and under control of its present government, there is no hope of its regeneration. [California's economic future] will demand a life, an impulse of energy, a fiery ambition, of which no spark can ever be struck from the soft sluggishness of the American Spaniard" ("California," 86). Nonetheless, this brand of jingoism still had room for a qualified pathos on behalf of the Californio. On this score, Dana's 1840 reviewer quotes a sympathetic condemnation of the Californio that will have a lasting impression: "'In fact, they sometimes appeared to me to be a people on whom a curse had fallen, and stripped them of everything but their pride, their manners, and their voices'" (325).

Some fifty-odd years later, these early observations of California persisted. The curse that Dana imagined from a secure, confident realm of Anglo-American racial superiority would come to underwrite concretely not only the Mexican-American War but also the ideology that accompanied the actual stripping of the Californio's elite economic and political status in California. By the end of the nineteenth century, all that was effectively left of Californio material culture was precisely "pride, their manners, and their voices." Their gradual disappearance was a matter of some concern. Both Mariano Guadalupe Vallejo and María Amparo Ruiz de Burton, one a former statesman and major ranch owner and the other a novelist and ranch owner as well, worried out loud about the survival of the Californio community. Elsewhere, the precipitous decline of the Californio represented a crisis for those like Bancroft who believed it was important for the future of California that its past be recorded. Californio voices were literally solicited to serve Bancroft's expanding archive, from which he meant to chronicle the actual transformation of Alta California into Anglo California.

At this same general moment, U.S. print culture still had a huge stake in California. This is clearly the case with the *Overland Monthly*, which originated in San Francisco in the midst of the gold rush, but also with a wide spectrum of eastern magazines, from *Atlantic Monthly* and *Harper's Review* to more science- or industry-focused magazines such as the *Massachusetts Plowman and New England Journal of Agriculture* or *Scientific American*. Magazine contributors such as Charles Howard Shinn and Helen Elliott Bandini expressed their concerns over the plight of the Californio community. While both were invested in an accurate history of California and expressed amply their concerns and admiration for Californio culture, they did so by lamenting the lack of Californio-told stories. Shinn is upfront in his desire and admiration for these stories, but to him Californios are reluctant storytellers. The Californios, he advises his readers, must be handled as delicate informants:

> The most attractive literary material left in California is to be found in the recollections and traditions of descendants of the pioneer Spanish families. But these men and women must be met with sympathy for their misfortunes, and with an unfeigned interest in the old ranch and Mission days. As soon as their confidence is fairly won they tell all they know, with almost childlike eagerness to help in the restoration of the past. One immediately observes the great stress laid upon family connections, the pleasure taken in stories of former times, and the especial reverence for the founders of the province, the governors and other officials, and the heads of the Missions. (377)

In retrospect, Shinn's admiration for the Californio is patronizing, and quite in keeping with Dana's much earlier observation of the Californio as indolent and childlike. Shinn nevertheless accurately observes the rhetorical style found whenever a Californio voice is recorded or translated. Bancroft's oral testimonios of Californios are largely shaped as if in response to a series of questions: who, what, when, where, and why. Even though family connections are also routinely exercised, the Californio elite was a relatively fixed number of families, families that were related by marriage many times over. It was inevitable that any answer to a who, what, when, where, and why would involve a family connection. Shinn was also correct in saying that the Californios were eager to restore their past. They too had an investment in recording the history of California, but as critics have noticed, the past they were anxious to record was also different than the history being produced by Bancroft. Bancroft's histories and those that imitated him confirmed the inevitability of an Anglo California. By contrast, in Mariano Guadalupe Vallejo's history of California, his sheer tome-like approach to writing history seems painfully unaware that his insistence on the historic significance of the Californio will have little impact.

Like the takeover of California itself, even the retelling of Californio history was a site of struggle, but as indicated also a curious colonial site of desire. With little or no access to English-reading audiences, Californio-told stories were few and far between. In a short amount of time, the actual telling of California history fell to Anglo-American writers. This demographic preponderance of Anglo-published history drowned out culturally the voice of the Californio. Its actual appearance in print was a rarity. Helen Elliott Bandini, writing for the *Overland Monthly*, actually goes out of her way to acknowledge the published historical sketch by a niece of Mariano Guadalupe Vallejo that appeared in the *Century Magazine*'s "The Gold Hunters of California" series.

"Ranch and Mission Days in Alta California"

In December of 1890 the *Century Magazine* published an insider's view of Californio history, a history that was considered rapidly receding and all too dependent on human memory for transmission. Earlier that same year, perhaps the most well-known and celebrated Californio, Mariano Guadalupe Vallejo, an iconic figure even before the Mexican-American War, died. Did the *Century* editors solicit a historical sketch from his niece Guadalupe Vallejo because there was a sense that a generational moment was about to pass and that it required an authentic voice to mark its passage? Or did they solicit her sketch "Ranch and Mission Days in Alta California" because it would confirm in their minds, as had Mariano Guadalupe Vallejo's death itself, that the historical moment of the Californio was truly over and that there was now nothing to worry about when it came to the Californio, either politically or culturally?

What motivated Guadalupe Vallejo to write the sketch? Was it the death of her famous uncle and his generation of Californios? Should we then treat this sketch like an elegy? But would calling it an elegy mean she's complicit with forwarding the demise of the Californio? Partly what makes her motivation intriguing is the relative paucity of published materials by Californios in English. While several Spanish-language presses, as evidenced by a number of newspapers, continued to operate after 1848 in California, English-language publications by Californios were few and far between. Anglo chronicler of the Californios Helen Elliott Bandini clearly laments the absence of more writing like Guadalupe Vallejo's: "It is a pity that one who writes so well, and must have such rich store of facts, romance, and tradition, to draw from should not oftener favor the public" (20). Even though Bandini clearly sees herself in her writings as a friend of the Californio, having married into an influential Californio family of San Diego, there is a hint in her validation of Guadalupe Vallejo's sketch as the seed of something troubling. Bandini's language of "facts, romance, and tradition" (20) indicates a generic preference for a Californio text that is potentially performative of an ethnic history and just that, not a preference for some kind of representation of Californios for California. Instead, "facts, romance, and tradition" identify a text that can be absorbed and appropriated rather than dialogued with or challenged.

In general, Guadalupe Vallejo's sketch mirrored much of what was already known and published about pre-Anglo Alta California, but if the historic contours of her sketch were familiar, scattered throughout the text there erupted a tone that was not. This tone, I would argue, indicates that she was not interested in entertaining Anglo readers: "It seems to me that there never was a more peaceful or happy people on the face of the earth than the Spanish, Mexican, and Indian population of Alta California before the American conquest. We were the pioneers of the Pacific coast, building towns and Missions while General Washington was carrying on the war of the Revolution, and we often talk together of the days when a few hundred large Spanish ranches and Missions tracts occupied the whole country from the Pacific to the San Joaquin" (183). This opening paragraph signaled a quiet but open break from the formal niceties that her uncle had insisted on from friends and family alike since the first grumblings that all was not well under the new U.S. government. By 1890 those grumblings had evolved to a new political fate, and while few Californios doubted the "truth" of the past, it was the future that was painfully doubtful. Yet the only way to negotiate that future, at least in print culture, was to insist on a historical reckoning with the California that Californios had built and claimed. This historicizing impulse was reasonable given the tremendous changes since 1848, but it encouraged a generic response that limited and circumscribed more "creative" writing. On the other hand, throughout the Southwest, there was little political room for creative writing by people of Mexican descent. Under a different set of social, racial, and political conditions, a Mexican American Bret Harte might have existed, but he or she did not. With a few exceptions,

Mexican American writing in the nineteenth century seemed fated to be historical and documentary in approach.

Given the Victorian protocols of the times, Vallejo's break with a "grin-and-bear-it" civility is startling and instructive of how we might read anew this period's Californio writings. Her text, despite its passive verb construction, "It seems to me...," manages an artful and radical distance from the presumed Anglo readers of the *Century Magazine*. While her sketch is hardly an all-out condemnation of the United States, the phrase "the American conquest," though also buried in the passive tense, shatters any pretense about the writer's ideological perspective. Read carefully, one can notice how Vallejo seeks to differentiate not just the past from the present but to dislodge momentarily from the present time of December 1890 an overwhelmingly celebratory Anglo-American claim on California. As she continues, she offers both a representation of Californio culture, as anchored in the visible institutions of the missions and ranches, and a verbal remapping of a territory that by 1890 was all but owned or controlled by Anglo-American ranchers and business interests such as the railroads.

While her nostalgic use of memory echoes many a Californio lament common at the time, Vallejo strategically maneuvers nostalgia beyond sentimentality and remorse, and instead, she reconstructs nostalgia so it shoulders both a critique of the Anglo-American period and the basis for a nativist regional pride. By the end of her sketch, Vallejo articulates an alternative regional exceptionalism: since the American conquest, no one has experienced the happiness the Californio once had, and no one ever will again. In short, if Alta California was Eden in the Américas, 1848 represents the region's fall from grace. Her reengineered nostalgia effectively claims a California frozen in time, and beyond political and cultural Anglo intrusion. (I have more to say about the role of nostalgia, its role in the Spanish fantasy heritage movement, and its potential for critique in the next chapter.)

At one level, her text can be read as a direct challenge to the presumed privileged status of the Anglo reader of the *Century Magazine*. There are a number of instances in the sketch where one detects a self-conscious attempt to resist Anglo-American hegemony, especially as it maligns the

Californio, but this kind of postnational reading that resists the ideological impulse to naturalize the ascendancy of the United States in the nineteenth century doesn't necessarily tell the whole story. More broadly, Vallejo's text illustrates quite well the complex set of power relationships and social identities Mignolo has identified over the years in his study of colonialism in the Américas. In particular, I would argue that her text displays several of the key concepts in Mignolo's work on coloniality.

Vallejo's sketch in the *Century Magazine* underscores a long-term Anglo print culture fascination of the Californio. As the presence of this sketch indicates, this fascination was not only about appropriation and colonial subordination of the Californio but also a complicated form of admiration. As such, print culture had established by 1890 a fairly dynamic discourse on the topic of Californios. Collectively, this discourse drove a curiosity about Californios that unintentionally produced and reproduced public rhetorical spaces for articulating and disseminating what Mignolo calls "colonial difference." With her "It seems to me . . ." introduction, Vallejo's sketch is a prime example of a text that erupts into the space of colonial difference. For Mignolo, this space is "where the coloniality of power is enacted," that is made visible, and simultaneously the space where there is a "restitution of subaltern knowledge" alongside the emergence of "border thinking" (preface, ix). Because the current state of affairs of the Californios is an unhappy one, Vallejo grants herself permission to engage overtly within this space of "colonial difference." This engagement is immediate, racialized, and highly rhetorical.

For example, Vallejo shows her generational difference with and defiance of her uncle when she groups "Spanish, Mexican, and Indian" into one regionally identifiable community of people. All three groups, she means to argue, were better off in the past than the present. Although rhetorically persuasive as nostalgia, her regional consolidation of pre-1848 communities belies the history of racial hierarchies that had produced a caste society long before the arrival of Anglo-Americans. Nonetheless, here rhetorically united people come together to confront the importation of a different colonial power matrix with its own set of hierarchies, mythologies, and histories. As if to make the point of "colonial difference" with another colonialist community all the clearer, she segues from her opening sentence to a validation of the Californio's European and Enlightenment credentials: "We were the pioneers of the Pacific coast, building towns and Missions while General Washington was carrying on the war of the Revolution, and we often talk together of the days when a few hundred large Spanish ranches and Missions tracts occupied the whole country from the Pacific to the San Joaquin. No class of American citizens is more loyal than the Spanish Californians, but we shall always be especially proud of the traditions and memories of the long pastoral age before 1840" (183). By unpacking the significance of her verbal confrontations in the sketch, one can demonstrate how her text not only deconstructs the coloniality that has allowed a printed Californio voice in the *Century*, but that the deconstruction itself points out different layers of coloniality between marked Anglo and Californio positions, and between these positions there is a deep interaction because of the dominant regional identification in the text.

Here, Mignolo's thinking on colonialism as a semiotic field is dramatically pertinent: "Colonial semiosis refers to a conflictive domain of semiotic interactions among members of radically different cultures engaged in a struggle of imposition and appropriation, on the one hand, and of resistance, opposition and adaptation on the other" ("Colonial Situations," 93). This kind of semiotic engagement is clearly evident in Vallejo's balancing of the sentence, "No class of American citizens is more loyal than the Spanish Californian," with the immediate caveat, "but we shall always be especially proud of the traditions and memories of the long pastoral age before 1840." Not to claim U.S. citizenship was not really an option for her. There was already a cultural and political mindset since 1848 that did not feel obliged to adhere to the tenets of the Treaty of Guadalupe Hidalgo, in particular those tenets negotiated to insure U.S. citizenship and all subsequent rights for thousands of people of Mexican descent throughout the Southwest and West. Vallejo's balancing act also reveals the depth of her desire not to jettison a past ethnic heritage in exchange for citizenship. In her mind, the two positions coexisted in the figure of the Californio quite well, and American loyalty did not require, as nativists of the 1890s claimed, the erasure of ethnic identities or cultural habits.

All the same, Vallejo's balancing act depends on her rhetorically maneuvering between the political and racial distance that exists between the understood meanings of "American citizens" and "Spanish Californians." It decisively turns on her deployment of the term "Spanish Californian" rather than "Californio" or even "Mexicano." It marks her attempt to narrow the radical distance that exists between her class of Americans and the Anglo readers of the *Century Magazine*. If two sentences before she meant to highlight the distance between her readers and her community by presenting a united ethnic front, here she narrows that cultural space in order to forward European credentials and to reassert an old racial superiority that favors the white logic of U.S. citizenship in the late nineteenth century. In this way, Guadalupe Vallejo resembles not only her famous uncle's admiration of Anglo-American style democracy and entrepreneurship but also her uncle's erstwhile compatriot and writer María Amparo Ruiz de Burton.

The term "Spanish Californian" concretizes for Vallejo the kind of "colonial semiosis" that would signal resistance even in a context of subjugation. Mignolo writes: "Colonial situations [the meeting-up of two ethnic communities of unequal technological advancement and adherents of different religions] are shaped by a process of transformation in which members of both the colonized as well as the colonizing cultures enter into a particular kind of human interaction, colonial semiosis[,] . . . conceived as a context of cross-cultural interactions, and territorial representations . . . [that] become a battle ground in which power is equated with truth and offers the possibility of circumventing the denial of coevalness by looking at the coexistence of similar semiotic practices" ("Colonial Situations," 94). Although Mignolo had more in mind the radical distance that existed between colonized indigenous communities in the Américas and colonizing Europeans when he conceptualized terms such as "colonial semiosis" or "colonial difference," Guadalupe Vallejo's semiotic renaming of the Californio as Spanish Californian recalls how hotly contested California was as a potential colonial territory by distinct European powers, from the Russians and British to the Spanish and Mexicans. It was inevitable that the original "colonial situation" of California, which was Spanish and Catholic, would be scrutinized for weaknesses and challenged by outsiders bent on creating their own "colonial situation." Interestingly, Vallejo alludes to this inevitably when she notes the end of the Californio pastoral period as 1840—not 1846, the start of the Mexican-American War, nor 1848, the signing of the Treaty of Guadalupe Hidalgo, and not even 1849, the beginning of the gold rush. Without any comment, she forwards this date. Unless she truly expected her *Century Magazine* reader to be conversant with the history of Alta California, there is no way an outsider could know that 1840 was the year of the Graham Affair.

According to Alan Rosenus, 1840 was the year Guadalupe Vallejo's cousin, the governor of Alta California, Juan B. Alvarado, ordered their mutual uncle, then commandant general of the territory, Mariano Guadalupe Vallejo, "to expel the would-be revolutionaries" such as Isaac Graham, who openly talked about "a Texas-style takeover" of Alta California (18–22). Thus, Guadalupe Vallejo embeds in her text, even as she professes the loyalty of Spanish Californians, a counter-discourse replete with dates, events, and places that directs the reader's attention to the evidence of discord and conflict left behind by Anglo-American adventurers and business interests. Though muted by the passage of time, Guadalupe Vallejo marshals out this evidence as a counterpoint to her own territorial mapping of Alta California as family history. While her stated goal is "to tell, as plainly and carefully as possible, how the Spanish settlers lived, and what they did in the old days" (183), she also makes it quite clear that she reveals the intimate details of Californio life, which "no modern writer"—her euphemism for the Anglo outsider—"can possibly obtain except vaguely, from hearsay, since they exist in no manuscript, but only in the memories of a generation that is fast passing away" (183). In short, she means to draw from not only what her mother has told her but also the recollections of her uncle, General Mariano Guadalupe Vallejo.

Viewing her sketch as a semiotic battlefield, Mignolo's colonial truth lies in Guadalupe Vallejo's strategically contesting Anglo-American appropriations of California on the one hand, but on the other forwarding the kind of "territorial representation" that would confirm the "colonial situation" in 1890. For Vallejo, her sketch is a territorial representation that coexists and is coeval with the U.S. mapping of the region as the thirty-first state of the union. As she concludes her opening section, Guadalupe Vallejo remembers the family's original patriarch, Don Ygnacio Vallejo, who was instrumental in the early efforts of colonizing Alta California: "The traditions and records of the family cover the entire period of the annals of early California, from San Diego to Sonoma" (183). Thus, in one sentence, Guadalupe Vallejo conflates with gentle ease family history with territorial designs; Northern and Southern California come together under one all-encompassing patronymic name: Vallejo.

Contesting Semiotics: English versus Spanish

In post-1848 California, the use of discursive space as a contested semiotic field with territorial designs is not unique to Guadalupe Vallejo, especially if and when that field locates the contest through tensions that momentarily suspend the real and symbolic power and authority of the Anglo-American presence in California. Not surprisingly, such contested fields might go undetected whenever the writer purposely conceals or belittles the semiotic field being represented by adhering to the protocols of the picturesque sketch *Century* editors called for at the time. This is precisely the case of Amalia Sibrian's clever use of nostalgia as cultural tool, if not weapon, to turn the tables. She inverts and deflects the typical condescending cultural gaze of Anglo writers of her time.

In her "Gold Hunters of California" sketch, entitled "A Spanish Girl's Journey from Monterey to Los Angeles," Sibrian recounts a seemingly simple tale of an actual journey that took place in the early winter of 1829. Sibrian's father took her and her mother on a trip to Los Angeles to acquire papers that named the father to a government appointment. Some sixty-two years later, what Sibrian remembers, what she wants to recount for the *Century Magazine* readership is basically the greenhorn behavior of a young American who did not know a word of Spanish. Having arrived in Monterey via Mexico City, the nameless young American asks her father if he might accompany the family in their journey to Los Angeles. The father agrees, and from then on, the American provides Sibrian one remarkable incident after another as they stop at the homes where arrangements have been made for lodging during the trip:

> He did not know a word of Spanish, and I have often laughed at some of his experiences on the road, owing to his ignorance of our ways and speech. At one house, the señora gave him some fruit, whereupon he handed her two reals, which she let fall on the floor in surprise, while the old don, her husband, fell upon his knees and said in Spanish, "Give us no money, no money at all; everything is free in a gentleman's house!" A young lady who was present exclaimed in great scorn, "Los Engleses pagar por todos!" ("The English pay for everything.") I afterward told the American what they had said, and explained the matter as well as I could, but he thought it a foolish thing that no one, not even servants, would take money for services. We several times met grown people, and heads of families, who had never heard any language except Spanish, and who did not know, in fact, that any other language existed. They were really afraid of our American, and once I was asked if there were any other people like him. (469)

This is a provocative incident to be sure, but what's interesting is Sibrian's lack of sympathy for the greenhorn American in 1829, as well as in 1891. Instead of forgiving his unknowing, erring ways, Sibrian holds him up for criticism for refusing to understand the code of hospitality toward strangers that was a marker of classed behavior among the Californio elite. Thus, the young lady's scorn highlights the American's boorish behavior as a byproduct of the relationship between the English language—the American by speech is English—and a capitalism that was associated by then with a Yankee commercialism that could purchase its way into foreign cultures. As if this scornful observation were not enough, Sibrian dramatizes the effect of the young American on the California populace by the threat that this American's English speech poses to Spanish speakers of the countryside. Their worry that there might be more like him has an ironic fruition in the actual readers of the *Century Magazine*, who, like their counterparts in California, represent the dominant citizenry of the nation.

This sketch is obviously meant to be humorous, but the next two incidents further underscore the hostile engagement between Spanish and English speakers that Sibrian chooses to memorialize: "The young American picked up some words in Spanish; he could say '*Gracios,*' '*Si, señor,*' and a few other phrases. One day we passed a very ugly Indian woman, and he asked me how to ask her how old she was. Out of mischief I whispered, 'Yo te amor,' which he said at once, and she, poor creature, immediately rose from her seat on the ground and replied, '*Gracios, Señor, pero soy indio*' ('but I am an Indian'), which gave us sport till long after" (469). Again, this incident raises many issues one might want to comment on, especially how the humor hinges on the racist portrayal of the elderly Indian woman, whose own indigenous language is absent on the page. All the same, Sibrian's mischief is clear; she meant to embarrass the American by committing him to a different social faux pas. The indigenous woman's response, "soy indio," to his supposed "I love you" reignites the colonialist caste system that was firmly in place in 1829, so ingrained that the indigenous woman, again supposedly, willingly subordinates herself through speech to the coloniality of power that regulates race relations, especially around sexuality, so as to explain why she cannot reciprocate the American's declaration of love. Sibrian goes on to describe how the American took his own linguistic revenge by tricking her into believing that the phrase "Dam-fools!" meant praise. A year or two later, she realized much to her consternation that what she took for "proper English" was in fact "bad words" (469).

All the same, other bad words are present as well. There are a number of mistakes in Spanish in this sketch, from conjugation to spelling to gendered endings. Although difficult to verify with any degree of certainty, they can be read as either simple editorial mistakes by the *Century Magazine*, despite the rudimentary Spanish invoked here, or some deeper word play by Sibrian herself meant to draw attention to the linguistic battle at play in her sketch and perhaps throughout the whole "Gold Hunters of California" series itself. Through these incidents, Sibrian makes use of the tension in the semiotic field not only to relay cultural differences between Anglos and Californios but to preserve and champion typical Californio values that were quickly disappearing with the demographic decline of the Californios as a landed class. Like Guadalupe Vallejo, Amalia Sibrian makes as much use of her textual presence as possible to wield nostalgia toward purposeful ends, reinserting a cultural map of Alta California that both predates the gold rush but also reattests to the sovereignty of that prior colonial territory.

Despite the intense curiosity of the Old California by documenting individuals such as Bancroft, periodicals such as the homegrown *Overland Monthly*, or fiction by writers as diverse as Josiah Royce, Frank Norris, Gertrude Atherton, and Helen Hunt Jackson, Californios or Californianas very rarely found, it should be stressed again, a public outlet for their voices or their stories in English. So opportunities for producing contesting semiotic fields in English were also few and far between. By contrast, the Spanish-language press did not have this problem, nor did its editors have to disguise their semiotic engagements. On the other hand, because the writing is in Spanish, its cultural influence circulates for sure, but the degree of its contestatory range is bracketed by its subordinated position as a minority newspaper. Thus, a satirical poem like "Un tipo" echoes many of the linguistic challenges found in Sibrian's sketch, but the focus is internal to the likely readership of this newspaper from Los Angeles in the early 1880s:

UN TIPO
A mi amigo Manuel F. Martínez

Aquí va un tipo, Manuel,
De aquellos que ni se sueñan;
Tipo ingertado de gringo,
Con resabios de canela.
Si digo algún disparate,
No le marques el alerta,
Porque entonces, caro amigo.
No leerás ni una cuarteta.
Comienzo pues con mi cuento.
Aguza tú, bien la oreja,
Y pon cuidado al asunto
Si es que en algo te interesa.
Conocí aquí en California
Una paisana muy bella,
Que coronaba su vida

Con diez y ocho primaveras.
Mas como estaba educada
En la americana escuela,
Inglesaba alguna frases
Que olían á gringo á la lengua
Con frecuencia se le oía
Llamar al cesto *basqueta*
Contar las cuadras por *bloques*,
A un cerco decirle *fensa*,
Al café llamarlo *cofe*,
A los mercados *marquetas*,
Al tendejón *grosseria*,
Y *tabla* á lo que era mesa;
A un compromiso *enganche*
Partida si había una fiesta;
Si iba á un baile era á la *bola*
Y á la *chorcha* sí era iglesia.
Una vez oí que dijo
A su amiga Filomena:
Por fin estoy *enganchada*
Con don Cosme de Varela,
Y es un *espaniar* que tiene
Muchos *bisnes* y muy buena
Porción que todas envidian
Y que corre hoy por mi cuenta.
Así pensaba y hablaba
La paisanita morena,
Que pintaba su semblante
Con carmín, para estar huera.
Y todo lo dicho, amigo,
No es una sombra siquiera
De este tipo que aquí abunda
Como en el caos las tinieblas.
Por nadie digo lo dicho.

A nadie mi pluma hiera;
Mas que se ponga este saco
Al que le ajuste o le venga. (Ruiz, *Hispanic Poetry*, 417–18)

The anonymous poet's caricature of the paisana's English-inflected Spanish reveals another dimension to the linguistic battlefield noted in Sibrian's sketch: the deleterious effect of the ever-growing presence of English in California on Castilian Spanish. Besides the corruption of Castilian Spanish speakers, there are, the poet also argues, additional cultural costs to this "gringo" influence in Los Angeles. Both the friend Manuel and la paisana have undergone deep changes: In line 3, Manuel is likened to a plant or fruit tree that has been spliced with another specimen to create a hybrid. In line 44, la paisana is faulted for applying cosmetics that whiten her "morena" face. This poet's satire and sarcasm about the destabilizing influence of American English on Spanish and Spanish speakers can be found in the Spanish-language press from New York and Philadelphia to Los Angeles and San Francisco. In fact, this kind of social criticism becomes a subgenre of the cultural and linguistic work these newspapers were meant to perform in the wake of 1848. If, in effect, Guadalupe Vallejo and Amalia Sibrian eventually have the means to argue in English for the past dominance and importance of the Californio in essence charting a prior sovereignty through nostalgia, Spanish-language newspapers through direct editorials or poems like "Un tipo" work to uphold a cultural sovereignty in the present by reconstituting the terms by which this Spanish-speaking community can imagine itself, especially as its proto-nationalist traits are being threatened by a hegemonic Anglo America.

By contrast, let's try to imagine that María Amparo Ruiz de Burton had written *The Squatter and the Don* (1885) in Spanish, something she could have easily done. She could have chosen to do what the Spanish-language press in California was attempting to do in the 1880s, to shore up Californio/Mexican identity from within. But she did not. I would argue she did not because she wanted to publish in English for financial reasons first and foremost but also because publishing in English allowed her to engage politically with the dominant powers of her world in the 1880s. Also, her status as a woman allowed only certain kinds of engagements in the public sphere through Spanish. Publishing novels in the United States as a woman by 1880 no longer had a severe public stigma attached to it; not so writing in Spanish. One risked social censure if publishing in Spanish as an upper-class woman. In this regard, a Californio man of letters would have a distinct advantage.

Mariano Guadalupe Vallejo's True Pioneers

While we know a fair amount of Mariano Guadalupe Vallejo's voluminous historical writings about California, *Recuerdos históricos y personales tocante á la Alta California* (1875), less focus has been put on the times that he wrote for public events with a live audience. As a man, his engagement in the public sphere was not limited to the printed page. When we do see him at public events, we see Vallejo ushered in and treated as a patriarch, and in that role he is often asked to narrate the history of California. Invariably he constructs a semiotic contestatory field that resorts to nostalgia, if only to empower a celebration of a Spanish heritage as the original foundation of civilization in California. Here too nostalgia merges with sovereignty to make the broad case of the national and global citizenry of the Californio, past and present. Such is the case when Mariano Guadalupe Vallejo was recruited to provide the history of the founding of Mission San Francisco de Asís for its centennial celebration on October 8, 1876. This was a task that he was more than prepared and willing to do, having just concluded the year before his five-volume memoirs on the broad historical topic of Alta California. Like his *Recuerdos históricos y personales*, this address before an estimated eleven thousand people at the Mechanics' Pavilion, an audience that included dignitaries such as Archbishop Alemany, California governor William Irwin, San Francisco mayor A. J. Bryant, and consul generals from foreign countries, was delivered in Spanish.[6]

In this public address, Vallejo employs the very same historical method as he does in his *Recuerdos*, a comprehensive memoir he wrote at the bequest of Bancroft, who was collecting documents and personal narratives from Anglo-Americans and Californios to write his own history of California. Marissa López reads Vallejo's *Recuerdos* as dialoguing and often at odds with

Bancroft's own method of writing history. In the context of nationalism, López distinguishes the difference between their methods as "history as a function of the economic consolidation of national identity and history as a rhetorical link to the past" (*Chicano Nations*, 69). In contrast to Bancroft, López argues that Vallejo "becomes the voice of a textual national community that recognizes its porous boundaries, its lack of centripetal force, and its contingent existence in relation to other nations" (69). Because of Californios' contingency to the nation-state, López further argues that Vallejo resorts to a historical method that can make use of his own personal history in the state, his family status, and extensive family relationships throughout California. Again in contrast to Bancroft, who insists on seeing the historian as an objective, depersonalized lens on the past, López finds Vallejo as resisting that claim and instead embracing the inherent biases that any writer of history brings to the text as a strength, not a weakness.

As a result, Vallejo's version of historical truth is predicated on his projection of himself as "bearing a synechdochal relation to the history of California" (74). Nevertheless, López astutely reminds us that Vallejo's subject position is not a trifling matter: "Vallejo's very present textual self and his reliance on letters, documents, and personal relationships in the construction of his narrative suggest the paternalism of the Spanish *hacendado*, who operated within a market economy structured around the patriarchal family" (75). All this is present in Vallejo's centennial address, with the added challenge of performing a history under the very scrutiny of those who actually control the future of the state.

In a rhetorical method that anticipates what his niece Guadalupe Vallejo will employ some fifteen years later, Mariano Guadalupe Vallejo saturates his address with a fluid density of historical dates, names, events, and places that make clear that European-descended people founded Alta California. By rehearsing a colonial history that predates Anglo-American hegemony, including social, legal, and economic institutions, Vallejo in effect is challenging the ruling colonial Anglo-American enterprise. Through subtle means, he obliges his audience, English and Spanish speakers alike, to interrogate their regional subject position under the logos of an Anglo America. In effect, Vallejo makes use of the anniversary to create what Matt Cohen calls a "publication event," a semiotic field in which there is a performance, "an embodied act of information exchange," a saturated and spatialized exchange where "the publication event presumes that its participants are aware that an act of communication is intended (though they may not be aware of the customs and rhetorics shaping it)" (7).

By inference rather than direct confrontation, Vallejo's address reasserts a colonial enterprise that has nothing to do with Anglo America:

> Honored by the cordial invitation tendered me by the Board of Directors of the present celebration, through the most Reverend Archbishop Alemany, I present myself before you for the purpose of narrating, in a few but significant words, the history of the discovery, occupation and foundation of this Mission of our holy Father, San Francisco de Asis, a name which it has borne with dignity since the time it was so called by the indefatigable missionary, Father-President Junipero Serra and companions, in respect and veneration for the founder of their Seraphic Order.
>
> Would that I were possessed of the necessary ability to do justice to the merits of those men, to whom is due the civilization of so many thousands of souls, and of numberless others that will succeed them.
>
> But, if my incapacity is great, my ardent desire to comply with the duty which has been imposed upon me, and which I have gladly accepted, is still greater. I only wish to ask your indulgence.
>
> I shall be as brief in my discourse as a subject of such great magnitude as this will permit. Before, however, entering into the particulars of our present subject matter, I may be permitted to give a condense synopsis of the events by which this port of San Francisco came into the possession of the Crown of Spain. (97)

Just over 9,200 words in length, Vallejo's address must have taken possession of his audience for at least an hour, if not more. Vallejo must have perceived this invitation as a singular opportunity. According to P. J. Thomas, among the eleven thousand present, "The Spanish, Mexican, and South American elements were largely represented in the immense throng, which was graced by the presence of many members of the clergy of the Province" (75). In other words, this audience was largely composed of a Spanish-speaking audience listening to a Spanish-spoken address.

When Vallejo finally gets around to narrating the founding of Mission San Francisco, his diction is that of a lay sermon, ever so mindful of a Catholic ecclesiastical history of Alta California in general and Northern California specifically. He again goes into great detail with dates, names, places, and events, many of which involve him or other family members. But it is also interesting how he actively omits certain kinds of references that would have been logical to make. Thus, he begins again, "On the 8th day of October of the mentioned year, 1776, the erection of the present temple of the Mission of San Francisco was commenced, and we to-day on this centennial anniversary, have met here, not only to honor the memory of those who dedicated it to the service of God, but also to show our admiration of the great principles by which they were impelled, namely, the faith of Him who died nailed to the cross for the redemption of man" (107). Vallejo, in most baroque manner, links the founding of Mission of San Francisco to the death of Christ on the Cross, joining divine sacrifice with colonial enterprise on the West Coast of the continent, totally ignoring the meaning of the other centennial text for that year: the Declaration of Independence, signed in Philadelphia. The significance of the year was not lost on the speaker previous to Vallejo, John W. Dwinelle, an elected official and Protestant. Though obviously respectful of the Catholic church, Dwinelle makes reference to the Declaration of Independence and resulting revolution to argue that the Catholic church is stronger in the United States precisely because of its territorial expansion into lands once claimed by Spain and France (94).

For his rhetorical turn, Vallejo suspends that other founding narrative, marginalizing it, as well as the territorial expansion of the United States. He continues, as López would argue, by interweaving family history with church history, and both with a spatial mapping that is local and global:

> Providence, which is infinitely wise and bountiful, has permitted that our venerable pastor should make mention of my father's being one of those brave men who aided and assisted the missionaries with his sword. Consequently, at the same time that I satisfy your desires, I

comply with a duty very satisfactory to myself in being the exponent of events that transpired one hundred years ago, the date upon which commenced the life and existence of San Francisco, which we can with pride style the Queen City of the Pacific. *Justitoe [sic] soror fides*—Faith is the sister of Justice. I shall be guided in my remarks by a pure and holy love for these two sisters. The invigorating breath of the gospel, as I said before, was given to us by some Franciscan Friars, who were indeed poor and humble Missionaries of Good, but rich in Faith and Hope in the success of their grand and arduous task. By this means were sown the prolific seeds of Christianity that has given such marvelous results during the one hundred years of its existence, which this rich and populous city counts; having written it to-day the Metropolitan Church, and which, by circumstances and coincidences that would be too lengthy to narrate, bears also the name of San Francisco. The Metropolitan Church, I said. Yes, it is the one over which our worthy Archbishop Alemany so honorably presides. (107–8)

Having wrapped the past and present in "Justitoe [sic] soror fides—Faith is the sister of Justice," his rhetorical hand is practically invisible as he reorients the meaning of Christianity when he renames Mission San Francisco as the Metropolitan Church, by which he means the larger diocese that bears the same name of San Francisco, which is also of course the "Queen City of the Pacific." If before he omits through ignoring the Anglo-American significance of 1776, here he omits through a thorough rendering of the Catholic foundation of San Francisco the city the simple fact that Catholics are a religious minority in San Francisco, as well as in the whole state in post–gold rush California. Nevertheless, in the context of this respatialized Catholic San Francisco, Vallejo encourages a meditation on the passage of one hundred years:

> Let us for a moment transport ourselves from this day to the former century, and let us compare the present gathering here to an assemblage of that epoch. The latter consisted of a handful of men who were brave Christians, armed to the teeth, and of another still smaller party of humble ministers of Christ, but gifted with wonderous fortitude

and a firm determination that nothing could change or oppose, as they had come to preach the Word of God and were resigned to take upon themselves the crown of martyrdom. Both of these parties were liable to become at any moment the victims of a rude crowd of naked savage gentiles, some of whom had come to them at first through curiosity, others prompted by a spirit of destruction, and all of them to obtain the presents which were given to them for the purpose of alluring them and inspiring them with confidence and have them hear for the first time the words of the Gospel. (108)

Striking on images that verge on the language of crusades but certainly reminiscent of Spanish conquistadores and priests who together sacrificed for "God, Gold, and Glory," Vallejo prepares his audience for the present as he proceeds from 1776 to 1876, carefully outlining each significant political period in between but one, the American period since 1846. Vallejo literally stops narrating the history of Mission San Francisco with that year. Instead, with great rhetorical flourish, he commends his audience more than once for representing the culmination of a hundred-year arc of historical significance.

The audience whom I have the honor to address on this occasion is a true representative of the high culture and advanced civilization of the nineteenth century, enjoying all the security and privileges which that state of society guarantees to them.

What a vast difference, gentlemen, between what was, and what we see to-day, in this centennial which we celebrate! Let us bear in mind that in the course only of one hundred years, this privileged place has taken a gigantic stride and fallen into the hands of a society worthy of prosecuting the work that was begun by those true Pioneers. The Mission of San Francisco, which at one time was situated on a desert, yet protected by the hand of Providence, to-day may be seen nearly in the centre of this populous city of the same name. (108)

Further, Vallejo visualizes on behalf of his audience the demographic extent of that centennial arc, calling attention not just to the number of people who resided in the region of Mission San Francisco but on their very Catholic identity. Having established through oration the present audience as the rightful sons and daughters of those "true Pioneers," Vallejo wants his audience, as Thomas wrote, mostly made up of "Spanish, Mexican, and South American elements," to take credit for the growth of its demographic and for its powerful cosmopolitan and commercial relation to Asia:

> I have occupied the attention of this intelligent audience so long for the purpose of giving a detailed narration of the primitive history of the Presidio, Mission and Pueblo of San Francisco, which up to the year 1846, did not count a population any greater than that within this fine hall—a weak fortification, one or two officers, a company of soldiers and a handful of resident settlers in twenty-five or thirty houses.
>
> What a change is presented to our view to-day! A great city, which, having absorbed the three points mentioned, has filled the entire peninsula with a population of nearly three hundred thousand inhabitants, dedicated to all the arts known to the highest degree of civilization. The harbor and city, protected by strong fortifications and well-equipped ships of war, situated on the most advantageous position, it is destined to become the grand commercial center of India, China and Japan, at the same time that it will be such for the entire northern coast of the Pacific. What shall be the destiny which the Supreme Benefactor has prepared for this portion of our beautiful native land for the next coming hundred years? I entertain the full conviction that the hand of the Great Creator, by which is guided the progress and happiness of mankind, will carry us to the highest degree of excellence in all the branches of knowledge. Then, it is to be hoped, that those who will celebrate that day taking a retrospective view of the present epoch, will remember with gratitude what this generation, by divine aid, has established for them, to carry on, until they reach moral, intellectual and physical perfection. (121–22)

With lofting language, he exhorts his Spanish listeners not to see themselves as a Catholic minority in a sea of three hundred thousand Protestants but rather to embrace the "divine aid" that has been bestowed on the region in anticipation of their presence. Through eloquence, manners, and family genealogy, General Vallejo, as he was presented to the crowd, takes on the role of prophet, a role he was quite used to, in fact, as he comes to a close: "And let us from this moment send cordial salutations to our fortunate descendants who will see the brilliant dawn of the second Centennial of the Foundation of the Mission of San Francisco de Asís" (122). Casting an eye toward the "brilliant dawn" of 1976, Vallejo projects himself and his audience, and their shared colonial Catholic heritage into a future, hoping for a generation descended from Californios that will remember what he and his generation had so painstakingly taken steps to preserve, a sense of progress based more on the glories of a regional past rather than wholehearted confidence in a national future.

On the Golden Shores of California

If Mariano Guadalupe Vallejo was worried about posterity's memory of him or the public reckoning with his generation's choices, he did not have far to go to pose those concerns. Indeed, much of his rhetorical legacy, which was all he had left by the time of his death on January 18, 1890, was in essence bequeathed to his surviving family members, in particular his son Platón Vallejo. Not long after his father's death, it becomes clearer and clearer to Platón that championing his father's legacy is increasingly difficult as the century comes to a close. Despite the many public and private moments of support—if not outright patriotism—for the United States, even the Vallejos could not help but register their frustration and anger at their declining social and political status. Writing on July 9, 1893, to William Heath Davis, who had written a memoir chronicling his time in California, *Sixty Years in California* (1889), Platón Vallejo found a sympathetic interlocutor. Indeed, Davis's sympathies ran deep. Mostly known as one of the founders of "New Town" in San Diego, Davis was one-quarter Hawaiian on his mother's side, and in 1847 he married María de Jesus Estudillo, daughter of José Joaquín Estudillo, whose land grant eventually became the town of San Leandro.

Because of these sympathies, Platón Vallejo believes he can complain freely about a census taker who had the audacity to question his nationality by identifying him as a foreigner. The census taker's official status is particularly painful, given that the Columbian World's Fair in Chicago, dedicated to Christopher Columbus's "discovery" of the New World four hundred years earlier, had formally opened the month before. Platón Vallejo stages his outrage in this manner:

> In the acquisition of this lovely California by the grandest of all nations of modern times my father (que en Dios descanse) may and can be truthfully said to have placed the diadem among the galaxy of stars that now adorn the fair brow of Columbia. And after this can I believe that anyone would or should have amiability to call me a foreigner?—Why I am an American by right of discovery, by right of conquest, by right of possession and by act of the *will* and not by accident or coercion. My people were heroes in the old country. These heroes discovered America. America has revolutionized the world. To land in America is to become a freeman. To set foot on the golden shores of California is equivalent to seeing the World's Fair all your life. ("A Letter," 101)

In memory of his father, Platón Vallejo treats his ancestors much like his cousin Guadalupe Vallejo did when she called settlers of Alta California "the saints and heroes of our history since the days when Father Juniper [Serra] planted the cross at Monterey" (183). In addition, this Vallejo pushes back on the census taker's definition of "American," expanding its origin and meaning beyond the exceptionalist ideology of the United States of the 1890s and returning it instead, like many before him, to its broader trajectory in the Américas earlier in the century.[7] Of course, he is also guided by an exceptionalist ideology. His exceptionalism mirrors an alternative regional coloniality that still seeks to compete with the Manifest Destiny that emerged from the eastern states. His claim "to land in America is to become a freeman" is not unlike that simultaneous suspension of disbelief and obfuscation in Ruiz de Burton's claim to whiteness in *The Squatter and the Don* when she exhorts, we "must wait and pray for a Redeemer who will emancipate the white slaves of California" (372). Both statements rely on their allegiance to settler colonialism's broad claim on behalf of Europe and of a self-evident natural ruling class to whom conquered lands are the spoils due to those heroes and saints willing to sacrifice life and limb.

It is hard to know what solace Platón Vallejo could draw from such a statement when it was well known that slavery and peonage existed side by side at the start of the settlement in Alta California. Nevertheless, any solace he could muster was fleeting and vulnerable to contemporary criticism: "But I fear that someone might read my letter and imagine that I was 'romancing.' I have not said one word about big pumpkins, nor the big trees, nor the treasures stored away in the vaults of the Sierras, and I do not wish to be thought to exaggerate" ("A Letter," 102). Here Platón Vallejo admits to the limits, if not dangers, of a fantasy Spanish heritage. Ripe for romance in the pages of the *Century Magazine*, in Helen Hunt Jackson's *Ramona* (1884), or even in the more regionally friendly hands of Gertrude Atherton's *Before the Gringo Came* (1894), nostalgia for Old California could easily be exaggerated and therefore dismissed as childish and inconsequential if it came from a Californio.

In the face of such resounding arrogance to override the voice of the speaking Californio or Californiana, like Miss Belle, with more "romancing," where could someone like Platón Vallejo go to get a hearing? I would argue he turns increasingly to what was already a known trope among Californios of his father's generation: California as Eden, a pastoral refuge. Sounding like John Muir, writing in that same period, Platón Vallejo finds a link with his father's generation through a love of place and ecology, thus departing from his father's exclusively historical arguments about the early settlement of California and moving instead to a long-term stewardship of those lands. So even as he complains to Davis about the census taker, he turns to this pastoral California for remedy: "To set foot on the golden shores of California is equivalent to seeing the World's Fair all your life. What a pity it would be if California were separated from the rest of the world! Where would you find another country like it! The beautiful hills and mountains. The bays and the grand ocean. And our glorious climate! If we could send these to Chicago—we'd never get them back I fear" ("A Letter," 101). These sentiments will increasingly occupy his reflections in the new century.

In his own memoirs (written 1914–15), Platón Vallejo would go on to labor against any hint of "romancing," insisting, as he does in this letter, that his regard for California and its wondrous attributes are something that people need to behold firsthand because they are "real" and unlike anything else in the world.[8] His passion to celebrate the Vallejo family history, San Francisco, and California, and all as a patriotic citizen of the United States, intensifies as the figure of the Californio endures increasing criticism for precisely those social, cultural, and political characteristics that were bound colonially and regionally to Atla California:

> It is said by some that the Hispano-Americans left no trace on the later institutions of California. With that statement I must beg to disagree. True, they were not able to show themselves at their best. Some yielded to the reckless temptations of the gold age. Others had their hands and brains occupied in litigation and squatter troubles, rowing out of the mighty influx of immigration. So, in a constructive way, they did not shine. They were not among the men who tore down mountains and performed other miracles. They did not build railways, construct transoceanic steamers or organize vast industries. All of this is true. (chapter 18, 52)

In other words, Vallejo concedes here to the charge that Hispano-Americans have not embraced the late nineteenth-century modes of capitalist production; as an ethnic group they have not enacted that brand of modernity that sought to capitalize on the territories won at the conclusion of the Mexican-American War. Given Vallejo's elision of ethnic labor history, his concession is more about the elite class of Hispano-Americans than actual laborers. They, the former landowning elite, have not weathered the new structures of coloniality well. Yet, as he concedes to one truth, he does so only to propose another.

His concession to the industrializing wonders of modernity allows him the rhetorical space to argue for a different but related form of cultural capital. For him, within the boundaries of the United States, which was all the more consolidated after the last hemispheric war, the Spanish-American War of 1898, the nation's accruing global standing nevertheless needs what only California can offer:

Nevertheless, the Californians left a deep impression on our social life, and I trust it may be permanent. You have all heard of the hospitality of California, which became famous through the world and is still one of the pleasant customs in our State. Do you know where that came from? It was neither more or less than a continuance of the broad, patriarchal, almost sacred habit of the Californians and of the early settlers from abroad to welcome the stranger within their gates. . . . There is no other country in the world where the word "welcome" is displayed so large on so many homes. It is this large brotherhood that makes us love our State; that makes the wanderer lonesome and eager to return. (chapter 18, 52)

To this structure of feeling that he equates with the status and importance of other social institutions, Vallejo broadens the meaning of hospitality to include the social arts like music, dancing, theater, and mirth making, but all within the orbit of the previous colonial, patriarchal space of Alta California. Altogether he insists that this shared ethic of living life was but a mirror of their physical environment: "Again, to the old Californians, everything in their beautiful young world on the Pacific coast looked bright, and, being by nature of a joyous disposition, they easily made their lives match their surroundings" (chapter 18, 52). In essence, his claims for an alternative mode of modernity lie in the very lifestyle and lifestyle choices that are typically considered pastoral and premodern. But instead of being antithetical to modernity, this ethic and lifestyle are precisely the means by which one can take refuge and pleasure when life becomes otherwise burdensome. The limits of modernity on the human psyche can only be addressed by returning to the natural laws of beauty and felicity, argues Vallejo: "If we have acquired from the Hispano-American something of our good fellowship, unknown elsewhere; if we have learned from him the trick of letting more sunshine into the dark corners of everyday life, he has indeed made an impression, has played a highly useful part, in a great social constructive scheme, more advanced than any other on the earth" (chapter 18, 52). So from his earlier language—"The beautiful hills and mountains. The bays and the grand ocean. And our glorious climate!"

("A Letter," 101)—Vallejo redirects well-known descriptions of the natural California, descriptions that are already feeding by this time the political economy of fantasy Spanish heritage, to be also proof of the Californio's contribution to modern civilization.

In this redirection, Platón Vallejo engages and enacts through writing an ethic of communal identity based on shared environmental values that Chicana eco-critic Priscilla Ybarra calls "goodlife writing": "Goodlife writing embraces the values of simplicity, sustenance, dignity, and respect. These are the four values I found to be consistent over the broad expanse of literature [by writers of Mexican descent in the United States, 1848–2010], and together they function to preserve mutually healthy relations among individuals and communities. The values in goodlife writing implicitly integrate the natural environment as part of the community, and thus cultivate a life-sustaining ecology for humans" (5). Echoing his father's projections into the future, Platón Vallejo's love for the California landscape, ecological wonders, and Californio-style hospitality as a civic institution form the basis of a regional environmental ideology that has come to replace what otherwise (land, social prominence, political control) has been lost since 1848. Ybarra argues that such a shift comes to identify a new iteration of patrimony. This revised patrimony does not depend wholly on the possession of land or control of the environment, but rather more on a spiritual and custodial relationship to land. Ybarra argues this shift is a fundamental response to Anglo-American hegemony after 1848. Ybarra writes: "Rather than allowing dispossession of the territories to comprise the center of their concerns, these writers reject the idea of possession itself as the bringer of misery, the practice that creates humiliation and subservience. . . . Simplicity, sustenance, dignity, and respect all benefit from the general principle of transcending possession in regard to human-to-nature as well as human-to-human relations" (6). All the same, while this shift may have produced necessary cultural work at the time, Ybarra argues two important points: "Mexican Americans lamented their loss of connection to the land in proportion to the degree to which they gained access to white privilege. These writers [of the early twentieth century] show the inner trauma caused when individuals choose not to delink from colonial/modern structures that alienate them from the land and from one another" (5). In this regard, Platón Vallejo will go on to instill in his daughter, Francisca Vallejo, not only a love for the "natural" California but a trauma over territorial loss, and its related prestige and wealth, altogether buoyed contradictorily by claims and access to white privilege.

As we shall see in the next chapter, through her own professed love for San Francisco and Northern California, Francisca Vallejo will continue to promote the family legacy and cultural patrimony, achieving a level of sophistication her father could have only dreamed of when he wrote: "This [San Francisco's potential realized], perhaps, I may not live to see, for though my heart is young, my years are many. But let us all unite, while time remains, to speed where 'manifest destiny' points" (chapter 16, 48). Like his father before him, Platón Vallejo holds out, even while facing his own mortality, that a partnership with Anglo America is still possible, but like his cousin Guadalupe Vallejo, he nonetheless suspects the family's better days are behind them. The next chapter takes up how and why Francisca Vallejo comes to claim a modernizing myth of California that was otherwise meant to be consumed first by the state and second by the rest of the nation, both at the expense of her own heritage.

2 Californio Settler History   Nostalgia as Patrimony

Remember me! When frozen, cold,
My heart forever sleeps;
And over my abandoned grave
The tomb-flower softly creeps.
Never more to see thee! But my soul
Of fire immortal cannot perish!
And through the night's mysterious calm,
Borne on the sighs of zephyrs—cherish
And hear the voices dear, that
Say to thee—Remember me!

In his sincere tribute to his deceased friend Dr. Platón Vallejo, George D. Lyman concludes his article for the California Historical Society in 1925 by quoting a poem that Mariano Guadalupe Vallejo wrote before his death.[1] Mariano Guadalupe Vallejo's granddaughter, Francisca Vallejo, had translated it into English so that Lyman could use it for his tribute to her father, Platón. By commemorating his friend through this poem, Lyman means to link Platón to his famous father, Mariano Guadalupe Vallejo. Indeed, through much of this loving portrait of Platón Vallejo, Lyman cannot help but also commemorate Mariano Guadalupe Vallejo. The two, for Lyman, are linked in the transition from colonial Old California to the thirty-first state of the Union. In his panoramic survey of the family's importance, he reifies by 1925 a broadly held perspective: "Beyond a doubt General Vallejo was the most notable and representative man of his people in the province, his position, during the Mexican rule, paralleling that of the proudest knights in Spain's heroic age" (284). But it is because of Platón Vallejo's education from the age of eleven on, first at Mount Saint Mary's College, Baltimore, Maryland, and later at the College of Physicians and Surgeons, Columbia University, New York, and his participation as battlefield surgeon during the Civil War that we also see Mariano Guadalupe Vallejo behave not only as a citizen of the United States but one with intimate access to the powers of the nation, an access that could explain how a family with so many regrets could nevertheless anchor their family's future with the Manifest Destiny of the nation (as noted at the end of chapter 1).

Underscoring this family's allegiance to the nation, Lyman finds it fitting to paraphrase from Platón Vallejo's own account of Mariano Guadalupe Vallejo's time in Washington DC where he met former friends, among them Generals Ulysses S. Grant, William Tecumseh Sherman, and Philip Sheridan. More important, though, he also met with President Abraham Lincoln. On more than one occasion, Mariano Guadalupe Vallejo displayed the kind of wit and foresight that had made him a regional leader in California:

> One day at a similar conversation after a long talk on the wonderful accomplishments of the California pioneers, a break came in the conversation and General Vallejo remarked in a musing way: "Mr. President, I hope a lot of our American people will go to hell before you and I get there." Doctor Vallejo was staggered at this unusual wish of his parent, but the President unperturbed, briefly asked: "Why?" "Because," said General Vallejo, "the Americans will change the climate, plant trees, introduce irrigation, build railroads, make everything cheerful and pleasant, and by the time we get there we can sit down at a marble top table and eat ice cream."
>
> President Lincoln thought so well of the General's opinion of Americans that he repeated this story several times. (288)

We can only speculate as to what motivated Mariano Guadalupe Vallejo to quip with Abraham Lincoln in such a manner. Perhaps, we are led to believe, it was to pierce through the president's melancholia over the war;

perhaps, it was an opportunity to do a bit of cultural work with the president to align himself, his family, and Californios to the broader, nation-building identity of pioneers; perhaps, and this is just as likely, he meant to link economic and political power in the East to the potential for its industrial expansion into the West.

Or was he too stricken with his own melancholia? Was it a melancholia that encouraged him to have some subversive sport with the president? Like Mark Twain's satirical short story "Captain Stormfield's Visit to Heaven" (1907–8), Mariano Guadalupe Vallejo's imagining a manicured heaven complete with an ice cream parlor, evidences an internal critique about the very same Manifest Destiny he otherwise supported when he argued for U.S. annexation at the junta (gathering) of Californio landowners and leaders in Monterey in May 1846. This firsthand and secondhand reiteration of a family anecdote at the center of national power during the Civil War bespeaks to yet another semiotic field with territorial designs in which the Vallejos are framed as participants. Through his quip about Manifest Destiny inevitably transforming heaven's landscape itself, Mariano Guadalupe Vallejo projects a kind of nostalgia into the future when one would remember a more pristine, untouched heaven. Renato Rosaldo has identified such memories as "imperialist nostalgia": what "agents of colonialism" yearn for "when they first encountered" the unaltered but soon to be colonized "place/space/people" of something new.[2] Rosaldo writes: "The peculiarity of their yearning, of course, is that agents of colonialism long for the very forms of life they intentionally altered or destroyed.... In any of its versions, imperialist nostalgia uses a pose of 'innocent yearning' both to capture people's imaginations and to conceal its complicity with often brutal domination" (107–8). But as this anecdote reveals, this "innocent yearning" associated with nostalgia need not be only about the past; it can be about the future as well.

This anecdote, I would argue, mirrors Mariano Guadalupe Vallejo's well-reported stance with U.S. annexation at the beginning of the Mexican America War.[3] Platón Vallejo writes:

> All the Californians spoke with frankness. The universal wish was to offer either annexation or alliance with some great maritime power,

able to insure protection and progress. But the members of the junta were divided as to which of the great powers it should be. A few—very few—favored Russia. More favored England, because she led in maritime power. Others favored France, because the French, like ourselves, were of the Latin race.

My father was the spokesman of the advocates of annexation to the United States. He was a student of all history, thought George Washington was one of the great figures of the world, believed in the American people and their high destiny. He made an argument that showed foresight in a high degree. Joined to any European power, he said, "California could never hope to be more than a province, a remote step-child, certain to be overlooked. Only by union with the United States could we hope to be a real part of a great nation.

"Sooner than anyone thinks," he exclaimed, "the American continent will be thickly peopled, from the Atlantic to the Pacific, and of that great country we Californians must form a part." (*Memoir*, chapter 12, 36)

As it turns out, Mariano Guadalupe Vallejo's continental vision was prophetic. Still no one foresaw the rapid growth of the state. Even Platón Vallejo, always loath to condemn Anglo-Americans outright or portray Californios as victims, cannot help but say the obvious about the gold rush: "Then came the mighty gold rush. It swept over California like a tidal wave, under which the native people were submerged. A more experienced race might well have staggered and gone down with the shock. Of the Californians, man, knowing little more than children of the big moving world and its ways, came to the end of their rope, there and then acquired the wild habits of the day, and often parted for a trifle with land that later came to be of immense value" (*Memoir*, chapter 16, 46). In the end, it was the very same character of ingenuity, risk-taking, and industry that the Vallejos always admired of Anglo-Americans that also came to undermine the prestige of the Californio. In 1846 Mariano Guadalupe Vallejo had argued in favor of U.S. annexation because he believed in that country's "destiny." He did not believe in, as championed by Pío Pico and others, a return to the monarchy under Spain. Nor did he believe that Mexico could ever right itself sufficiently to provide a hemispheric vision that safeguarded and promoted Alta California. Instead, he chose to believe in the outward signs of modernity that favored technology and commerce on a continental scale. Like other Californios, even fictional ones like Don Mariano Alamar of *The Squatter and the Don*, Mariano Guadalupe Vallejo never imagined a modernity of subtraction. If he perceived a "dark side" to this U.S. modernity, he did not think it was meant for him.

Of course, over time his perception changes. Marissa López captures the double-edged sword of modernity, how it subtracts even as it "progresses," when she observes in a letter to his wife, Mariano Guadalupe Vallejo's chilling realization of how the use of miraculous technology, in this case the railroad, can all the same produce human tragedy on a unprecedented scale: "Vallejo was not blind to the dehumanizing effects of those modern marvels, nor was he unaware of the racialization and proletarianization of California's Mexican American population that followed in the wake of conquest and modernization" (*Chicano Nations*, 60). And yet, it takes the third generation to truly understand the family burden of a fully staged Californian modernity. His granddaughter, Francisca Vallejo, will shoulder the burdens of her Californiana heritage by navigating how best to present family history as a claim on regional sovereignty. And she will strive to do so with one of the newer storytelling technologies of the twentieth century: radio. Her task will be additionally burdensome because of the omnipresent demands of a Spanish fantasy heritage industry that was by then deeply institutionalized by the state of California.

This chapter examines the role that nostalgia plays for the Vallejo family of Northern California in their attempts to contest and intervene on an Anglo-American hegemony that seeks not only territorial and cultural claims on California, but its superior claim to history itself. Evolving notions of family identity and claims to place reveal a deep initial subtractive response to modernity in the aftermath of the Mexican-American War. Place, property, race, and memory are the vectors of this chapter's focus on settler nostalgia and its deployment to make claims on a sovereignty based on settler history and culture. These vectors intersect with the subtractive elements of a modernity that is alternatively pegged to the successes, failures, and eventual disappearance of those Californios who welcomed the American invasion in 1846. Having lost the claim to land through the infamous Land Commission, squatters, and debt, Francisca Vallejo's bid in her 1930s radio show is to make a critical argument through history about sovereignty. Here sovereignty refers not to ownership or possession in a legal sense, but a sense of patrimony.[4] This patrimony as sovereignty becomes a discursive vehicle to invest and reinvest in related concepts like tradition, heritage, and family lore. In this context, nostalgia becomes a perfect affective mechanism for making memories public—memories that would otherwise remain private, individual, or familial about a Californio homeland.

The primary texts examined here for this nostalgia are Francisca Vallejo's 1936–37 radio transcripts. Her program, "Padres, Gringos, and Gold," for the radio station KYA San Francisco anchors the argument that the Vallejo family, like other Californio families, participated in the "fantasy Spanish heritage," but cautiously so, in order to forward their nostalgia as critique and proof of themselves as the original unalienable Californians. Through three generations, the Vallejo family, culminating with Francisca, makes the case that not only is California an exceptional place and space for the evolution of Western civilization, but that Californios, like themselves, had a proprietary and guiding hand in nurturing this exceptionalism well before Anglo-Americans arrived.

"This Is Francisca Vallejo Speaking"

On the night of May 25, 1936, at 7:45 p.m., on radio KYA, Francisca Vallejo began her first episode of a radio program to which listeners could dial in three times a week to hear her narrate old Californio stories. Perhaps such listeners would do so to forget for a moment the economic depression they were enduring. Perhaps they dialed in to drown out the news of mass deportations of Mexicans and Mexican Americans on the one hand or the unprecedented numbers of Okies and Arkies migrating from the drought-stricken Dust Bowl of the Great Plains states on the other. Or perhaps they dialed in just curious to hear what the granddaughter of Mariano Guadalupe Vallejo had to say:

Buenas noches, amigos, good evening, friends! This is Francisca Vallejo speaking. It is my privilege to announce that I shall bring to you a series of programs which I have written around the history and romance of our wonderful California. We shall dip into her lore and legend, play her traditional music and learn to know her with a deeper understanding and affection! Occasionally, I may present one of my own compositions, and from time to time, I shall speak to you of Chamberlain's Lotion, which is sponsoring these programs. I know you are going to share my enthusiasm for this splendid product; just give it a trial.[5]

For the rest of 1936, and into 1937, Francisca Vallejo will regale her listeners with stories of Old California: its discovery and the establishment of the mission system, tales of bandits, romances, native legends, and seminal moments like the Bear Flag Revolt. Along the way, Vallejo writes episodes devoted to the flora and fauna and ecosystems, reminding her listeners of the national treasures of California. We would call it environmental writing today. Local tribes are also featured, as well as details about ranch life and domestic homemaking by the doñas. Hers is an insider's journey into a past well trodden by historians of that period. Whatever novel content she provides is by virtue of her family genealogy and intimate access to her father's, Platón Vallejo's, rich recollection of Mariano Guadalupe Vallejo. Embedded here and there are Francisca Vallejo's subtle but clear family grievances, grievances she literally airs over the airwaves: squatters, land grant disputes, and unscrupulous lawyers find their way eventually into her program.

All the while, Francisca Vallejo navigates a social sphere that expects civility, cosmopolitanism, and erudition of its doñas, even if bereft of its once prominent landholdings. In this vein, Francisca Vallejo writes and speaks, again literally, as she were not only the granddaughter of Mariano Guadalupe Vallejo, but the granddaughter of María Amparo Ruiz de Burton. Having said that, Francisca Vallejo, like Ruiz de Burton, regularly expresses her owning class privileges, which also include an ideology that sees herself and her family members as Spanish Californians, and Castilian

Spanish speakers. While she evidences a pride for all things California, some Californios are clearly, in her opinion, of better breeding and class than others. So too her views on race with regards to "native" peoples and the "Chinese" in San Francisco are mixed, racist at times, and always paternalistic. Indeed, reading through her radio transcripts one can intuit her heartfelt and earnest devotion to a patriarchal, Catholic, Spanish colonial worldview that she is now the spokesperson for and the defender against the ravages of time, neglect, and cultural amnesia.

Vallejo's efforts in San Francisco are not unlike those found in Los Angeles in this period. As Eileen Wallis's historical work on women's clubs in Los Angeles has demonstrated, there was a broad-based network of Californio- and Mexican-descended women who actively challenged Anglo-American cultural authority when it came to a Spanish past in California. According to Wallis, this type of challenge often occurred at the highest social circles of Los Angeles: "In 1933 a female reporter from the *Los Angeles Times* covered a fashion show for her paper. Local club women dressed in satin gowns, and mantillas represented 'the olden, golden California days. Each garment, each shawl, each mantilla was redolent with romance. The very scent . . . carried one back to the days of Ramona'" (133). Because of the tremendous economic and demographic growth of the city since the 1880s that included Mexican immigrants, there were generally more such events in Los Angeles than in San Francisco (see Wallis, "Introduction"). Wallis finds in Los Angeles a patterned and consistent attempt to remind the public "that previous generations of Californianas had been witness to and players in state and national history" ("Keeping Alive," 134). Women, descended from Californio elite families and those from more modest backgrounds, collaborated to make sure their histories were not "pushed aside in a rush to celebrate the 'Spanish' past" (142). All the same, theirs was not an effort to stop or diminish such celebrations of a Spanish past; they just wanted to be included and be accorded respect as cultural insiders: "Because they were elite or middle-class, and in many cases they were either married to Anglos or they were the daughters of Anglo fathers, they did not directly challenge the 'Spanish fantasy past' version of regional history. Instead, they asserted their own and their familiar places within that history and strove to keep things as 'authentic' as possible" (143).

Like these club women in Los Angeles, Francisca Vallejo's radio program, "Padres, Gringos, and Gold," also participated in and contributed to what Californian historian Carey McWilliams would later identify as the "fantasy Spanish heritage" thesis. All the same, there is something unusual in the appearance of this radio program, both as a historical event—these programs were aired for thousands of listeners in the Bay Area—and as a preserved object in an archive. That these radio transcripts exist in the Bancroft Library at the University of California, Berkeley, begs the question, by its sheer uniqueness, what other radio programs by a Californio-descended individual or New Mexican or Tejana/o exist as a record of cultural production in English for an English-listening audience? Especially programs produced during the economic and social upheavals of the Great Depression, a period that was virulently hostile to people of Mexican descent and other communities of color? In short, Francisca Vallejo accomplished a unique intervention into California history even as she also participated in her own subordination to an ever-powerful Anglo-American re-narration of "Old California." Trading on the quixotic nature of nostalgia itself, Francisca Vallejo leverages her family genealogy to remind and, at times, to lecture her audience about the importance of the original settlers of the region, and specifically to continue what had become by then a multigenerational Vallejo tradition: to enshrine and promote the centrality of Mariano Guadalupe Vallejo to the unfolding future of the state of California. Francisca Vallejo was engaged in a project she had inherited from her father, Platón Vallejo, but also shared with other members of the extended Vallejo family, which was to adapt and transmit, whenever possible, the cultural capital of a privileged, colonialist past into the nation-building apparatuses that were constructing California as the Golden State of the Union. Even if by 1936 family fortunes had waned considerably, losing thousands of acres to squatters, lawyers, and debt, when even the ancestral home, Lachryma Montis, could not be saved, the Vallejos wanted the world to see them as the First Family of that Golden State, and through their eyes, words, and feelings, they wanted the world to acknowledge the meaning of the real California.

Coloniality of Nostalgia

As Vallejo's radio transcripts make clear, a more expansive understanding of settler nostalgia—the histories, myths, and representations that come to rationalize the violent occupation of land by a Europeanized people after 1492—makes visible the demands of territorial designs at any particular historical moment. For example, mimicry of preconquered Californio subjects and culture, as in the adoption of a Spanish fantasy aesthetic, becomes essential for capitalist consumption in the early twentieth century of California. Based on the "narratives and cultural practices that emerged in the latter half of the nineteenth century" (64) and reimagined by such cultural productions like Jackson's *Ramona*, Alberto Varon writes, "Spanish fantasy heritage manifested across the social and cultural landscape in demonstrations of public holidays ('Spanish Days'), in the education system (curricular changes to include the Spanish pioneers), and on the physical topography (in a 'mission' revival: architecture style)" (66–67). In this manner, though counterintuitive, settler nostalgia lends itself to the continuous mapping and remapping of previous territorial designs ever secure in its performance of an inevitable victorious Anglo-American nation. So too is there a gendering and regendering that accompanies the Spanish fantasy heritage. Especially among elite women circles at the turn of the century and well into the early twentieth century, the Spanish fantasy heritage becomes a kind of cultural marriage that joins two competing colonial projects. Think here of the cultural work of someone like Adina de Zavala, whose advocacy led to the preservation of the Alamo and other missions in San Antonio, Texas, for historical posterity.[6] Also think here of the literary marriage plots from novels like *Who Would Have Thought It?* to *Caballero* that dramatize the union of distinct colonial projects. In all these contexts, settler nostalgia, even as it makes visible the competition between colonial projects, works to maintain the overall logic of coloniality.

Given the disruptive and dissenting discursive practices that the Vallejo family had engineered over three generations as a primary example, I introduce *coloniality of nostalgia* as a specific type of colonial difference, a discursive field where one can actually perceive a collision of colonial projects; here the collision is between an established Spanish/Mexican regime and an emergent Anglo-American one. Nostalgia, despite its conservative tendencies, provides the Vallejo family with both a platform for critique and a basis for demanding local and national inclusion. Citing Raymond Williams, Rosaldo argues "that not all nostalgias are the same; under different historical circumstances, they mean quite different things" (116). He goes on to assert a fluid understanding of nostalgia that helps us reconcile the divergent aspects that can be found in its aesthetic and political deployment: "The memories that evoke moods of imperialist nostalgia both reproduce and disrupt ideologies. . . . It is in their inconsistent plenitude that memories eventually unravel the ideologies they so vividly animate" (121). I take Rosaldo's notion of disruption as a key element in both defining the significance and effect of settler nostalgia, but also as a means of reading this nostalgia for its ideological content. It is when this disruption emerges from multiple competing or overlapping sources of settler-colonial ideological content that the concept of a coloniality of nostalgia explains how one settler nostalgia can be used to contest a more formidable settler nostalgia without ever exhausting the ideological, and hence symbolic, content of either.

To invoke the former, Alta California, always entails invoking the latter, California, as the Golden State, especially since the overall modus operandi of settler colonialism, writes Patrick Wolfe, is to replace what has been destroyed or displaced with an imprint of its settler inevitability (388). The Vallejo family recourse to nostalgia is then a refusal of a settler process that seeks to eliminate the "native" in favor of the colonizing settlers. Collectively the Vallejos refute this process on two points: refusing to see 1) Californios as "natives" excluded from the white privileges of modernity or Californios as the targets of coloniality, and 2) Californios as "settlers" who failed as colonial rulers. In this dynamic, the Spanish fantasy heritage reflects what Wolfe observes in general: "settler colonialism does not simply replace native society *tout court*. Rather, the process of replacement maintains the refractory imprint of the native counter-claim" (389). The Spanish fantasy heritage is "the imprint of the native counter-claim," a discursive space where Californios like the Vallejos enter and exit in contradictory ways because this is what is available to them, and unlike the actual indigenous of a region, whether called Alta California or California the Golden State, Californios and Californianas have access to a coloniality of power that still recognizes them as colonizers, even if history also records their colonization.

Because they refuse their elimination under the logic of settler colonialism, we can see more clearly how a deployment of Californio settler nostalgia was designed to refute a loss of sovereignty, a loss of homeland to a newer class of settlers. This refusal has some surface commonality with what Audra Simpson has written about settler colonialism and its offer of state recognition through forms of consent with coloniality from indigenous people, especially as the structures of settler colonialism and structures of refusals "manifested [themselves] in the games of settler colonial governance."[7] All the same, this Californio refusal never means to negate or forget its settler-colonial privileges. Lorenzo Veracini writes that a "special type of sovereign entitlement" belongs to "a specific class of settlers: those who have come to stay, those who will not return 'home'" (53). This "intention to stay" Veracini calls "animus manendi," which is "manifested by residency, suitable reproduction, and possession" (53). Veracini's latter term, possession, is particularly important in unpacking the vexed significance of a Californio nostalgia that is deployed to reckon against the loss of Californio landownership, while simultaneously recording a righteous dispossession of indigenous peoples of their lands, their homelands. Veracini's definition of corporate sovereignty as "a concept contiguous with self-government and suzerainty ... and not as primarily concerned with establishing state institutions" describes extraordinarily well how the previous colonial administration of Alta California understood sovereignty with its well-defined regional culture as limited self-autonomy from Mexico City (54). Because of the absence of well-defined state institutions, Alta California had always been perceived as vulnerable to foreign colonial takeover. Ironically, this very same vulnerability due to its history as a corporate sovereignty is what allows Californios like the Vallejos to make claims on California as homeland outside of well-defined state institutions.

It is safe to say that this more expansive view of nostalgia complicates the literature on this topic in Chicanx studies. Indeed, the critique of colonialism during the Chicana/o Movement was thorough and, in many ways, uncompromising to a fault. The critique, while useful and strategic for presentist agendas, obliged everyone, but especially academics, to take a hard line with historical figures of Mexican descent who did not mirror the revolutionary ethos of the movement. Nowhere was this hard line more evident than in the way that Chicana/o scholars reiterated Carey McWilliams's analysis of the Anglo-American coopting and repackaging of a Spanish Mexican past into a commercially friendly "Spanish fantasy heritage" in California and the Southwest in general (see *North from Mexico*). McWilliams's critique of this Anglo-American conquest of Spanish Mexican culture influenced how Chicana/o scholars viewed individuals like Mariano Guadalupe Vallejo, former governor and general of Alta California and also a major player in California's early state history, or later Miguel Antonio Otero Jr., first territorial governor of New Mexico. In the Chicano Marxist manifesto *Fan the Flames*, individuals like Otero were described as part of a small group of "opportunists who sell their people out to the oppressor nation. . . . This class of feudal landlords became transformed into a comprador bourgeoisie, who acted as middlemen for the imperialists in selling the region's resources and the people's labor for super-exploitation."[8] Because of their overall conciliatory relations with Anglo power brokers, such post-1848 figures were viewed with disdain by the emerging new histories of Chicanas/os. They were the historical "sell-outs," as opposed to their contemporary counterparts who were too willing to work within the system, people such as Hollywood character actor Leo Carrillo, who was often faulted for his stereotypical depictions of Mexicans, or Congressman Henry B. González of San Antonio, for his public attacks on Chicano militants. Overall the adoption of McWilliams's analysis led to a sophisticated guilt by association on the one hand, but on the other hand there was also a more rigorous recognition of the colonial privileges that some elite members of pre-movement communities enjoyed before and after 1848 and the roles they played in the labor struggles that followed, from the hacienda to ranching, from farming to migrant picking of crops.

Altogether this colonial critique of the pre-movement period limited what and who could be resurrected for a "usable past."

Yet, as the Recovery Project has demonstrated for the last thirty years, the whole idea of a "usable past" for Chicanx studies is incomplete without a thorough reckoning of its archival record. Given that this is the ultimate goal of this project, it is important to chart and meditate on the role that literature, or radio storytelling in the case of Francisca Vallejo, plays in representing and negotiating the burdens of modernity. More specifically, the task is to grapple with the consequences that followed a literature deliberately shouldering the limits of telling a story very few—until lately—wanted to hear. I focus here on a family collection of writings about Old California and Californios that find a new format of expression in radio. For there is in the Californio archive ample evidence that the Vallejo family, not just Mariano Guadalupe Vallejo, participates in something like a homespun discursive industry to promote a Californio history, even as the family's own efforts invariably licensed more romanticized and culturally suspect portrayals of a "Spanish" California. The Vallejos' published and unpublished Californio writings bear the rhetorical markings of texts that seeks to curry favor with Anglo readers while still retaining an unassailable ethnic, regionally bound identity. Because this regional identity locates its center in the past rather than in the present or future, the Californio use of nostalgia has been often viewed as either political escapism or political accommodation.

Instead of this narrow definition of nostalgia, I argue that a Californio nostalgia of coloniality serves a whole range of ideological and rhetorical purposes, some of which are escapist, accommodating no doubt at times, but always demonstratively about engagement with the new regime of colonial masters. Californio nostalgia in the service of a "fantasy Spanish heritage" concretizes what Mignolo identifies as the larger cultural role of "colonial semiosis" as the discursive meeting ground of differentiated communities, which have been brought into contact with one another because of colonialism, and in this case because of competing colonialisms (similarly explored in chapter 1). It is this engagement, what Mignolo refers to as the human interactions between two unlike people in the context of colonialism that gets recorded in language at some point that is at the crux of what I mean by a *coloniality of nostalgia*. Because of their experience and memory of a previous, shared coloniality of power, colonial elites, like the Vallejo family, could not help but articulate their radical difference even while actively seeking to narrate their new subject positions as inhabitants of the United States. It is because of their demotion from their prior colonial status that their post-1848 declarations of selfhood and place-making become increasingly suffused with a modernity of subtraction. Theirs is a modernity desirous but ambivalent about being included in a political, social, and aesthetic system of values so ready to belittle, if not jettison, a Spanish/Mexican colonial past.

Much like the images or discourses of the "noble savage" that underwrote a mythic narrative of nation-building for the United States, the vanishing Californio provided the emergent Anglo culture in California a usable past from which to launch a regional narrative of statehood. To be sure, Anglo-American relations with Californios or Californio-Mexicans in the beginning were not so crass as the above statement. The historical record is full of intermarriages, joint capital ventures, and shared local and national events (the gold rush, the Civil War, the continental railroad). But over time, Anglo-Californio relations began to take on a nostalgic, museum-like quality. A kind of romanticism for a Spanish Californio past slowly but surely seeped into a renovated California imaginary. Antonia Castañeda writes:

> The mission revival movement, which imitated a Spanish-Mediterranean architectural style for public and private buildings, dates from this period. Historical societies and journals published histories of the missions and *pueblos*, along with reminiscences of the halcyon days in the former Spanish *adobes*. Leading Anglo denizens in towns up and down the state organized "fiesta days" that included parades, music, food, rodeos, and a *fandango* (dance) or two. In Santa Barbara, Helen Hunt Jackson's novel *Ramona* was converted into a play that was performed year after year. Some of the descendants of California's "best Spanish families," who aided and abetted both the creation and the perpetuation of the Spanish myth, joined these celebrations. (12)

The figure of the Californio had a role to play in an evolving California history, but until fairly recently its symbolic role was to exist as an artifact of the past, much like the surviving missions of Fray Junipero Serra's ecclesiastical vision for Alta California. It is precisely this symbolic role I am invested in interrogating. Rather than refuting its cultural work as yet another manifestation of U.S. colonialism, I seek to intensify our knowledge of its colonial production. I am interested in reexamining what Californio-told stories, histories, anecdotes say in response to an emergent discourse they helped to establish even as they were in no way empowered to stop their eventual subordination to a more powerful Anglo-American cultural imaginary. I argue for the need for renewed attention to what was actually written, recorded, and published. While I certainly believe that strategic silences and gaps contain at some final level the "real" story of Californios, as Genaro Padilla and Rosaura Sánchez have suggested, I nonetheless believe that extant texts by Californios still offer us a wealth of interpretive possibilities despite being deeply conditioned to register as nostalgic and hence not threatening, not threatening to the status quo.

As mentioned, the Californio nostalgia I survey has mostly been understood, with some exceptions, as complying with nation-building discourses that forwarded the United States as the vanguard of Western culture. Here, I follow the critical lead and example of F. Arturo Rosales, who studies the Bandini family archive and argues that if "Californios adhered to 'Spanishness[,]' they did so following their own agenda—one that predated the Anglo takeover" (82). In other words, Californio nostalgia does not overtly contest the legitimacy of U.S. colonialism of former Mexican territories. Rosales would agree. On the whole, Californio texts rarely register the kind of opposition, resistance, or political analysis that is more commonly seen in the works of someone like Cuban revolutionary José Martí or much later in the writings of Chicanas or Chicanos during the Chicana/o Movement. Instead, they have been interpreted as too accommodating of American ideological forces and, at times, even as apologists for U.S. exclusionary politics. Their nostalgia is not unlike other examples found throughout the Southwest, whether in a figure like Miguel Antonio Otero Jr. or even Jovita González. Until very recently, Chicana/o scholars tended to be very critical of the aristocratic Californios, treating them as either dupes of American imperialism or race traitors because of their very public attempts to cozy up to American centers of power. Critics of such figures, argues Rosales, have "confused Californio eagerness to establish regional Hispanic superiority with their embracing the commercial Anglo inspired myth [of a fantasy Spanish heritage]" (82).

In addition, I would argue that much of Chicanx studies' criticism of the Californios evolved from a critique of their symbolic role in Anglo-Californio accounts of California history. Chicana/o critics of the Californios unintentionally sided interpretatively with the nineteenth-century Anglo-American use of their nostalgia—a nostalgia that actually rewrites their historic presence in California in tamed terms, such as colorful, honorable, even gracious, but in the end anemic in its ability to colonize the land, its resources, and its indigenous population. Such a Spanish fantasy heritage, Varon argues, "isolated, alienated, and disempowered Mexican Americans by separating Mexican immigrants and residents from a Europeanized, imagined past" (65); this de-linking in turn underwrites increasing "Jim Crow-style restrictions on Mexican Americans' political participation" in California and elsewhere in the Southwest (65). Californio nostalgia was framed discursively from the very beginning as telling a history that required rescuing from its dead-end trajectory. The subliminal proof of this cultural reading was in the very basis of the phenomenon that extirpated the Californio and Californiana from his and her elite status: the gold rush.

If it had not been for the extraordinary set of circumstances that launched a massive immigration of mostly Anglo-Americans and Europeans to California, the territory, barely showing signs of its newer colonial status as Mexican, would probably have evolved more along the lines of New Mexico and Texas, which is to say, if it had not been for a demographic explosion of outsiders, the Californio elite would have weathered Anglo-American influence differently, and their own cultural and political cache would have probably lasted longer. Instead, Californio nostalgia bears all the signs of this extremely rapid transformation of Alta California with duress and poignancy. Nowhere are the signs of this transformation as clear as when Californios and Californianas broke from the cultural script that allowed them to speak history only in the service of U.S. hegemony and instead articulated a history that was driven by a love of place, and a love for the social relations that existed in place before the American period.[9] Varon concurs: "Mexican Americans utilized the cultural phenomenon [of the Spanish fantasy heritage] to assert themselves as agents of political change and as part of the social landscape" (64). Nevertheless, their articulation of a Californio place is also a conqueror's history. It is a history tied up in acts of colonization and oppression of the indigenous, whose nuances beg to be understood on their own terms, terms not readily familiar to Anglo-American readers back then but remarkably available to us now, precisely because of the force of their clarity when it comes to claiming California as a sovereign Californio homeland.

"The California Citizen of Yesterday and Today"

From the late nineteenth century through the 1930s, a fantasy Spanish heritage seems to have spoken to middle- and upper-middle-class women. It seems to have linked Anglos and Californios and Mexican Americans in the broad context of the New Woman of this period. Looking back, for all its obvious racial and class privileging of whiteness and U.S. imperialism, at home and abroad, a fantasy Spanish heritage often appears in the archive as potentially progressive, especially if we consider it as a cultural sphere where women are actively negotiating the demands for inclusion and recognition in the political realm. The settings for enactments of a fantasy Spanish heritage may be genteel, polite, and even cosmopolitan, but such settings are nonetheless often underwritten by a wealth and authority in direct contrast to experiences and labor of the lower classes. The fantasy Spanish heritage was undoubtedly marked by class privilege, but precisely because of its status, it also evidences a kind of citizenship akin to the power and responsibility inherent in voting rights or legislative acts of the state. Helen Hunt Jackson's *Ramona* for all its flaws, which are legion, nonetheless proposes a progressive politic on behalf of Native Americans. As an answer to the Indian Question, Jackson's proposal sits squarely on the foundation of a Spanish fantasy past as if that nostalgia alone could secure the necessary sentimentality to move a nation, as it happened with Harriet Beecher Stowe's *Uncle Tom's Cabin* (1852) and the question of slavery.

Although further research is required to understand how Francisca Vallejo's radio show came about, there was no doubt of her qualifications. She was by the start of the program a well-known regional figure in her own right. She was sixty-one years old, a composer, poet, and writer, and she was in possession of key family, and hence state, memorabilia. She was well connected to the upper social circles of San Francisco. Gertrude Atherton, who had known the Vallejo family for years and who even based her protagonist Diego Estenega in *The Doomswoman* (1893) on Mariano Guadalupe Vallejo, wrote a foreword to Francisca Vallejo McGettigan's volume of poetry *Along the Highway of the King* (1943). In keeping with the fantasy Spanish heritage she helped to invent and promote, Atherton cannot help but introduce her protégé through a nostalgic Californio history: "California has contributed more than her quota of authors to American literature, but none other, perhaps, with the unique background of Francisca Carrillo Vallejo, for, if the world ever *had* an Arcadia, a 'Terrestrial Paradise,' it was California in the days of the Dons, from whom this writer derives both her forbears and her inspiration" (5). Once again the territorial designs of nostalgia show themselves quite clearly. Francisca Vallejo is a living descendant of those "days of the Dons" that had anchored an earthly Eden on Earth, and through her Atherton assures the readers of this volume they will not be disappointed. Laying out her genealogy as betwixt and between the grandfather, who was the "Lord of the North," and her grandmother Francisca Benicia Carrillo, who was "a cultured musician as well as modeled wife and devoted mother," Atherton asks, "How could their grand-daughter, Francisca Carrillo Vallejo be other than gifted? How could she escape the inheritance of that pictorial, dramatic epoch? We know that she did not. She is the voice of California, an authentic poet and composer" (5–6). Atherton's description of Francisca Vallejo in her book's foreword could easily have been her introduction for the more than one hundred episodes of her radio program, "Padres, Gringos, and Gold." Three times a week, for thirty minutes at a time, she was literally the voice of California's past and present, with a future that included her father and grandfather very much on her mind.

The timing of her program, which began on May 25, 1936, could not have augured a better start. Francisca Vallejo was tapping into what was then in the state of California an annual economic and cultural fascination referred to as "fiesta time." In San Francisco, this period of late spring into early summer had a particular resonance with the cultural elite. In *The Spectacular San Franciscans* (1949), Julia Cooley Altrocchi writes: "San Franciscans never missed an old Spanish *fiesta* if it occurred within a reasonable radius of 800 miles. Coronado and San Diego were not too far. Santa Barbara's Old Spanish Days Annual Fiesta and Monterey's Founding Festival and San Juan Bautista's anniversaries were and are a natural part of San Francisco's social life" (329). Indeed, just eleven weeks into her program, having covered topics such as the founding of San Francisco, Padre Junipero Serra and the missions, a famous courtship, and "Indian legends" that she learned from her father, Francisca Vallejo, on June 19, 1936, reminds her listeners that fiesta time had arrived. She even produces the same cultural mapping that Altrocchi does: "Fiesta time in California arrives in May and with its round-ups and barbeques, its rodeos and meriendas, whirls merrily along through the summer months from Mendocino to San Diego, flaunting its multi-colored skirts it shawls and castanets and singing the songs of old Spanish-California Days with affectionate gusto!" Since recordings of her program have not been found and may not exist, we can only imagine her voice, its timbre and tone, by what remains textually on scripts typed on onionskin paper and very often filled with editorial marks and side notations that guided her live performance.

Like the many accounts of Mariano Guadalupe Vallejo's oratory prowess, there are so many tantalizing places to go when considering Francisca Vallejo's live performance of a fantasy Spanish heritage on the radio in 1936. Reading through her extant radio transcripts, one gets a feeling of layers of semantic possibility because of the medium of radio and its obvious privileging of sound and voice. Her notations on the page indicated conscious attempts to heighten sound and voice to aesthetic levels. Not only would she read her own poetry, but she would begin and end each episode with a musical rendition of "La Paloma." Although it is unclear from her transcripts whether she performed "La Paloma" or played a sound recording of it, the song had been so popular and for so long that most aficionados, from California to Latin America, accorded it a regional appreciation even though it was composed by Spanish composer Sebastián Iradier and written when he was in Cuba in 1863. Part of its appeal was no doubt the highly romanticized idea, captured in the lyrics, that the figure of the dove could represent love from a distance—the greater the distance, the greater the ardor of that love. It is not hard to see Vallejo purposely mapping the emotional drama of "La Paloma" onto her cultural script about Old California, in effect wooing her listeners with a love affair between Old and Modern California.

As she does in the above quote, Vallejo peppers her radio scripts with Spanish words, with a word selection that often intimates a deeper meaning or social context. So, when she says "meriendas," this is not simply to say a Spanish-style light afternoon snack but to gesture toward a cultural habit that organizes differently the day's meals of the day and hence work time. It is not Anglo-American, and this is why it is appealing, because it offers an alternative to Anglo-American time itself. She makes specific use of "fiesta time" to introduce both the topic for that evening's episode but also a forthcoming event at Mission San Juan Bautista that very weekend: "Tomorrow, the twentieth of June and the following day, Sunday, the twenty-first, A Mission Pageant titled 'The Twilight of the Dons' will be enacted at San Juan. The story is written around characters who once lived in the San Juan Valley, and with their loves and hatreds wove a colorful pattern into the robe left by them as inheritance to their children" (program 12, 1–2). Although her text here and the history of this mission that follows evidences pride and enthusiasm, the title of the pageant play nevertheless betrays a wistful combination of nostalgia and pathos in the word "twilight."

The play itself was written by regional playwright Lucy Cuddy, and it turns out that Francisca Vallejo wrote the music for this play, which remained memorable for more than a decade.[10] Altrocchi writes:

> When, in 1936, San Juan Bautista, with the plaza restored, celebrated with especial emphasis its 139th anniversary, San Franciscans were

there with all their famous fervor. *The Twilight of the Dons*, written by Mrs. John Cuddy and General Vallejo's gifted granddaughter, Francisca Vallejo McGettigan, was presented to an enchanted group. There were also a horse show, polo with William S. Tevis, Jr., descendant of Governor Pacheco, as Captain of the Burlingame team, a *baile* or old Spanish dance, "the guests retiring on and off and reappearing in fresh costumes as in old days," tea in the Zanetta house near the Mission, and "open house" in all the fine old Spanish ranches in the vicinity, now almost all Anglo-Saxon-owned. (329)

Within all the markers of this event's high cultural significance, Altrocchi inadvertently ends up echoing a phenomenon Platón Vallejo had identified in his 1914–15 family memoir: "So far as name goes, the Hispano-Americans have already lost much of their identity. Their daughters have married largely with the later-comers. They left many descendants, but they are no longer known by Spanish name; they are Smiths, Brown and Whites. The small boys are no longer Juans, Joses and Pedros. But you can still trace in their bright young faces the old Castillian type. And you will find, no young people of our generation more proud of their country, more ambitious to make good, than those who claim a kinship with the followers of Father Junipero Serra" (chapter 18, 52). Platón Vallejo might have had his own daughter in mind when he wrote this, because there is no doubt of her dedication to the memory of Junipero Serra.

On the other hand, the cultural attitude beneath Altrocchi's offhanded, unironic comment that the old Spanish ranches are now mostly "Anglo Saxon-owned" (329) or the attitude that's captured in Altrocchi's description of dressing up like dons and doñas could not have gone unnoticed by General Vallejo's granddaughter. If this is so, Francisca Vallejo shed her bitterness in small doses, channeling anger, regret, or remorse through stylized moments of family acts of patriotism. Though she purposely advertises *The Twilight of the Dons*, she highlights the forward-looking nature of the dons by rehearsing her grandfather's allegiance to the United States, nowhere in better display than when he argued in favor of annexation by the United States in 1846:

Then Mariano Guadalupe Vallejo, hardier, more cosmopolitan, clearer visioned arose. He conceded Pico's point that they could no longer look for protection from Mexico; he asserted that the Californians in electing their own governor had already taken the first step toward independence. Continuing, Vallejo said: "There is another step to be taken, I will mention it plainly and distinctly, it is . . . annexation to the United States! Why should we go abroad for protection when this great nation is our adjoining neighbor? When we join our fortunes to hers, we shall become not subjects but fellow-citizens, possessing all the rights of the people of the United States. California will grow and prosper and her citizens be happy and free. Look not with jealousy upon these hardy pioneers who scale our mountains and cultivate our unoccupied plains, but rather welcome them as brothers who come to share a common destiny." (program 12, 3–4)

In his climactic confrontation with Pío Pico and his supporters, who advocated a return to the Spanish monarchy, Francisca Vallejo retraces the events of that day that her father had written about (*Memoir*, chapter 12), but when she quotes her grandfather's words, she does so through a careful editing of Mariano Guadalupe Vallejo's speech as recorded by Joseph Warren Revere (28–30). Mariano Guadalupe Vallejo uses the word "pioneers" to describe Anglo settlers in California here and later in life with frequency, in part because it was a description that also acknowledged the settlers of Alta California. Both Platón and Francisca Vallejo would each invest in the same term, thus accurately identifying a broad feature of European settler colonialism no matter the country of origin to their regional identity. All the same, while on the surface this "common destiny" to share with "brothers" seemed to be self-evident during "fiesta time," this was not always the case. This colorful patterned robe that was left as an inheritance to future generations needed an advocate, and the means of that advocacy lay in manipulating the fantasy Spanish heritage wherever she could.

On July 20, 1936, in program 25, Vallejo manages in an episode devoted to the domestic world of the Californiana to reintroduce into public sphere an older Vallejo voice, her cousin Guadalupe Vallejo from the *Century Mag-*

azine of December 1890. She quotes her cousin directly, seemingly just to underscore that "Spanish-Californian women were splendid (expert) housewives":

> "It seems to me" says Guadalupe Vallejo, niece of the General and daughter of Jose de Jesus whose acres spread far and wide on the eastside of our great San Francisco Bay, "that there never was a more peaceful, happy people on the face of the earth than the population of Alta California before the American conquest. In the New England States the War of the Revolution was in progress but on the Pacific Coast, peace and contentment filled the hearts of Californio's children, and the bells of its many Missions rang out their messages to Spanish Don and Indian neophyte alike." (program 25, 2–3)

Following in her cousin's footsteps, Francisca Vallejo reiterates and reorients the subversive language of 1890 but in the service of adding another layer of cultural capital to her descriptions of adobe homes, elegant furnishing from England and France, and beautiful costumes: she emphasizes a scene of peace and prosperity in California, while in Protestant New England revolution and war was being waged.

While civilization had arrived with the Catholic padres long before it did in New England, it had been up to the Californianas like her grandmother to make it a reality. Whatever feminist impulse we can ascribe to Francisca Vallejo's broad claims on behalf of Old California, we find it in moments like this where she joins herself to her cousin's words, only to embed that 1890 regionalist critique of the nation within the domestic realm of her grandmother's patriarchal, Catholic and colonialist universe: "My grandmother, Francisca Benicia Carrillo, was a splendid housewife and manager. My father would often speak of the smoothness with which their large household was run. Mammá was always at the helm and overlooked every thing from the beautiful rose garden to the huge pile of mending that the Indian girls struggled with each week" (program 25, 5). Although primarily referred to in print, in her own time and later, as the wife of Mariano Guadalupe Vallejo, the granddaughter represents her by her maiden name, Francisca Benicia Carrillo, forgoing for the moment the

Spanish custom of adding the husband's surname after "de." Her grandmother's own maiden name is not only linked to the town of Benicia that Mariano Guadalupe Vallejo founded and named after her but a name that also recalls the Carrillos of San Diego. Hidden beneath the affectionate "Mammá" sleeps a deeper matrilineal history that records the extraordinary story of the maternal great-grandmother, María Ygnacia López de Carrillo, who after the death of her husband, Joaquin Carrillo, in 1836, moves the entire family to Sonoma to live with her married daughter, Francisca Benicia. With the help of her two Vallejo sons-in-law, she begins Rancho Cabeza de Santa Rosa, which is eventually confirmed as a land grant in 1841. Learning to speak the local indigenous language, she employs indigenous labor and manages successfully a farm and livestock. Although she dies before seeing the political fruition of all her labors, her grandson José Antonio Romualdo Pacheco Jr. becomes the twelfth governor of California in 1875, the first native-born governor of California, and the first and only governor of Mexican-Californio heritage. In her own time, María Ygnacio López's resourcefulness and ingenuity were most probably taken for granted given what it took to establish the political economy of a rancho in general. Nonetheless, one wonders what knowledge and skills were passed on from daughter to daughter, especially given that María Ygnacia López's own mother, María Feliciana Arballo, was a member of the much celebrated Juan Bautista de Anza expedition to Alta California in 1775–76, an expedition that concluded with the land survey for what would become Mission San Francisco de Asís and the presidio.

So in the twenty-fifth episode of her program, we can see a bit more clearly how Francisca Vallejo forwards her own maiden name as Francisca Vallejo at the beginning of each episode not only to emphasize a Vallejo genealogy but also to signal a matrilineal narrative.[11] In such moments, Karen R. Roybal argues, the archive "expose[s] the matrilineal dimensions of property ownership and herencia—inheritance, legacy, and heritage—*and* the resistance and negotiation by women of Spanish/Mexican descent after 1848" (*Archives of Dispossession*, 3). As such, her inaugural episode on May 25, 1936, featuring the Anza expedition and its role in the founding of San Francisco, for all its outer celebration of patriarchy, also entails a quieter but equally pioneering matrilineal genealogy. By renaming her grandmother Francisca Benicia Carrillo over the airwaves, Francisca Vallejo was also covertly uttering the histories of her great-grandmother María Yngacia López de Carrillo and her great-great-grandmother María Feliciana Arballo, while simultaneously, we must also notice, displacing her own mother, Lily Poole Wiley, originally from Syracuse, New York.[12]

Although she grew up in Sonoma, California, surrounded by her extended Vallejo family, it is perhaps easy to understand how a non-Vallejo like her mother could be displaced. Francisca Vallejo was ten years old when her mother died at the age of thirty-seven in 1885. By contrast, her father would live on another forty years. She was roughly fifteen and sixteen years old when her grandparents died in 1890 and 1891. But perhaps the displacement of her own mother is a measure of what Roybal finds in the post-1848 archive: that "culture increasingly becomes not only the site of contest and struggle against further Anglo American incursion and appropriation but also the gendered site of agency and intervention against dispossession" (*Archives of Dispossession*, 3). As we have seen in the *Century Magazine* and Platón Vallejo's letter to William Heath Davis, the 1890s seems to be the decade the Californios were noticeably losing their influence and political capital and yet ironically becoming the mythic figureheads of a lost era of Spanish California, an era that was accruing commercial and cultural significance for the state of California.

As her cousin Guadalupe Vallejo did in her *Century Magazine* article, Francisca Vallejo eventually finds a way to explore this topic of dispossession through cattle and ranching in program 37 on August 17, 1936:

> Buenas noches, amigos; good evening[,] friends; this is Francisca Vallejo speaking, bringing you episodes of California history and romance under the auspices of Chamberlain's lotion.
>
> Conditions in California were favorable to only one industry when the Spanish settlers first came here under Gaspar Portola, and that was the oldest industry in the world—that of the keeper of herds.
>
> Every advantage was present to encourage the raising of cattle and sheep, while lack of a proper market demand gave no incentive to the

pursuit of the manufacturing or agricultural industries, save to the extent justified by the needs of the colonists themselves....

This, then, was why the rancheros petitioned for the California Land Grants, and this the main reason they were so readily granted them. The colonists needed land for their cattle, ranges for their herds, and land lay idle everywhere—why not grant it to her colonists? So thought Spain and Mexico followed in her footsteps. Indeed there is no subject in California history more vital in import or more interesting in outcome than the litigation that concerned the private land grants issued during the Spanish and Mexican eras.

To the early settler they were the basis of his wealth and prosperity; [to] the American—the foundation upon which their later titles depended. At the present day, nearly every farm deed in California traces back to a title dated from Madrid or the City of Mexico. Most of our ranches are but divisions of some one of the famous Grants given by either Spanish or Mexican Governor up to the time of the American Conquest.

Some were recognized by the United States government, others were thrown aside, and many a descendant of an old grantee feels his birth-right was wrested from him by ways that were dark and means most peculiar. (1–2)

Once again, one would love to know her tone as she launched into the topic of land grants. Was there any noticeable upset in her voice? Was there any detectible sarcasm at the idea that some grantees lost their birth-right "by ways that were dark and means most peculiar"? Was there any self-consciousness or irony when she claims the lands were idle? In other episodes, including this one, she takes great pains to direct our attention to the indigenous lore learned by her father, or the many instances she acknowledges indigenous labor as an integral part of the Californio economy. All the same, her phrasing is clear and direct: "Indeed there is no subject in California history more vital in import or more interesting in outcome than the litigation that concerned the private land grants issued during the Spanish and Mexican eras" (program 37, 1–2). As if to heighten the importance of this statement, she refers not to the U.S. annexation of Alta California but to the "American Conquest" (program 37, 2) as the defining moment that will make these land grants the issue for all Californios.

Given her general genteel approach captured by the radio transcripts, Vallejo's directness here is curious, and made all the more curious by the absence of the previous six radio transcripts, which might have shown some thematic buildup to this one. All the same, she takes full advantage of this episode to make an economic argument about conditions before the "American Conquest" that seems to be setting the record straight:

> Then was the period of early California's greatest prosperity, from 1828–1846. The market for tallow and hides flourished with both England and the United States.[13] It was then that the Dons made the tremendous fortunes that have been in a few instances only, passed on the third and fourth generations.
>
> Before the American occupation, which really was the Pastoral Era of California, cattle raising was by far the biggest, in fact the only industry engaged in, and live-stock furnished not only the principal item of food but also the necessities of life and luxury that came into their simple manner of living.
>
> Hundreds of Indians were employed on the various ranchos, usually under the supervision of a white mayor-domo, though occasionally an Indian over-seer was employed.
>
> On Wednesday evening, we will continue with a description of the Pastoral Period in California and what effect the long years of living close to the soil had upon her people.
>
> Until Wednesday evening, then, at 7:45 I bid you all Buenas noches, hasta la vista! (program 37, 4–6)

Within the periodization of the Californio's greatest prosperity, from 1828 to 1846, roughly the beginning of the secularization of mission lands to the beginning of the Mexican-American War, Vallejo provides an alternative timeline to understand the previous wealth and industry of the Californios. She names it the "Pastoral Era of California" as if to indicate its difference from the industrial economy that characterizes the East, but one suspects that "pastoral" is also being used as a wedge against the phrase preceding it, "before the American occupation." Like "American Conquest," this phrase "before the American occupation" stands out rhetorically, I would argue, to make some claim to sovereignty implicated in her use of the pastoral. Even though the term "pastoral" would suggest some kind of premodern activity, Vallejo accurately sets forth its colonialist connotation under modernity when she nonchalantly mentions the use of indigenous labor as yet further proof of an advanced society.

As she promises, Vallejo continues the conversation about "the Pastoral period in California and what effect the long years of living close to the soil had upon her people" (program 37, 6) in program 38, August 19, 1936. Like her father before her, who entertained out loud whether Hispano-Americans left any "trace on the later institutions of California" (*Memoir*, 52), Francisca Vallejo also carefully makes the case for understanding a claim to sovereignty based on culture rather than property or political representation:

> The social customs of Spain and Mexico left a lasting imprint upon the California citizen of yesterday and today rather than the political policy of the two Latin governments. In the daily life of the Spanish Californian of a hundred years ago, we find much that appeals to our own love of life in the great out-doors, and, in the hospitable spirit and unconcern of the Californian as the petty restrictions that bind our Eastern countrymen, we can trace the care-free assurance and open-hearted hospitality of our Spanish California forbears.
>
> Simplicity was the key-note of life in the pastoral period of California and scarcity of luxuries, the absence of money, together with a certain austerity natural to the Spanish make-up, made the early California born colonist a character that was native to California alone, and one that had and *has* a strong appeal to the more calculating if more energetic Anglo-Saxon race. (program 38, 1)

By sliding from one phrase to another, "the California citizen of yesterday and today" to "Spanish Californians of a hundred years ago," and collapsing the differences between each, Vallejo concedes the political differences between the United States and Spain and Mexico. But she makes this rhetorical move only to make an exceptionalist claim about an "open-hearted hospitality" that is uniquely rooted to California as a place. Accordingly, because of a regional austerity, Spanish Californians were able to construct a culture that is the antidote to the "petty restrictions that bind our Eastern countrymen." Like Platón Vallejo, his daughter understands the pastoral character of Old California as different but not antithetical to coloniality and modernity; in short, without knowing to call it as such, Francisca Vallejo identifies a racialized "structure of feeling" that was recognized as appealing by "the more calculating if more energetic Anglo-Saxon race" and which was no doubt a deep-rooted basis for the fantasy Spanish heritage.

If Vallejo felt urgent about unpacking what she meant by her racialized analysis about the origins of a fantasy Spanish heritage, she does not display it on the airwaves. For the next twenty-three episodes, she entertains and lectures her audience about rodeos, pirates, the Bear Flag Revolt, bullfighting and bears, and fur trappers such as Jedediah Smith before returning to this topic in her episode about squatters. While nonetheless carefully laying out the legal context of disputes that arose from imperfect titles, it is on the topic of squatters that Vallejo sheds another layer of cosmopolitan gentility:

> Conditions were particularly favorable for the birth and spread of "squatterism," and immigrants, knowing nothing of the nature of Mexican claims looked upon any land that was unoccupied as legitimate material for acquisition and upheld their right with the old adage "possession is nine tenths of the law." In their careless manner of reasoning, it was a simple step from possessing the land to claiming the produce of its acreage and any stray cattle that wandered within the range of their appropriation.
>
> Many of the early immigrants roamed the country at random, living [in] their wagons, making the gathering of unbranded calves their chief means of livelihood. In a few years abounded in squatters of every nationality but chiefly, Americans. They paid scant regard to any legal technicality and did not hesitate to challenge the oldest land-grants

in California. Their particular activity as seizing upon unfenced or unguarded lots in the many growing townships without the least compunction as to prior rights held by other individuals. (program 61, 2)

Squatterism as Vallejo describes it has an uncanny resemblance to the challenges endured by Californio protagonist Don Mariano Alamar in *The Squatter and the Don* (1885). This resemblance may have to do with how Ruiz de Burton modeled her Don Mariano after her good friend Mariano Guadalupe Vallejo, especially since they shared a problem with squatters. Without saying so directly, Francisca Vallejo all but calls these squatters— the majority of them Americans—thieves. She goes on to assure her listeners that legal steps were taken to investigate the legitimacy of land grants, most of which, she declares, were found to be in "conformity to the law" (program 61, 2) by William Carey Jones's report. But her sense of injustice does not stop here:

> This [Jones] report was of course, quite out of step with the wishes of the immense army of American squatters. From the view-point of the American pioneer, it was quite beyond reason that a few hundred contented, un-energetic Spanish Californians should hold title to the most desirable lands in the country to the exclusion of the bona fide farmer of Yankee extraction! What right had the Arguellos the Peraltas and the Vallejos, yes—even Captain John Sutter to vast estates of eleven or more leagues? Did not land lay as rightful reward to the hardy pioneers who braved the dangers of desert and sierra? (program 61, 2–3)

Vallejo deals with the mythology of Californio indolence and idleness head-on, clearly using sarcasm and incredulity to counteract the unspoken Manifest Destiny that led Anglo-American pioneers to believe a God-given right to land west of Mississippi just because they "braved the dangers of desert and sierra." Thus "un-energetic" is simply a "view-point of the American pioneer," not fact, especially when even large grant holders like Captain John Sutter, of gold rush fame, were also vulnerable to the charge of "un-energetic" from squatters. Although she will go on to admit that "not *all* the squatters were deep-dyed villains" (program 61, 4) and that it was a legitimate ploy to claim land recorded in a grant, she nonetheless surveys the innumerable ways Californios lost their lands to imperfect surveying methods, shady lawyers, and the proliferation of the "professional squatter" (5) who could hold a landowner hostage by the sheer threat of a land claim and whose vote was nonetheless courted by politicians. Recourse to the courts was all but ineffective:

> Numerous original owners of California lands, guaranteed protection by the United States were subjected to gross mistreatment and indignity actually despoiled by the harassing activities of squatters and their unscrupulous lawyers. The California rancheros were no match for these sharpers who on one pretext or another took out loans and mortgages and made fore-closures that cannot be doubted were fraudulent and unworthy.
>
> The proceedings of the law were utterly baffling to the average ranchero, and the litigation entailed both drawn-out and ruinously expensive. Valuable lands fell into the hands of rascally lawyers and long terms of probation for recordings and clearance of title resulted in complete loss of the property, many times the owner dying before the suit was settled.
>
> It is on record that one claimant had to wait thirty-five years to have his claim recorded and its title cleared. Then you hear the query— "Why was it that the Spanish Californians could not hold their lands?" (program 61, 5)

So, she ends this on October 12, 1936, having given a fairly thorough structural analysis as to why the Californios could not hold on to their lands. Again, the radio transcript offers little emotive charge to this episode beyond the semantics of the text. Between her question here and the program's concluding lines is a gap, leaped over to announce the next program: "Wednesday evening we will hear of the episodes that led up to the building of the great cross-country American Rail-roads. Until then we bid you all Buenas noches, hasta la vista!" (program 61, 6).

Trading Nostalgia for Cultural Sovereignty

But one wonders how this talk of squatters and displacement and greed, because of that other unspoken matter in this episode, must have sat with her listeners, whose lives in 1936 were also about contending with the Great Depression. At that very moment in California, great economic and racial disparities were daily fare. News of deportations of Mexican and Mexican American migrant labor and the onslaught of Arkies and Okies from the Dust Bowl to fill the needs of the state's agribusiness had been gripping news for months. So much so that John Steinbeck chronicled these events in a series of articles, published in the *San Francisco News*, October 5–12, 1936, collected later under the title *The Harvest Gypsies*. In the muckraking tradition of journalism at the time, Steinbeck exposes the human tragedy in the making because of greed. If May began the annual pageantry of "fiesta time" for the socialites of San Francisco, Steinbeck draws the city's attention to a wholly different annual period, mapping along the way a political economy of the state that stood in dark contrast to polo matches, costumed teas, and open houses at Californio ranches now Anglo-Saxon owned:

> At this season of the year, when California's great crops are coming into harvest, the heavy grapes, the prunes, the apples and lettuce and the rapidly maturing cotton, our highways swarm with the migrant workers, that shifting group of nomadic, poverty-stricken harvesters driven by hunger and the threat of hunger from crop to crop, from harvest to harvest, up and down the state into Oregon to some extent, and into Washington a little. But it is California which has and needs the majority of these new gypsies. It is a short study of these wanderers that these articles will undertake. There are at least 150,000 homeless migrants wandering up and down the state, and that is an army large enough to make it important to every person in the state. (October 5, 1936)

Was Francisca Vallejo aware of these articles? Did she read them? Was her own show on October 12 deliberately attempting to make some common cause with Steinbeck, or at the very least broaden the discussion of "wanderers" back to the nineteenth century? Steinbeck makes the possibility of a coincidence seem highly unlikely:

> To the casual traveler on the great highways the movements of the migrants are mysterious if they are seen at all, for suddenly the roads will be filled with open rattletrap cars loaded with children and with dirty bedding, with fire-blackened cooking utensils. The boxcars and gondolas on the railroad lines will be filled with men. And then, just as suddenly, they have disappeared from the main routes. On side roads and near rivers where there is little travel the squalid filthy squatters' camp will have been set up, and the orchards will be filled with pickers and cutters and driers. (October 5, 1936)

Steinbeck's squatter camps are nothing like the land-hungry squatters of Californio land grants: they have little or no political support, live in poverty, and are homeless. All the same, Steinbeck's observations of the harvest gypsies' living and working conditions speak to a large-scale agriculture industry where the ever-increasing consolidation of ranches and farms with fewer owners has produced extra-legal means of controlling the economy and social policy. It is here one finds a resonance with Vallejo's episode on squatters.

Writing about how migrant labor in the state had been previously "Filipinos, Japanese and Mexicans," (October 5, 1936), Steinbeck explains why that pool of labor changed: "If they attempted to organize they were deported or arrested, and having no advocates they were never able to get a hearing for their problems. But in recent years the foreign migrants have begun to organize, and at this danger signal they have been deported in great numbers, for there was a new reservoir of which a great quantity of cheap labor could be obtained." Although one would think that race politics would favor the new migrant labor from the Dust Bowl, Steinbeck makes clear that class identity can still trump race:

> Thus, in California we find a curious attitude toward a group that makes our agriculture successful. The migrants are needed, and they are hated. Arriving in a district they find the dislike always meted

out by the resident to the foreigner, the outlander.... The migrants are hated for the following reasons, that they are ignorant and dirty people, that they are carriers of disease, that they increase the necessity for police and the tax bill for schooling in a community, and that if they are allowed to organize they can, simply by refusing to work, wipe out the season's crops. They are never received into a community nor into the life of a community. Wanders in fact, they are never allowed to feel at home in the communities that demand their services. (October 5, 1936)

While Steinbeck makes clear he is writing about this whole new underclass of white Americans, his analysis for the state's love-hate relationship is, in fact, based on the state's treatment of the foreigner, "the outlander." Although Filipino and Japanese migrant labor is significant, those groups' combined numbers do not compare with those laborers of Mexican descent in the fields or the cities. In this context, especially because of the infamous deportations of Mexicans and Mexican Americans in this period, it is difficult not to see Francisca Vallejo willingly weighing in on a topic that was invariably about a much larger debate—about race, class, citizenship, and the increasing identification of the "Spanish Californians" with the much larger population of Mexicans.

While it is also clear, based on her radio transcripts and her other writings, that Francisca Vallejo understands herself and her family's legacy as a class apart and even regionally different from Californios in Southern California, she nevertheless also acknowledged a Mexican heritage, as had her father and grandfather before her. Like others, including Ruiz de Burton, this Vallejo also makes use of a prior Mexican citizenship: "The treaty of Guadalupe Hidalgo gave to Mexican citizens a guarantee of security and protection in the enjoyment of 'liberty, property, and religion'" (program 61, 1). That this guarantee on behalf of Mexican citizens was never fully enacted is precisely the point of her episode on squatters and perhaps the larger point of the contemporary social conditions in California in 1936. A pathos lurks here in this episode and others that begins to outline the shadows of using a nostalgia with such limited cultural and political capital. Even though she displays a deep regard for the possibility of trading nostalgia, as linked increasingly for her in the landscape and ecology of California, for a kind of cultural sovereignty, there is nonetheless a sense of vulnerability in such transactions.

About a month later, on November 11, 1936, she offers a wistful meditation on the California sequoia that speaks to such vulnerability:

> Our subject tonight is the California Sequoia, and as an opening I will read you an original sonnet entitled The Violet to the Sequoia: the violet speaks.
>
> Oh, Patriarch, incline your ear all knowing
> Bend down your boughs that brush against high heaven
> And pause but for a little in your growing
> To point the obscure way to earthly leaven.
> From boundless spaces, planes unknown above us—
> Lean low, and let your hoary wisdom tell us
> For what we bud and bloom that man may love us
> But to be trampled, torn, or culled to sell us!
> Why so obscure *our* lot? Not all our striving
> Has served to lift us far above the sod,
> While you, a growth prodigious contriving
> Have reached the heights where rests the foot of God!
> We would be strong; we would the centuries see!
> Bend down your boughs, lean low, and *speak*, oh Tree!
>   (program 72, 1)

If the majestic Sequoia represents the patriarchal history that colonized Northern California, Vallejo then seems to be bemoaning the collective fate of her family's legacy in particular and the Californios' in general. Under fantasy Spanish heritage, the old Californio has been accorded an exotic and beautiful niche within the political ecology of the state, but just like the violet, the old Californio can be "trampled, torn, or culled to sell." Even the memory of someone like Mariano Guadalupe Vallejo, a family equivalent to the sequoia, can be diminished and erased because of avarice: "In ancient times, great groves of trees were venerated and revered as sacred; used as halls of council and worship. Here in California, when the Calaveras Grove was discovered, one of the grandest trees was cut *down* for the sake of the stump! The vandals had looked upon the Earth's greatest growth and forsooth—must dance upon it!" (program 72, 5). The violet pleads to the sequoia in hopes that its age will offer some wisdom about how to navigate the present to be strong for the future. In this manner, the violet asks the sequoia to speak, to give witness not unlike El Mesquite does in Elena Zamora O'Shea's long story *El Mesquite* (1935).

Like O'Shea, Vallejo frames her discussion of history, colonialism, and vulnerability within a dialogue for her listeners. After unpacking the violet's plea to the sequoia, it is the sequoia's turn to speak:

THE SEQUOIA TO THE VIOLET
The heights are chill, and deep within my heart
I feel the pang of loneliness. Alone
And high above my kind and kin has grown
This age-old trunk whose planting played a part
In that Fourth Day of the Creator's plan.
But I am weary and with you would rest
Close to the Earth, as on a mother's breast,
Yielding not strength—but sweetness unto man!
So must we bide! Your fragrant breath a sigh
With plea for immortality, and I—
With grandeur sated, towering—free of fears—
Fling Death disdainful challenge through the years!
What worth *are* we? What value can we give
To living,—you, that die, and I—that live! (program 72, 5–6)

If the sequoia's words were meant to be solace to the violet, they in fact offer only more pathos. The ability to tower above the rest of nature and a long historical memory seems to be of little consolation to the sequoia. The patriarchal sequoia would seemingly give up immortality for rest "close to the Earth, as on a mother's breast." Even though she admits to a weariness through the figure of the sequoia, Vallejo would go on to revise these two poems and include them in her 1943 volume of poetry, *Along the Highway of the King*. Even in the midst of pathos, she continues to promote her father's profound regional allegiance: "Upper California is today the most pleasure-loving section of all the world, where people live more in accord with what seems to me the natural laws" (*Memoir*, 52). To this she adds, as an epigraph to the volume: "'To thee, California, of gold is thy heart!'"

As in her radio program, Vallejo means to once again celebrate and translate an old Californio past into the present. But she is also quite aware of the precarious nature of her project. Even as she closes her opening poem, with the same title as the volume's *Along the Highway of the King*, she cannot help but articulate a self-deprecating awareness: "Oh, Padres of the Past! To rue / Your passing ridicule might bring, / Yet . . . would I walk the ways you knew, / Along the Highway of the King!" (11). Despite the challenges of her time, its incredulity, its racism directed at lower-class Mexican Americans and upper-class "Spanish Californians" alike, Francisca Carrillo Vallejo's body of work connects her not only to others in California like her distant cousin and Hollywood actor Leo Carrillo, who will re-create his family's Californio past, brick by brick, in Carlsbad, California, or Los Angeles's socialite, club woman, and writer Ana Bégué de Packman, but even more suggestively to women such as Fabiola Cabeza de Baca, Nina Otero Warren, Cleofas Jaramillo of New Mexico, and in Texas to Adina de Zavala and Jovita González, all at work in the pre–Chicana/o Movement period, similarly and yet differently and for the most part independently of one another, to recover and make a better permanent reckoning of those families, communities, and histories that began for better and worse before 1848.[14]

Though all these women did this work—and for years—it took less than a generation for their efforts to be all but forgotten. So forgotten and displaced in California, for example, that Lorna Dee Cervantes writes in 1981:

I run my fingers
Across this brass plaque.
Its cold stirs in me a memory

of silver buckles and spent bullets
of embroidered shawls and dark rebozos,
Yo recuerdo los antepasados muertos.
Los recuerdo en la sangre,
la sangre fertile.
What refuge did you find here,
ancient Californios?
Now at this restaurant nothing remains
but this old oak and an ill-placed plaque.
Is it true that you still live here
in the shadows of these white, high-class houses?
Soy la hija pobrecita
Pero puedo maldecir estas fantasmas blancas.
Las fantasmas tuyas deben aquí quedarse,
Solas las túyas. ("Poema para los californios muertos," in
    Emplumada, 42)

In contrast to the mission-style track homes, an architectural aesthetic under revision and reinvention since the late nineteenth century, Cervantes observes the uncanny interplay once again between memory, nostalgia, and simulacra. The Spanish fantasy heritage has become itself a version of material reality in California, so much so that one has to distinguish between the Anglo (white) ghostly imitations of the past from the real Californio ghosts. So refuge from what becomes the driving question of the poem. Refuge from violence? Refuge from injustice? Refuge from anonymity? With no other trace than an enigmatic plaque—no history, no books, no voices—Cervantes resorts to the essentialism of terms made available by the Chicana/o Movement: blood memory. It is recorded in the blood she claims, and within that fertile blood lies the truth of Californio fantasmas, which she prefers. Fortunately, we no longer have to depend on blood memory alone, and although Francisca Carrillo Vallejo might have agreed about the fertility of blood, she herself also believed in leaving behind a record, a material presence, in her compositions, her writings, and in her voice still speaking to us from her days on radio KYA, San Francisco.

3   Game of Modernities

Coloniality and
Racial Loyalty in
the U.S. West

His Majesty and I, in his name, will receive you with complete affection and charity. [The people who are with me] will leave your wives to you and your children at liberty, without imposing servitude, so that they and you may do freely whatever you may wish and may think wise. [This will be] as nearly all the *vecinos* of the other islands have done. Besides this, His Majesty will extend many privileges and prerogatives to you and will make you many grants.

If, [however], you do not do [what I ask] or you maliciously delay [doing] it, I assure you that, with the help of God, I will attack you mightily. I will make war [against] you everywhere and every way I can. And I will subject you to the yoke and obedience of the Church and His Majesty. I will take your wives and children, and I will make them slaves. As such, I will sell and dispose of them as His Majesty will order. I will take your property. I will do all the harm and damage to you that I can, [treating you] as vassals who do not obey and refuse to accept their lord and resist and oppose him. (*Requerimiento*, Alonso de Ojeda, 1514 or 1515)

In his seminal work *The Spanish Frontier of North America*, David J. Weber narrates the intellectual, cultural, and psychic terrain that framed the initial contact in 1540 between the exploratory force of Francisco Vázquez de Coronado and the Zuni people who met to resist him in what is now New Mexico.[1] Having tried an ambush that failed, the Zunis treated the encroachment of the Spaniards as if it were a cosmological event: "With sacred golden cornmeal, Zuni warriors drew lines on the ground, warning the intruders not to pass beyond them" (15). By contrast, Coronado responded with the discursive and ideological weight of the requerimiento, a formal declaration of conquest that was meant to be understood in sacred and secular terms: "The requerimiento demanded that native peoples accept the dominion of the Spanish Crown and embrace Christianity. If they resisted, their lands would be taken from them and they would be killed or enslaved" (15).[2] While neither system of communication produced its intended effect, Weber notes it is the Spaniard's superior weapons of guns and steel that ultimately wins the day for Coronado and his men: "The vanquished defenders fled, leaving behind storehouses of corn, beans, turkeys, and salt, to the delight of their hungry visitors" (15–16). Notwithstanding Weber's tongue-in-cheek characterization of "hungry visitors," he makes it clear that these storehouses of foodstuffs were a far cry from the illusions of gold, silver, jewels, and fame that underwrote Coronado's expedition.

Although a failure in one sense, Coronado's expedition succeeded in the overall scope and drama of the Spanish colonization of the New World. It succeeded by ignoring what the Zuni had plainly and clearly set before them: that the land was already marked by human habitation, including language, culture, and history. If not claimed in a European sense, it was already understood in sacred terms, albeit not in a Christian manner. Coronado trespassed, not unlike those conquistadors before and after him, over the sacred cornmeal on the land, a system of knowledge claimed by the Zuni, but rendered through colonial violence as erasable and obsolete and therefore subject and subjugated to the assumed superiority of the logic of the requerimiento, a communication on paper that was meant as a deed to a land presented to its rightful owners. Although already well practiced by the time Coronado entered this Zuni village, the requerimiento and the indigenous resistance to it should be treated as the genesis of the legal, symbolic, and psychic trauma that will echo and morph in the centuries to come, especially as the land and the peoples who inhabit it come under increasing pressure from a modernity/coloniality matrix that seeks total domination.

Richard Flint and Shirley Cushing Flint quite clearly establish how the requerimiento emerged out of "strong ecclesiastical complaints about the abuses of natives of the New World by conquistadores and *encomenderos*" (616), complaints that led to reforms known as the Laws of Burgos in 1512. Nonetheless, the legal finding of the requerimiento established "the conditions under which war could legitimately be waged against [natives]" (616). For the next sixty years after 1513, "conquistadores were required to read this document, through interpreters and in the presence of notaries, to native leaders before hostilities could be opened against them" (616). Despite the complaints that led to its formulation, the requerimiento represents and unmasks the unbridled eagerness of Spain to colonize in the sixteenth century. If Walter Mignolo is right when asserting that the indigenous response from resistance to accommodation to adaptation to European modernity/ coloniality constitutes colonial difference, and that such strategies for engaging with European colonization underwrite border gnosis, then where do we, as academic knowledge producers, align ourselves with colonial violence, given the darker side of modernity, especially given how coloniality is constantly at work to disguise its power, as well as constantly compromising our ability to critique, whether from the inside or the outside?

For us who take seriously the settler-colonial dimensions of U.S. literatures, it is important to avoid any hasty answer to the question of whether we critique from inside or outside. For us in Chicanx studies, the vexed responsibility that comes with representing a community that evidences a deep colonial and settler history, a community that is also later colonized, ethically obliges us to explore the burdens of modernity, whether under the sign of colonizer or colonized or both. And if this responsibility is complex to grasp and complex to execute, the requerimiento also makes clear that not all burdens of modernity are the same, nor equally endured, nor equally represented in history or preserved in archives. Indeed, the requerimiento is a stark reminder of the colonial history that privileged such families as the Vallejos in the first place.

It is also critical to dispel any belief that the requerimiento speaks only to Spanish colonization in the Américas. The requerimiento belongs to modernity and as such is connected to a wide array of other texts authorizing, validating, and naturalizing the inevitability of settler colonialisms globally. To be sure, there are many texts to consider in the evolving genealogy of the requerimiento. John L. O'Sullivan's 1839 essay, "The Great Nation of Futurity," is one such text:

> Yes, we are the nation of progress, of individual freedom, of universal enfranchisement. Equality of rights is the cynosure of our union of States, the grand exemplar of the correlative equality of individuals; and while truth sheds its effulgence, we cannot retrograde, without dissolving the one and subverting the other. We must onward to the fulfillment of our mission—to the entire development of the principle of our organization—freedom of conscience, freedom of person, freedom of trade and business pursuits, universality of freedom and equality. This is our high destiny, and in nature's eternal, inevitable decree of cause and effect we must accomplish it. All this will be our future history, to establish on earth the moral dignity and salvation of man—the immutable truth and beneficence of God. For this blessed mission to the nations of the world, which are shut out from the life-giving light of truth, has America been chosen; and her high example shall smite unto death the tyranny of kings, hierarchs, and oligarchs, and carry the glad tidings of peace and good will where myriads now endure an existence scarcely more enviable than that of beasts of the field. Who, then, can doubt that our country is destined to be the great nation of futurity? (429–30)[3]

Famously connected with the concept and coining of Manifest Destiny, O'Sullivan voices here an exceptionalism all too common in settler-colonial narratives. Unlike the foundation of the requerimiento in the divine right of kings and an ecclesiastical certainty in the righteousness of Christianity, O'Sullivan's logic depends on the Enlightenment's promise for delivering the "equality of rights" to all those who believe in tenets that include freedom of speech, the right to bear arms, and freedom of religion. In light of calls for territorial expansion, O'Sullivan's futurity restages these tenets in the vein of a birthright disguised as a set of democratic principles.

O'Sullivan's belief in the concept of nation signals the forwarding of new political structures predicated on the establishment of boundaries even as the country expands westward. Although veiled in a rhetorical tradition only mildly removed from that of John Winthrop's 1630 lay sermon "A Model of Christian Charity," O'Sullivan's "city upon a hill" has become the site of futurity itself, where the United States sits as a moral beacon and exemplum for the world (Winthrop, 91). By solely occupying a future in which the United States is the "salvation of man" and the collaborator with "the immutable truth and beneficence of God," he maps the ultimate boundary, the ultimate horizon, for a U.S. exceptionalism as the heavens themselves (430). For O'Sullivan, Manifest Destiny requires an evolving moral obligation to bring "the life-giving light of truth" to "beasts of the field," to those peoples he considers as existing outside of modernity itself (430). Thus, he returns us to the basic staged conflict of settler colonialism: civilization versus barbarity, an opposition that relies on violence as the means of executing an exceptionalism posing as liberty and freedom. To refuse this exceptionalism is to deny yourself membership in O'Sullivan's future, and without this future there is no existence.

Some three centuries after the Zunis' refusal of Coronado and after the Mexican-American War (1846–48), the territories conquered by the United States became a site of heightened contestation between older and newer forms of settler colonialisms; this site became known as the West. Caught betwixt and between the contestations of older Spanish/Mexican colonialisms and the emergent imperialism of Manifest Destiny are the numerous indigenous peoples that had been under the pressure of modernity ever since conquistador Francisco Vázquez de Coronado and his army— composed of Spaniards, creoles, Catholic priests, Mexican indigenous allies (men and women), and Africans (servants, free and enslaved)— set out to discover and conquer the fabled Seven Cities of Gold in 1540.[4] Although credit of actual colonization of what Coronado claimed on behalf of the crown was bestowed on a different conquistador, Juan de Oñate y Salazar, and much later, in 1598, Coronado's expedition nevertheless set in motion the processes of modernity and coloniality that would introduce and impose a European understanding of the universe. From this imported understanding of the universe would result hierarchies of power, knowledge, gender, and identities that will become inscribed in a range of oppressive structures that govern everyday life from political subjugation to slavery to genocide.

This chapter focuses on one of those enduring inscriptions of modernity and coloniality, the contested nature of race and racism in the U.S. West. The aim here is not to prove their existence nor origins in modernity but rather to argue where and how it is possible to see these processes well past their genesis. To that end, I examine writers, some born in the nineteenth century, whose words and writings greet the early twentieth century with pathos and angst. Some of the writers featured in this chapter evidence settler hybrid identities. Such writers struggle to negotiate the promises of modernity with the realities of coloniality, always amid the presence of an indigenous resistance troubling their racialized futures. Over time, those inscriptions of modernity and coloniality that displaced indigenous livelihood in favor of settler nationhood become the mechanism for a settler consolidation of power over land, race, and racial superiority. Evidence of such colonial inscription, the echoing of the kind of deadly drama enacted between Coronado and the Zunis, abound throughout the Américas. To foreground such a complex network more locally, this chapter means to resituate one historical figure—Geronimo—and one historic event—the Lincoln County War—both often treated as synonymous with the rise and consolidation of the U.S. West. To better understand how a modernity of subtraction works in terms of constructions of race, racism, and, most important, raced communities, and the interplay between them after 1848, this chapter highlights how racial loyalty operates regionally as an index for competing settler-colonial regimes in territorial and cultural arenas where indigenous refusal of their colonial subjugation is ongoing.

Not surprisingly, the U.S. military plays a central role in this chapter, for not only did it forward the policies of Washington DC, but it also had the distinct task of negotiating those policies in places that were territories of the federal government. As such, those living in those territories came under its jurisdiction for all sorts of issues, legal, economic, and social. The military was, in short, the instrument of territorial expansion and territorial occupation, as well as the primary vehicle for disseminating the discourses of the evolving nation of the United States, especially on matters of race and segregation of raced communities. The military, as both symbol and actor, had a deep role to play in the transition from one Spanish Mexican settler-colonial system to an Anglo-American one, and its reach was everywhere, reshaping the everyday experience of race, gender, class, and settler violence. The myths and legends that have emerged from the settler West are very often predicated on the presence of the U.S. cavalry. In one form or another, these myths and legends represent the lasting cultural memory of a coloniality of power that continues to underwrite Manifest Destiny as an inevitable heroic narrative of progress. But a closer scrutiny of such heroic narratives reveals quickly not just the constructed nature of those tales but the reality that those actual historic moments were as complicated as the historic actors involved.

In what follows, I develop an analysis of Geronimo's autobiography for the ways his story complicates our set opinions about race in the U.S. West. I follow the general argument found in Martha Menchaca's *Recovering History, Constructing Race* (2001). Menchaca argues that part of the cultural strategy to disenfranchise former Mexican citizens after 1848 was to racialize their mixed-race heritage as indigenous. In this context, a modernity of subtraction for people of Mexican descent tracks their demotion from a preferred privileged status under coloniality. I then reexamine the Lincoln County War in New Mexico during its territorial period through a racial analysis of the conflict's various participants. The primary text under consideration is the republished biography by Miguel Antonio Otero Jr., *The Real Billy the Kid* (1998 [1936]). In his attempt to rehabilitate the popular mythologies surrounding Billy the Kid by the 1930s, Otero invariably renarrates a complex set of racial relationships that existed after the Civil War. The Lincoln County War drew in every conceivable raced community at the time; this included not just Nuevo Mexicanos or indigenous peoples of the area but also African American soldiers of the Ninth Cavalry. Otero's biography of the Kid is actually a territorial biography, inadvertently pointing out, as does Geronimo's story, how archives need to be reexamined not just for singular raced communities but for how those raced communities interacted with one another. Together, both texts clarify why we need to desegregate how we think about minority ethnic archives and how to be open to the possible racialized networks they might reveal.

Race Loyalty after 1848

Because of the layers of violence and displacement over the last five centuries that have been visited upon indigenous peoples throughout the Américas by way of modernity and coloniality, it is often difficult to perceive when one version of coloniality ends and another one begins. Further, there is no region or indigenous culture or indigenous language that has not been crisscrossed by more than one colonial enterprise or another. This crisscrossing is certainly true of the Southwest and West. Geronimo's and Otero's texts are examples of Mary Louise Pratt's notion of the "contact zone," and as such, these texts provide us with new ways of thinking about the emergent West of the nineteenth century and its embedded histories of multi-raced communities.[5] But rather than revisit the contact zone as initiated and dominated by European travelers, merchants, and conquistadors, I investigate through Geronimo's and Otero's texts the later evolutions of the contact zone for signs of racial loyalty. As the histories and effects of European colonialism in the Américas demonstrate, there was no singular contact zone, nor was any one contact zone particularly more static or fluid than another. Indeed, over time all contact zones underwent transformations in accordance with the later stages of colonialism. These transformations are particularly evident when and where one raced contact zone overlaps or suddenly encroaches the raced contact zone of another.

A focus on racial loyalty provides a more thorough mapping of the cultural, political, linguistic, gendered, and historical connections between individuals and groups of any particular contact zone, as well as disconnections between individuals or within groups of any particular contact zone. Of interest here is the range of expression of and reaction to the "coloniality of power" and all other manner of registered forms of "colonial semiosis," especially those instances in texts and histories where in retrospect one can perceive through a comparative analysis a network of correspondence. As Roland Greene has argued in "Not Works but Networks" about the "networks of colonial and postcolonial studies," these networks of correspondence can be found across race, ethnicity, nationality, gender, and class, as well as circuits and flows of ideas, discourses, resistances, alliances, and alternative identity formations between allies and non-allies alike (222). The evolving nature of the metropolis as found in New York City, Philadelphia, New Orleans, San Antonio, Albuquerque, and San Francisco is ideal as a place to imagine the mutability and multiplicity of the contact zone, but so too are places repeatedly visited by violence and forced displacement, hence Geronimo's tribal homeland and the Lincoln County War.

In *Mohawk Interruptus*, Audra Simpson captures what is at stake for indigenous people in accepting the logic of settler colonialism, be it the legacy of the requerimiento or Manifest Destiny or both, as well as how to understand the complex social orders that must be navigated nonetheless:

> In this there is acceptance of the dispossession of your lands, of internalizing and believing the things that have been taught about you to you, that you are a savage, that your language is incoherent, that you are less than white people, not quite up to par, that you are "different," with a different culture that is defined by others and will be accorded a protected space of legal recognition *if* your group evidences that "difference" in terms that are sufficient to the settlers' legal eye. (22)

Because acceptance of the "settlers' legal eye" is akin to accepting the logic of what Patrick Wolfe has identified as elimination, Simpson's decolonial ethnography surveys all the ways the Mohawks refuse to participate in their own elimination. Simpson writes: they "simply refuse to stop being themselves. In other words, they insist on being and acting as peoples who belong to a nation other than the United States or Canada" (2). All the same, continues Simpson, what lies beyond the settler construction of difference is "the position that requires to 'coexist' with others, with settlers, with 'arrivants' in the parlance of Jodi Byrd (2011)—meaning formally enslaved or the indentured who did not voluntarily come to North America—and to live tacitly and taciturnly in a 'settled state'" (22). It is within such settled states where indigenous refusals of the settler nation overlap in tacit coexistence with settlers and arrivants that racial loyalty also finds expression.

Through a philosophy of liberation, Nelson Maldonado-Torres has called attention to the epistemological and ontological structures of such settled states. He has developed what he calls a coloniality of being in order to establish the Western philosophical origins for the imposition of racism, slavery, and violence as fundamental features of settler colonialism.[6] For Maldonado-Torres, under the aegis of modernity and coloniality, the instruments of colonialism required the creation of a system of constant warfare against the Other, the non-European. To be a racialized Other is to be subject not only to the racial superiority of the European but to the violent maintenance of that racial superiority. Building from Maldonado's coloniality of being, but ever mindful of Simpson's articulation of indigenous refusal within the realities of a settler state, I forward racial loyalty as a concept that sheds light on the historic interplay between the maintenance of a European racial superiority, the construction of race and racism, and the manipulation of nonwhite and white communities in support of a settler nation.

I define *racial loyalty* as part of a kinship system derived from the racial hierarchies imposed by modernity through European colonization of what would become the Américas. As an outcome of modernity and maintained by coloniality, racial loyalty is often expressed by acceptance, accommodation, tension, or resistance with the forwarding of European whiteness as the global, universal standard for recognizing authority, power, civilization, and history. I argue that racial loyalty is, in fact, an enduring feature of settler colonialism in which gender plays a key role in reinforcing racial loyalty through patriarchy, Christianity, and the rise of the settler state. Thus, racial loyalty is deeply embedded in quotidian life and, as such, also deeply embedded in artistic and philosophical production. In this context, racial loyalty is not only historically found in the past, but it is in fact a component of what Aníbal Quijano calls "coloniality of power." Or, as Jodi Byrd argues in her article "Still Waiting for the 'Post' to Arrive," just as there is still no post, as in *postcolonial*, racial loyalty as a feature of social constructions of race and racism is ongoing.

Mark Rifkin's insights into the myriad ways that geopolitical notions of a people or peoplehood or population have been manipulated by the settler state to control and subjugate indigenous people on the one hand and to justify the legitimacy of the settler state on the other are key features of the biopolitics also inherent in the kinship dimensions of racial loyalty. Rifkin writes:

> In particular, a focus on kinship can aid in illustrating and developing that double-sided critical movement, since it functions as an ideological switch point between biopolitics and geopolitics. Kinship provides an idiom through which to cast the operation of the state apparatus as merely an extension or recognition of instinctive familial bonds of affection and care. As a term and concept, kinship emerges out of a Euroamerican anthropological tradition that seeks to remake Indigenous social formations as an older/other version of the social sphere of family, measuring the former within the normative frame of the latter. (152)

The invention of race and racism that condition Rifkin's kinship as idiom, I would add, is not only a settler feature framing indigenous communities but also a feature of other nonindigenous raced communities occupying, contesting, and negotiating the same geopolitical space under pressure since 1492 and, beginning in 1848, increasingly so in what becomes the U.S. West. While the coloniality of power of the settler state always favors those communities that reify the centrality of all things Euroamerican, biopolitics nonetheless condition their communities in a hierarchical relation to one another. Race and racism cannot exist without the imagined or actual presence of the racialized Other, or for that matter the idealized figure of superior whiteness.

It is here in this geopolitical but also temporal space, opened by a serious study of racial loyalty, that we can begin to understand how the Recovery Project by virtue of constructing an archive that tests our resolve to be open and compassionate but also critical of and outraged at the divergent displays of racialized settler power, as perpetrator or victim or both, makes possible a critical praxis that is neither about flattening the relevance of historic wrongs nor simplifying matters into an us-versus-them mentality. Further, the aim here is to intervene in what Byrd in her 2011 *The Transits of Empire* has identified in current critical praxis: "Simply put, prevailing understandings of race and racialization within U.S. postcolonial, area, and queer studies depend upon an historical aphasia of the conquest of indigenous peoples. Further, these framings have forgotten, as Moreton-Robinson has argued, that 'the question of how anyone came to be white or black in the United States is inextricably tied to the dispossession of the original owners and the assumption of white possession'" (xxvi). Exploring racial loyalty as a concept requires a similar acknowledgment: that we understand how people of Mexican descent became Mexican American, Chicana/o, Nuevo Hispano, Tejana/o, and Chicanx in the United States is invariably tied to the dispossession and displacement of Native peoples of their lands and livelihoods. This history of becoming settler hybrids evolves from a history of entangled relationships to indigenous peoples: as friends, foes, neighbors, and, at times, family members. At other times, these entangled relationships travel through uneven notions of mestizaje and through the migration of Mexican indigenous people to the United States since 1848.

This prioritizing of entangled colonially raced relationships aligns with the critical charge that Maylei Blackwell, Floridalma Boj Lopez, and Luis Urrieta Jr. outline in their call for critical Latinx indigeneities: "We are conceptualizing Critical Latinx Indigeneities as an interdisciplinary analytic that reflects how indigeneity is defined and constructed across multiple countries and at times, across overlapping colonialities. This includes thinking through the colonial legacies at play across the transregions created by Indigenous migration.... The continual experience of dispossession, not solely across time but also across space and borders has pushed us to develop Critical Latinx Indigeneities as simultaneously both a local and a hemispheric approach" (126–28).[7] Thus, unpacking racial loyalty, even when racial lines of loyalty are subverted to make common cause across race, can create a critical opening within colonial difference through the mutual recognition of the violent processes that underwrote all racialized communities in the United States, be they indigenous, arrivant, migrant, or any hybrid iteration of the three. In this context, a modernity of subtraction not only marks the demotion of privilege for people of Mexican descent under the settler state, it also reveals the opportunity to notice when that prior privileged status and its complicity with the settler state is interrupted, contested, and complicated. Only after such revelations can Recovery critics hope to aspire to produce a decolonial scholarship worthy of the archive it draws from.

Geronimo's Autobiography as Homeland Narrative

Long before his surrender in 1886, the life of Goyaałé, popularly known as Geronimo, of the Bedonkohe Apaches had been the stuff of frontier fears and legendary feats, as well as a moving target for two nations, Mexico and the United States. Between 1905 and 1906, already in his late seventies, Geronimo agrees to narrate his autobiography. Among the many things memorialized is Geronimo's lifelong animus toward Mexicans and Mexico: "It has been a long time since then, but still I have no love for the Mexicans. With me they were always treacherous and malicious. I am old now and shall never go on the warpath again, but if I were young, and followed the warpath, it would lead into Old Mexico."[8] For Anita Huizar-Hernández, "it is no coincidence that Geronimo dedicates more pages of his autobiography to his raids against Mexican as opposed to U.S. settlers. He never apologizes for his hatred of all Mexicans" because he continues to harbor the hope that he can secure the return of himself and his people to their lands, that the United States can still be an ally (60). By contrast, history and popular culture have consistently framed Geronimo as a leader of renegade Indians who were marked for capture and execution if need be by the U.S. Cavalry. In other words, his capture helped to naturalize further the logic and legitimacy of Manifest Destiny. To paraphrase Jodi Byrd, Geronimo became a transit figure of empire to those who celebrated his imprisonment. Geronimo's pursuit and capture were demanded by a culture seeking to nation-build. And yet what matters to Geronimo are the racialized narratives over land, his particular racial loyalties, and his antagonism against the racial loyalties of Mexican settlers that predate his surrender to the U.S. Calvary.

Western historians have long paid attention to Geronimo's raids against Mexican settlements and Mexican troops, and that he spoke Spanish, and that his popular name, Geronimo, was begrudgingly bequeathed to him by the Mexican settlers who, fearing his warrior prowess, prayed out loud to San Geronimo (Saint Jerome) for protection. Over time, the appellation Geronimo became so synonymous with Goyaałé that it became his nom de guerre. Much less attention has been paid to the fact that he was born under one national flag (Mexican) but died under a totally different one

(U.S.).⁹ Though U.S. culture might prefer to claim Geronimo as a U.S. Indian, his orally transcribed narrative is clearly interested in not forgetting Old Mexico. Indeed, this transcription exists, according to S. M. Barrett, who had to seek permission from President Theodore Roosevelt to produce his autobiography, because Geronimo took to confiding in him only after Barrett told of the incident of his having been shot by a Mexican: "As soon as he was told this, he came to see me and expressed freely his opinion of the average Mexican and his aversion to all Mexicans in general" (39). Barrett and Geronimo were able to communicate because they both spoke Spanish.

The task here is to present Geronimo's life story as a homeland narrative, belonging not to the United States nor the Republic of Mexico but to Goyaałé himself, and to those his text imagines as the occupants of a geography filled with his and his people's history and experience. His narrative reoccupies, replenishes, remaps a geography with the lived presence of Goyaałé and his people that was rendered blank under U.S. military and government policy.¹⁰ Juliana Barr in "Geographies of Power" explains, "It is important to know how Indians understood territory and boundaries, how they extended power over geographic space, and how their practices of claiming, marking, and understanding territory differed not only from Europeans but also from each other's. Then scholars may better understand how ideas of sovereignty became translated into social and political practices on the ground, extending power over real places" (9). This claim "over real places" repeatedly reveals itself as Goyaałé becomes Geronimo. It is Geronimo who exists discursively and historically for two nation-building projects that competed with each other and later collaborated in the pursuit of Geronimo and his people. As such, his homeland narrative presents opportunities for investigations that shed specific light on how settler borders, including knowledge productions such as maps, histories, and surveys, have impinged on the geographic histories of indigenous peoples of the Southwest.

In what follows, I demonstrate why the Recovery Project should include texts like Geronimo's autobiography under its purview of study. Up to now, nativos appear in recovered primary texts and scholarly works with some frequency, but for the most part as either peripheral to the plot of a novel, say Ruiz de Burton's *The Squatter and the Don*, or as part of a broader racial analysis of the period, as in much of the work that has been done so far in recovering Mexican American literature since 1992. Nativos have yet to appear under the aegis of the Recovery Project as their own primary subjects. While Geronimo's text evidences a resistance to any kind of adoption under the nationalist sign of Mexico (or for that matter the United States as well), it is nevertheless possible to consider Mexico as a cultural and colonial signifier that dialogues with Geronimo's text. It is after all the settlers of a Mexican frontera who name Geronimo, and it is Mexico, and before that Nuevo España, that condition his Apache long-term resistance to repressive regimes of colonial power. Because of these colonizing conditions, one should not confuse Geronimo the historic figure and his autobiography with the term *Hispanic*, but on the other hand, there's a danger in not admitting that people like Geronimo in North America lived for a while in a Hispanic-dominated world. Not admitting this history risks furthering the "historical aphasia of the conquest of indigenous peoples" that Byrd urges us to contravene on (xxvi). Likewise, the presence of indigenous people like Geronimo meant something to communities we would now consider Hispanic.

In her book *Recovering History, Constructing Race*, Martha Menchaca argues and demonstrates that any historically driven initiative to recover Mexican American history necessarily dovetails with a simultaneous need to comprehend racial constructions at any given time. As the earlier quotation also makes clear, in Geronimo's mind there's an Old Mexico that exists in 1905–6 south of the border, but before 1848 there was no Old Mexico. Everything was just Mexico. Born in the early 1820s, Geronimo spent his early life as a nativo under Mexican rule. During this period, the Mexicans are the primary colonizers, the primary oppressors. Again, he spoke Spanish, and well into old age. Geronimo's autobiography presents Chicanx and Latinx scholars with an opportunity to engage as literary and cultural critics with an aspect of Mexican American history rarely dealt with. I believe the Recovery Project gives us a critical context from which to investigate the Other as indigenous that existed prior to the United States, as well as how this Other transitioned as Mexican hegemony was dismissed and submerged after 1848. Geronimo's autobiography is one extant and vibrant example of a world that refuses to be forgotten, refuses to be ignored.

As those in global studies have demonstrated, under the project of modernity, the spread of capitalism, reinforced by imperialism, often linked one isolated region to others far beyond their mutual borders. In an astute analysis of race, masculinity, and U.S. imperialism, "The Rough Ride through Empire," Curtis Marez adroitly links the Spanish-American War in 1898 with its domestic version in New Mexico. Calling attention to overlapping expressions of cultural and colonial mimicry the war enabled, Marez cites Theodore Roosevelt's earlier emulation of the Mexican vaquero in 1888, the vaquero's style and ranching methods, a copying that in even Roosevelt's estimation, in fact, underwrote Manifest Destiny out West. This copying, as Marez puts it, "would reemerge a decade later as agents of imperial expansion" (32). Central to his argument is Roosevelt's coopting of the Mexican vaquero alternates with a figurative and political displacement of the figure of the Mexican as well. This alternating manipulation of the term *Mexican* created a cultural space for the subjugation of the Nuevo Mexicano and indigenous in the regional imaginary of Anglos in New Mexico. Marez writes: "Local Anglos used the U.S. victory over Spain to retroactively justify the expansion of white power in New Mexico. Put another way, the U.S. displacement of Spain as the ruler of Cuba both echoed and reconfirmed the substitution of a U.S. empire for a Spanish one in New Mexico" (33).

But Anglo consolidation of its hegemony in New Mexico does not come without reaction and subversion. According to Marez, as "Anglo power brokers" entrenched themselves in the territory, "Hispano competitors/collaborators, working-class mestizo villagers, and Pueblo Indians... variously engaged in struggles over hegemony in the New Mexican territory" (33). Crucial to these struggles were "performance practices involving intercultural mimesis." In short, Anglos playing Spanish or Mexican in turn forced the hand of elite Hispanos to be more Spanish, while the mestizo and Pueblo communities agreed to perform an old folk dance, "Los comanches," which narrates the defeat of the Comanche by the Spanish. Again, cultural identification, cooptation, and displacement all served to align groups, once in opposition with one another, now united to contest Anglo territorial rule: "The play, in other words, potentially enabled working class mestizos to ritually reproduce antipathies to the territorial rulers in 'Spanish' drag who rode into state power on the heels of U.S. imperial triumphs in 1898." By extension, Pueblo Indians leveraged this critique of Anglo rule as they simultaneously revived their much older feud with the Comanches.

Yet the performance of intercultural mimesis that Marez cites as pivotal in the military period that precedes the U.S. war of imperialism in 1898 is in the same historical moment in which the U.S. government seeks to subjugate rebellious indigenous tribes in the West. While Wounded Knee continues to serve for Western historians as one end point of the Indian Campaigns, in New Mexico and Arizona it is the final surrender of Geronimo that allowed both Mexican American and Anglo communities to assert themselves along the border between Mexico and the United States.[11] Thus, before the Spanish-American War, there is an intense cultural and military collaboration to rid the U.S.-Mexican border of its Indian problem.[12] It's hard to ignore in Geronimo's text, for example, that his own hatred and warpath against Mexicans begins curiously around the same time there is an increased Anglo-American presence in the area. In turn, Geronimo's capture by Anglo troops coincides with the Mexican government's own intensification of hostility to chase out the Apaches from its northern territories.[13]

After his father's death and his mother's decision to stay with the tribe, Geronimo becomes the head of the family. Whether because of his father's death and his change in family status or simply because of his age, Geronimo's life as a warrior commences: "In 1846, being seventeen years of age, I was admitted to the council of warriors. Then I was very happy, for I could go wherever I wanted and do whatever I liked.... I could go on the warpath with my tribe. This would be glorious. I hoped soon to serve my people" (*His Own Story*, 81). Of course, it is hard not to notice that Geronimo's life as a warrior starts precisely as the Mexican-American War begins, a period of a conflict that also destabilized whatever set of relationships, good and bad, had been established under the Mexican government since the country's independence in 1821. Despite the fact that the Mexican constitution of 1824 conferred citizenship on all residents of Mexican territories, including the indigenous, the government in Mexico City and in the northern territories paid little or no attention to that detail.

Geronimo never takes up Mexican citizenship as a legal concept in his story. Instead, he makes clear that with his new warrior status he is able to ask to marry "the fair Alope, daughter of No-po-so" (*His Own Story*, 71) and to provide her father with a herd of ponies to seal the deal. Geronimo paints a tender picture of domestic life: "Not far from my mother's tepee I had made for us a new home. The tepee was made of buffalo hides and in it were many bear robes, lion hides, and other trophies of the chase, as well as spears, bows, and arrows. Alope had made many little decorations of beads and drawn work on buckskin, which she placed in our tepee. She also drew many pictures on the walls of our home." In quick strokes, Geronimo establishes himself as a traditional member of his tribe, his status as warrior balanced with his status as husband and provider, and soon as a parent, together with Alope, of three children: "We followed the traditions of our fathers and were happy." However happy they may have been, the ongoing colonial battle for mastery of the region would soon undermine the simplest aspect of traditional life.

Of the many interesting clarifications one finds in Geronimo's story, one stands out: his becoming the figure of Geronimo of Western legend was really a process that began with a massacre of members of his tribe, the Bedonkohe Apaches, including his wife, children, and mother, deep in Mexico, in Sonora near Casa Grande, at a Mexican town the Indians called Kas-ki-yeh. It was the summer of 1858, and Geronimo's tribe had traveled south to trade with Mexican settlers. Unbeknownst to them, the trade had been a lure to make it easier to either execute them outright or capture individuals for forced servitude.[14] Upon discovery of the massacre and their extremely vulnerable situation, Geronimo's chief, Mangus-Colorado, "gave the order to start at once in perfect silence for our homes in Arizona, leaving the dead upon the field" (*His Own Story*, 77). The murder of his family left Geronimo stunned and incapacitated: "I did not pray, nor did I resolve to do anything in particular, for I had no purpose left. I finally followed the tribe silently, keeping just within hearing distance of the soft noise of the feet of the retreating Apaches" (77–78). After much effort, the tribe finally arrives at their home, and days later, Geronimo is finally able to measure the depth of his loss: "There were the decorations that Alope had made—and there were the playthings of our little ones. I burned them all, even our tepee. I also burned my mother's tepee and destroyed all her property.... I was never again contented in our quiet home" (78). Perhaps because their bodies were left behind, the only solace Geronimo finds is at his father's grave: "True, I could visit my father's grave, but I had vowed vengeance upon the Mexican troopers who had wronged me, and whenever I came near his grave or saw anything to remind me of former happy days my heart would ache for revenge upon Mexico" (78). Although he vows revenge on the Mexican troopers responsible for the murder of his family, it is Mexico that represents for him the source of his heartache; he vows war against a settler country to the south.

Having secured the consent of his council and Mangus-Colorado, his chief, Goyaałé of the Bedonkohe Apache seeks the support of their kinsmen, the Chokonen (Chiricahua Apaches) and their chief Cochise and the Nedni Apaches and their chief Whoa, and to each he made the case to go on the warpath: "'Kinsman, you have heard what the Mexicans have recently done without cause. You are my relatives—uncles, cousins, brothers. We are men the same as the Mexicans are—we can do to them what they have done to us. Let us go forward and trail them—I will lead you to their city—we will attack them in their homes. I will fight in the front of the battle—I only ask you to follow me to avenge this wrong done by these Mexicans—will you come? It is well—you will all come'" (*His Own Story*, 79). He wins their support, and in the summer of 1859, almost a year later, as he notes, he leads them into Mexico. Because of his terrible loss, he is given the honor of leading them into battle against the soldiers who killed his people at Kashiyeh (79–83).

After a brutal two-hour battle with many casualties, spears against rifles, knives against sabers, Geronimo stands victorious with a soldier's saber in his hand, looking for more troopers to kill, but there were none: "Still covered with the blood of my enemies, still holding my conquering weapon, still hot with the joy of battle, victory, and vengeance, I was surrounded by the Apache braces and made war chief of all the Apaches. Then I gave orders for scalping of the slain. I could not call back my loved ones, I could not bring back the dead Apaches, but I could rejoice in this revenge. The Apaches had avenged the massacre of 'Kas-ki-yeh'" (*His Own Story*, 83). As he readily admits, although he had avenged the massacre of Kas-ki-yeh, his hatred for Mexico never abated. He goes on to narrate numerous incursions into Mexico, setbacks and victories, details about how his people were often kidnapped and held captive, and vice versa, how Mexican men, women, and children were held captive. His last battle against Mexican troops is in 1885 (107–10).

But his blood feud with Mexico is also shadowed by the U.S. Cavalry: "This was the last battle that I ever fought with Mexicans. United States troops were trailing us continually from this time until the treaty [his surrender] was made with General Miles in Skeleton Cañon" (*His Own Story*, 109–10). In fact, as he goes on to clarify, Anglo-American presence in what would become Arizona began to increase drastically just about the same moment that Geronimo's notoriety as a warrior was being noticed: "About the time of the massacre of 'Kaskiyeh' (1858) we heard that some white men were measuring land to the south of us" (113).[15] And even though it would be officers of the United States that come to hunt, imprison, and exile him and his people from their native lands, for Geronimo, it would always be Mexico, and Mexicans, who deserved his warrior wrath: "During my many wars with the Mexicans I received eight wounds.... I have killed many Mexicans; I do not know how many, for frequently I did not count them. Some of them were not worth counting" (110).

When Mexicans Are Also Indians

As Geronimo's text underscores, indigenous people were pursued until contained or executed on either side of the U.S.-Mexico border. In that same period, a different kind of Indian policy was also emerging, targeting people of Mexican descent. To reiterate, Martha Menchaca observes that part of the cultural and legal strategy after 1848 was to disenfranchise former Mexican citizens by racializing this conquered constituency as indigenous. I understand this type of racialization is also the means by which U.S. colonialism attempted to re-territorialize people of Mexican descent as racialized bodies de-linked from their traditional settler lands. This Indianization of Mexicans worked unevenly with a preexisting racial caste system that had evolved for centuries under Spanish and then Mexican colonial rule. Since one of the outcomes of the Mexican-American War was to question the legitimacy of previous colonial land claims from Texas to California, the newly conquered peoples from these areas, areas of conflict for centuries for indigenous and colonists alike, soon had to deal with the new Anglo-European markers for race, language, and land ownership.

While this form of racialization was new, Menchaca also argues that it echoed older colonial versions in the casta system. Looking back, one can see that early Mexican American culture is clearly in the grip of this racial drama. It's folklore often reflects how racial loyalty unites regimes of racism and settler kinship networks. Although regionally associated with colonial Texas, the folk song "Los inditos," for example, could easily be thought of as the standard experience and beliefs of colonizing Mexicans in the northern territories of Mexico:

Ahi vienen los inditos
por el carrizal
ahi vienen los inditos
por el carrizal.
¡Ay mamita! ¡ay papito!
Me quieren matar
¡Ay mamita! ¡ay papito!
Me quieren matar
Ahi vienen los inditos
por el carrizal

THE LITTLE INDIANS
The little Indians are coming through the canebreak.
Oh, mommy! Oh, daddy! They want to kill me. (in Paredes, *A Texas-Mexican Cancionero*, 47)

Américo Paredes cites "Los inditos" as the only song he knows that has survived from the pre-1848 period of the borderlands, the region between present-day Texas and Mexico. For him songs composed in the post-1848 period represent the intercultural conflict that appeared with Anglo immigration to the region starting in the early 1800s. He argues that before 1848, compositions tended to focus on floods, droughts, and conflict as well, but the conflicts "were accepted as problems of daily life that unsettled but did not threaten the existence of the colony" (21). Here too, "'Los Inditos' preserves the ranchero's memory of raiding Indians living nearby the canebreak" (21), but the conflict memorialized here, according to Paredes, was of a certain order not to be confused with what came after 1848: "Indian raids were a terrible thing to the frontier Mexican, but they did not create an 'ethnic' resentment against Indians, such as was caused by Anglo penetration. Individual raids might be remembered with grief and rage, but the general feeling was that Indians were 'natural' beings it was in their nature to fight and raid. Their depredations were classed with other natural calamities, such as fires and hurricanes" (22). By contrast, Paredes argues, Anglo-Americans, despite their claims to Christian behavior, were actually hypocrites who established a system of laws that aggressively and covertly contested the frontier Mexican, acting "worse than the Comanches" (22).

As with his seminal study, *"With His Pistol in His Hand"* (1958), Paredes continues to make the case with "Los inditos" that the border region between Texas and Mexico saw its greatest violence and injustice with the imposition of Anglo-American rule. In his dedication to this collection of border folksongs, he writes: "To the memory of my father, who rode a raid or two with Catarino Garza; and to all those men who sat around on summer nights, in the days when there was a chaparral, smoking their cornhusk cigarettes and talking in low, gentle voices about violent things; while I listened." His thesis on border conflict makes little or no room for the colonialization, and hence treatment, of indigenous people in the same region. Without any disclaimers, Paredes repeats Rousseau's noble savage theory as a way to identify and explain how Indian raids were comprehended by the frontier Mexican. By downplaying the colonial conflict actually cited by the song, reducing it to the equivalent of a fire or hurricane, Paredes unconsciously privileges the coloniality of power of the frontier Mexican, preferring to view "Los inditos" as a kind of nursery song with ogres or bogeymen (22).

By contrast, even though he quite clearly establishes the widespread notoriety of the song, "widely known throughout the frontier areas, and even down into the interior of Mexico" (21), the power of the song to indoctrinate, to establish racialized fears of the Indian as Other, to reinforce a kinship identity among the Mexican settlers, and to set up a political unconscious ever ready to retaliate against the raiding Indian is lost on Paredes as a significant aspect of cultural analysis. Also lost here, as Menchaca's work has demonstrated, is the complex nature of race and racial politics in the pre- and post-1848 period of the Southwest and West, where friend or foe and opportunity or calamity often rested on racialized identities, racialized kinship networks that shifted according to the colonial script of the region.

As made clear in his dedication, much of Paredes's interest, if not analytical focus, stems from a personal regional memory of his father and his father's generation of men. His reference to chaparral marks this memory at a time before industrialized agriculture succeeded in eradicating the local flora, including the chaparral.[16] Because of this loss, a loss of place, and the positioning of the border rebel, Catarino Garza, as heroic kin, Paredes's memory cannot help but be nostalgic. As in the previous chapters, nostalgia is once again a vehicle for critique, but his analysis of "Los inditos" points to the limits of that kind of critique. What is important to notice is not the nostalgia per se but rather the intervention needed to recognize Mexican Americans' burdens with modernity as not always stemming from conflict with Anglo America alone. Especially on the topic of race and racial subject formation, the modernity of subtraction experienced and represented by writers of Mexican descent before 1948 often portrays a complex network of processes, events, and resolutions.

Indeed, a quick return to "Los inditos" provides a glimpse into how an earlier Spanish Mexican settler moment could be fused with the process of "Indianization" after 1848:

Compónte tu chimal
Y vámonos a pasear,
compónte tu chimal
y vámonos a pasear.

Me ves que estoy enfermo
y no me puedo levantar,
me ves que estoy enfermo
y no me puedo levantar.
Compónte tu chimal
y vámonos a pasear.

Straighten up your *chimal*, let us go for a walk.
You can see that I am sick, and that I cannot get up. (47)

It is an odd stanza, and an odder companion to the opening stanza, which focuses more on the direct threat of violence at the hands of Indians. Its oddness increases in the context of Paredes's headnote to how the song should be played: "Use a *huapango* strum when playing this piece on the guitar, but do not play it too fast. It should have a tempo of a baby bouncing on his parent's knee. If you are singing it to a child, it is best to do so without accompaniment. That is the way it was sung to children among our people" (46). Like this headnote, Paredes's reading of the second stanza is also odd, but equally revealing. He uses it to support his contention that conflict with indigenous people did not create "ethnic resentment" of the kind that became commonplace with Anglo-Americans: "The very real and terrible cry of frontier times, '¡Ahi vienen los indios!' loses its threatening character when transformed into 'Ahi vienen los inditos.' The child, of course, becomes a little Indian himself, as he dandled on his parent's knee and told in song to straighten his *chimal*. It is worth noting, however, that we have no songs saying 'Ahi vienen los rinchitos' or 'Ahi vienen lost gringuitos,' identifying our children with little Texas Rangers or little Anglo-American invaders of the Southwest" (22). What holds this reading together for Paredes is his contextualization of the word "chimal," which he establishes as a Náhuatl word for a round shield. He explains that such shields were commonly used by Plains Indians, likely the tribes identified by the song (21). According to Paredes's logic, by wielding the shield, the child is placed in the position of the Indian; he becomes like an "Indian," because he acts like one with the chimal. In my mind, whether or not Paredes's reading of the chimal is correct or not is not the issue. The real issue lies in that his reading is the culturally assumed reading that he learned from his elders: "I learned it ['Los inditos'] from my mother, who learned it from my paternal grandfather" (21). The song's meaning was passed on to him. Also, the presence of the Náhuatl word for round shield, "chimal," points to an intercultural, hybridized, linguistic space where indigenous and nonindigenous aspects start to blur. Further, given the practice of kidnapping in these border regions, by Indian tribes and Mexican settlers alike, and the fact of centuries of miscegenation in these regions, who is the indito and who is not also starts to blur because of phenotype.

Paredes's instructions for how to perform "Los inditos" to children speaks to a kind of cultural indoctrination that became so naturalized as to achieve the status of tradition, a means by which a community, "our people" (46), could be marked and made familiar, if not familia, through a frontier lullaby. Nonetheless, in the context of the new Anglo-American regime, Indianization of bodies and lands had the overall effect of suppressing indigenous identities even further in Mexican American communities, contributing to their settler hybrid identities. It also had the effect of isolating and separating indigenous and mestizo Mexicans from white Mexican Americans, creating a social mechanism for internalized racism against dark-skinned Mexican Americans and a renovated racism against indigenous people. These parallel processes will get increasingly played out on the border states all the way to the end of the Mexican Revolution in the early 1920s.[17]

Yet the new Anglo-American order could not erase all previous colonial racial structures overnight, or always maintain strict segregation between Mexican and Indian communities. In some cases, memories of conflict in the prior colonial past get recorded and transmitted through performance, as in "Los inditos" or "Los comanches." But one can also find traces of less conflicted, but no less colonialized, relations. For example, as treated previously, the Californio Vallejo family writings are replete with Indian lore, events, and personages. Apart from instances of conflict, they also narrate a political economy that is significantly depends on indigenous labor.[18] This reliance on indigenous labor was no accident since Californio land grants were largely composed of former mission lands, where Christianized natives were forced to work. For this reason, when one reads Guadalupe

Vallejo describe ranch life, she invariably records the labor and lives of the indigenous who worked for the family. In fact, because Californio ranches had to be so self-sufficient, Californios and indigenous people lived, worked, worshiped very closely together: "In these days of trade, bustle, and confusion, when many thousands of people live in the Californian valleys, which formerly were occupied by a few Spanish families, the quiet and happy domestic life of the past seems like a dream. We, who loved it, often speak of those days, and especially of the duties of the large Spanish households, where so many dependents were to be cared for, and everything was done in a simple and primitive way" (191). As she proceeds to tell her reader of a "'wash-day expedition' to the Agua Caliente," a hot spring, one gets an idealized picture of a rancho community of Californio children, young and old Indian female servants, and the doña working together in procession with an oxen-driven carreta to wash "great piles of soiled linen" (191). The "women put home-made soap on the clothes, dipped them in the spring, and rubbed them on the smooth rocks until they were white as snow" (192).

On the other hand, in her portrait of women's labor around washing, we learn that the whiteness of the linen, and in particular the white dresses of doñas and their daughters, were treated with special care and concern since whiteness was a marker of the "Spanish ladies of the upper classes in California" (192). Perhaps to further this regional identity as opposed to a Mexican one, she takes care to rehearse how they traveled to Agua Caliente: "We climbed in [the carreta], under the green cloth of an old Mexican flag which was used as an awning, and the white haired Indian *ganan*, who had driven the carreta since his boyhood, plodded beside with his long *garrocha*, or ox-goad" (191). Besides distancing her class from anything Mexican, she reinforces her racial and class difference from the "Indian," whose peon status and identity is anchored in his precise labor for the rancho as the driver of the carreta.

But Guadalupe Vallejo's anecdote does not end with the labor that ultimately separates the settler and the indigenous women but rather with their shared piety: "To me, at least, one of the dearest of my childish memories is the family expedition from the great thick-walled adobe, under the olive and fig trees of the Mission, to the Agua Caliente in early dawn, and the late return at twilight, when the younger children were all asleep in the slow carreta, and Indians were singing hymns as they drove linen-laden horses down the dusky ravines" (192). Of all the memories available to her as a member of the Vallejo family, this is how she chooses to end her article for *Century Magazine*. Echoing Fray Junipero Serra's vision for Alta California, she remembers a Catholic world order that was brought to bear on a region to Christianize the indigenous. She remembers the indigenous women singing vespers, specific Catholic prayers for the end of the day, and it is these prayers that unite them as one rancho. No doubt, Guadalupe Vallejo invokes a romanticism that we should be wary of, one that should alert us that Catholicism was also a colonizing agent of modernity. All the same, Vallejo's memory is powerful for her and a powerful contrast to the "trade, bustle, and confusion" (191) of 1890. I would argue that this memory is so powerful precisely because of the particular kind of segregation between indio, Mexicano, Californio, blanco, moreno, negro, and so on that came about after 1848. However subtle, Vallejo ends her article with yet another critique of Anglo America, of its modernity and its subtractive prerogatives.

In sum, one area where modernity demanded a response from people of Mexican descent after 1848 was in their collective denial of ever having shared an indigenous heritage or ever having had shared livelihoods with indigenous people in a settler-colonial community. This demand becomes certainly true for those settler hybrids who leverage the past as a hedge against new forms of discrimination in the early twentieth century. They were legally and culturally encouraged to compensate and sublimate for their buried indigenous origins or shared cultural and religious practices by overstating and lamenting the loss of their status as colonizers. Such is even the case with Jovita González, who in an attempt to articulate a viable regional non-Anglo identity cannot help but reproduce in stark terms the racialized divide between colonizer and colonized:

Escandón era un capitán español que vino a Texas en 1748.

España quería colonizar la tierra entre el
Río Grande ye el río Nueces

> Esta tierra estaba infestada por los indios
> bravos, algunos de los cuales eran caníbales.
> Aunque muchos españoles vivían en el nuevo mundo
> ninguno quería venir a la tierra de los Texas,
> como llamaban a Texas en aquel entonces.
>
> España estaba ansiosa por colonizar esta tierra,
> por temar que los franceses en Luisiana
> adquirieran esta tierra
>
> El rey de España buscaba un conquistador
> valiente para que hiciera esto.
>
> Por información de vir[r]ey de la Nueva España
> se dío cuenta de un capitán español que vivía
> en Queretaro, Mexico, que era muy conocido
> Al llamado del rey de España Escandón fue[19]

In this unpublished sketch entitled "¿Quiénes Somos?" González answers the question of who we are by rehearsing the Spanish colonization of the region—and, interestingly, just like Paredes would later do in *With His Pistol in His Hand*. The answer to "¿Quiénes Somos?" revolves around the figure of Capitán Escandón. Spanish and conquistador, Escandón enters the temporal frame of 1925 as the Spaniard who colonized the frontier just south and north of the Rio Grande, and by doing so, he helped delay the encroachments of the French in Louisiana.

In 1925 though, González resurrects him to create yet another wedge of colonialidad, but this time against the encroaching Anglo-Americans who are intent on capitalizing on and industrializing el Valle de Texas and the border towns. The imposition of Anglo-American modernity onto people of Mexican descent post-1848 did not just re-enforce the political and economic colonization of once-held Spanish/Mexican territories; it also made it more difficult to notice the relationship of colonialism to modernity, especially, as we see here, when specific expressions of colonialidad of power are deployed as critique. For the settler hybrid, the project of modernity is thus vexed in terms of race and doubly vexed in terms of gender at those geopolitical moments when it is confirmed that one set of colonial masters has been replaced by imperial ones, and that no liberation strategy outside of modernity itself is available.

By contrast, we can say that Geronimo's twice-narrated story bears the geopolitical markings of layered modernities. His memories and oral narrative are in dialogue with his and his people's place of origin in the borderlands of Arizona and northern Mexico, a homeland overdetermined by European-inspired waves of colonization since Coronado's expedition in 1542. Geronimo's autobiography serves as an essential reminder that any attempt to locate modernity in Mexican American writing from this same border region should not come at the expense of reinventing colonial power relations, neither the previous Spanish racial casting of gente de razón y gente sin razón nor the later Mexican republic of Mexicanos y indios. To recover modernity alongside Geronimo's representation of history and place is well within Mignolo's understanding of how to mark the extent and limits of colonial power in the Américas. As in the previous chapters, Geronimo's narration of particulars establishes not just the shifting contact zones of his and his people's lives, but also their reactions, the character of living in a place. As James Taylor Carson might say, Geronimo's text presents "native landscape as both a cultural and moral space, a place where mythical beings, ancestral spirits, daily life, and geopolitical concerns coexisted and interplayed" (783).

Thus, Geronimo's text should be read as a prime example of how one individual found a way to represent the "conflictive domain of semiotic interactions among members of radically different cultures engaged in a struggle of imposition and appropriation, on the one hand, and of resistance, opposition and adaptation on the other" (Mignolo, "Colonial Situations," 93). Not only does Geronimo's text give evidence of this dynamic engagement, more precisely it does so within territorial representations that name European colonial intrusions that work to erase and silence indigenous inscriptions of their place in the world. As Mignolo observes, throughout the Américas, these territorial representations are a form of colonial semiosis that work to undermine the denial of settler-colonial semiotic practices, a "denial of coevalness" that always means to occlude indigenous presence, especially in terms of place and time (94). By "denial of coevalness," Mignolo generally means the denial of ideologies of racial and cultural superiority that underwrote European colonialism in the Américas. Seen in the context of subversive semiotic practices, Geronimo's text promotes justice through truth-telling from the perspective of a contested place like the borderlands between the United States and Mexico. Geronimo's text confirms over and over again how natives like himself and his people were targeted and exploited to make way for colonialism and modernity.

One gathers, as one reads along in the text, that it is the nearness of his death and the nearing genocide of his people that compels Geronimo to narrate his story. Early on he acknowledges his motivation: "We are vanishing from the earth, yet I cannot think we are useless or Usen would not have created us. He created all tribes of men and certainly had a righteous purpose in creating each" (*His Own Story*, 69). Geronimo's deathbed memory and desire for the warpath rekindles the contact zone of his and his tribe's historical moment that dealt with Mexican settlers and their Mexican government's desire for control of the northern territories. Hemmed in militarily by the Mexican republic on one end and the United States on the other, it should surprise no one that his declared faith in Usen and his hope for the future comes in the opening section of his story, which means to narrate for posterity the origins of the Apache peoples. Geronimo's positioning of the origins tale establishes the primacy of their place-based identity. This is an idea that Geronimo returns to at the end of his story, when he appeals to President Theodore Roosevelt for the return of his people to their ancestral lands:

> We are now held on Comanche and Kiowa lands, which are not suited to our needs—these lands and this climate are suited to the Indians who originally inhabited this country, of course, but our people are decreasing in numbers here, and will continue to decrease unless they are allowed to return to their native land. Such a result is inevitable.
>
> There is no climate or soil which, to my mind, is equal to that of Arizona. We could have plenty of good cultivating land, plenty of

grass, plenty of timber and plenty of minerals in that land which the Almighty created for the Apaches. It is my land, my home, my fathers' land, to which I now ask to be allowed to return. I want to spend my last days there, and be buried among those mountains. If this could be I might die in peace, feeling that my people, placed in their native homes, would increase in numbers, rather than diminish as at present, and that our name would not become extinct.

I know that if my people were placed in that mountainous region lying around the headwaters of the Gila River they would live in peace and act according to the will of the President. They would be prosperous and happy in tilling the soil and learning the civilization of the white men, whom they now respect. Could I but see this accomplished, I think I could forget all the wrongs that I have ever received, and die a contented and happy old man. But we can do nothing in this matter ourselves—we must wait until those in authority choose to act. If this cannot be done during my lifetime—if I must die in bondage—I hope that the remnant of the Apache tribe may, when I am gone, be granted the one privilege which they request—to return to Arizona. (173)

In case I have given the wrong impression, I am not advocating that we consider Geronimo's life story "recoverable" along the lines of the Recovery Project on behalf of Chicanx studies. According to Angie Debo, even at his deathbed, Geronimo "relived the youthful tragedy of the massacre of his first family and his hatred of Mexicans" (440). He was not one of them, the "Mexicans," nor of course does his life story ever claim an identity other than that of his people. In his final days, he petitions, like a Moses of his newly adopted Christianity, to have him and his people granted the freedom to return to their homeland. Even as race and racism increasingly segregated one community from another, Geronimo's biographical facts suggest that nonetheless there is a coloniality that links Anglo-Americans, Mexicans, Mexican Americans, and Apaches. This coloniality shaping raced communities is recoverable and germane to the Recovery Project. As Geronimo's text demonstrates, there exists a critical horizon where the recovery of

Mexican American history and print culture will prove incomplete without grappling how it overlaps with the histories and cultures of other groups, especially the indigenous of the Southwest and West. It is in this context that I believe the Recovery Project can play a respectful and purposeful role in U.S. Native studies.

The Lincoln County War in New Mexico

In 1936 former territorial governor of New Mexico and descendant of a powerful colonial family in the region Miguel Antonio Otero Jr. publishes a text that is part memoir, part ethnography, but overtly a biography of the infamous outlaw Billy the Kid.[20] This curiously crafted text saw limited publication in its time, but subsequently, in the cottage industry that surrounds Billy the Kid, it has become a mainstay of information for Kid scholars. All the same, the text's Hispanic importance, like the author himself, languished in the margins of archival purgatory for decades. Fortunately, in 1998 the Recovery Project republished the Otero text.[21] In his introduction, John-Michael Rivera makes two key arguments about Otero and his text: One, he re-situates the importance of Otero to Chicanx studies. During the Chicana/o Movement, Otero was routinely one of the historical figures much maligned as an apologist for the U.S. takeover of the Mexican Southwest. Like other figures in the nineteenth century, Otero was no simple vehicle for U.S. hegemony, Rivera argues, but rather an astute politician for Nuevo Mexicanos, who nonetheless believed in the democratic institutions of the United States. Second, in this complicated context, Rivera reads Otero's interest in Billy the Kid as a cultural project that allows him to critique U.S. colonialism, narrate the "real" Billy the Kid, and simultaneously contest a monolithic Anglo-European mythology about racial superiority in North America (xi).

My interest is not only to expand Rivera's argument that Otero consciously makes use of a border figure, like Billy the Kid, who cuts historically across language, class, and nationalist sympathies, but to call attention specifically to the multiple raced narratives in Otero's text. In particular, I argue that multiple raced narratives underwrite Otero's repeated attempts to assigned "truth" to his telling of the Lincoln County War of 1878. Beyond his obvious rehabilitation of Billy of the Kid as a local hero, Otero, as Rivera observes, never lost sight of incorporating Nuevo Mexicanos as part of the rhetorical *people* who hailed Billy the Kid as one of their own: "Billy was a good boy, but he was hounded by men who wanted to kill him because they feared him. He was always on the defensive'" (Paulita Maxwell Jaramillo, Fort Sumner, qtd. in Otero, 133). "'Billy was a perfect gentleman and a man with a noble heart. He never killed a native citizen of New Mexico in all his career; the men he did kill, he had to in defense of his own life. He had plenty of courage. He was a brave man and did not know what fear meant. They had to sneak up on him in the dead of night to murder him'" (Don Martin Chavez, Santa Fé, qtd. in Otero, 133). Indeed, as these quotations make clear, Billy the Kid was very respected if not championed by local citizens, as Don Martin Chavez puts it. Further, again as Rivera observes, of all the contemporary Anglo eyewitness reports of Billy the Kid, only Otero makes clear how Hispanicized Billy the Kid was in fact. Besides his ability to speak Spanish, Billy the Kid repeatedly made use of his popular reputation among Nuevo Mexicanos and Mexicanos south of the border to disappear among them when it suited him. Billy the Kid's own Hispanicized life, his settler hybridity, is thus a regular feature of the biography, but he is not the only settler hybrid in Otero's text.

By 1936, although memory of the Lincoln County War—and the Santa Fé Ring that made use of the law and lawlessness alike, depending on the circumstance—was quickly fading, Otero reinvests in the open-ended character of New Mexico's territorial period. Far more provocative than the Kid's Hispanic mannerisms are Otero's narrative threads that weave a multiracial cast of characters—good guys versus bad guys, of course— some Anglo, some Nuevo Mexicano, some Native American, and some even African American at the height of the Lincoln County War. If in the territory west of New Mexico, Geronimo and his people were being persecuted by the U.S. and Mexican cavalry, here in New Mexico in the 1870s monied interests are busy consolidating economic opportunities, where even gunmen like Billy the Kid have a role to play in the transformation of New Mexico into a territory suitable to join the union. The racial loyalties represented in Otero's text are both familiar in their rigid constructions and oddly fluid given the economic motivations that underwrote the Lincoln County War. For example, Billy the Kid's whiteness in Otero's narrative ebbs and flows depending on his kinship and economic ties with people who knew him. By contrast, the racial status of Nuevo Mexicanos and Pueblo people are more static, but interestingly, African American soldiers enjoy a very situated celebrity status in the region.

Because Billy the Kid and the Lincoln County War have had a continual hold on popular culture and historians alike, I am going to rehearse only the essential details about this local conflict that grew out of a desire to control the markets that opened up in the years following the end of the Mexican-American War.[22] In this period, not unlike other regions in the West, business opportunities (like the railroad monopolies in California), electoral politics, and law enforcement were often institutions corrupted in the pursuit of money-making schemes by individuals, but more often by groups. In this case, you had the overarching nemesis in the so-called Santa Fé Ring, "a political constituency affiliated with the Republican Party in Washington, D.C." but of course headquartered in Santa Fé, New Mexico (Rivera, xxx). This cartel, as Rivera calls them, sought the monopolistic control of the cattle industry, railroads, and federal contracts in the whole territory of New Mexico. This cartel in turn supported as an ally the Murphy, Dolan, and Riley families who controlled Lincoln County in the south of the state. These families represent the true villains of the Otero text.

Into this dubious environment arrives one John H. Tunstall from England. Shortly after his arrival in 1875, Tunstall becomes friends with and a business associate of the Otero family and, more important, a business partner of lawyer Alexander A. McSween. Together, Tunstall and McSween open the first bank in Lincoln County and a merchandise store that competes with the one run by Murphy and Dolan. Because of a previous break over refusing to defend cattle thieves who actually worked for Murphy and Dolan, McSween was approached and befriended by John Chisum, cattle king of the southern New Mexico region. His large spread was often raided by cattle rustlers that supplied Murphy and Dolan, and hence the Santa Fé Ring.

Three years later, in 1878, it's clear to all that Tunstall and McSween, supported by Chisum, the Oteros, and other Nuevo Mexicanos, are definitely prospering. Targeted because of their insistence on living within the letter of the law, Tunstall and McSween soon fall prey to the machinations of Murphy and Dolan. By this time, too, Billy the Kid, who had previously worked for Murphy, is now in the employment of Tunstall as a cattle hand. In fact, it is the outright murder of Tunstall by the Lincoln County Sheriff William Brady and his men that, as Otero writes, "was the one spark needed to start the Lincoln County War into a blaze" (39). Of Billy the Kid, Otero purports the following: "Standing at the open grave, The Kid muttered savagely: 'I'll get every son of a bitch who helped kill John if it's the last thing I do.'" After Tunstall's burial, both sides basically prepare for a civilian armed conflict that is steeped in personal animosities but also acutely about managing the political and economic future of the territory.

In hindsight, the most interesting aspect about this episode of vigilante hostilities is how revealed the colonial mechanisms of power are that were brought to bear on New Mexico in the decades after 1848. Not so unlike María Amparo Ruiz de Burton's novel *The Squatter and the Don* (1885), which critiqued the willingness of monopolists to subvert democratic and legal institutions in the name of profit, Otero's rendering of the *real* Billy the Kid lifts the shroud of mythology off the Lincoln County War to expose how the continuing logic of Manifest Destiny undermined any pretense that the new Anglo regime was bettering New Mexico. Rivera writes:

> What is ultimately seen through *The Real Billy the Kid*, then, is a distinctive contestation narrative written from the perspective of an elite Hispanic in New Mexico, one that attempts to reinscribe the cultural history of Nuevomexicanos through historical biography. Otero thus challenged the image of Billy the Kid and the history of the Hispanic Southwest as rendered by historians representing the Euroamerican colonial power structure. It is no wonder, then, that Otero's text was not as popular as [Pat] Garret's or any other Anglo-American representation of Billy the Kid's life and that it has taken over eighty-five years to introduce his voice to the public. (xvii)

I would add that Otero's text also makes clear how the continuing logic of Manifest Destiny over time blurred the line between colonizer and colonized under the nation-building project of the United States and its civic and financial institutions. Such blurring is fundamental to understanding how settler hybridity evolved in Mexican American communities. In the case of families like the Oteros, the post–Civil War politics of Manifest Destiny aggravated racial loyalties that were already submerged, intertwined, and complicated through hundreds of years of Catholicism and miscegenation by 1848. The elites of New Mexico owed their status and wealth in the region to their ancestors who colonized and oppressed the indigenous peoples in the area since the Oñate Expedition in 1598. Emblematic of the political unconscious of this colonial legacy, Otero's text on Billy the Kid is virtually silent on the topic of colonial relations with indigenous peoples.

By contrast, Otero's text is alert to the historical presence of African American soldiers at nearby Fort Stanton. Their role in the Lincoln County War is yet another instance of how greed and avarice manipulated the racial groups in the area and in a complexity more recognizable in the late twentieth century. Nonetheless, the following is part of the historical record: Unlike the more celebrated Gunfight at the O.K. Corral in Arizona, or even the distinctly regional Massacre at Mussel Slough in California, the events surrounding the Battle of Lincoln, a siege of the McSween home in Lincoln, are less known despite the over-the-top violence it wreaked on the locals. Over a four-day period, the town of Lincoln is divided by armed combatants. Holed up in the McSween home is Billy the Kid, a number of other Anglos, including wives, but also, significantly, quite a number of Nuevo Mexicanos. Opposing them is the Murphy, Dolan, and Riley group. A stalemate develops because each side is equally armed and provisioned. To break the stalemate, the Santa Fé Ring collaborators decide to call upon their ally Colonel Nathan A. M. Dudley and his troops, the Ninth Cavalry, "a negro regiment," (102) as one of Otero's informants (George Coe) remembers.

Writing about this moment and the complicated set of relationships among those involved, Otero narrates:

At this time, blustering Colonel N. A. M. Dudley was commander of Fort Stanton. He was one of those officers whose principal duty seemed to be to consume the good liquor furnished by Murphy Dolan, and Riley. A friend of the Murphy-Dolan-Riley faction, he did not feel that he could refuse Peppin's summons. [Peppin succeeded William Brady as sheriff after Brady's death at the hands of Billy the Kid and other Tunstall/McSween allies.] He dispatched his orderly, gathered a troop of cavalry, a squad of artillery with a Gatling gun and a twelve-pounder, and started on the double-quick for Lincoln. Colonel Dudley himself took command. (54)

McSween takes the presence of the cavalry as a hopeful signed that some kind of truce could be negotiated. Instead, the Murphy-Dolan-Riley faction take advantage of the confusion that the cavalry's entrance onto the scene caused and set fire to one of the back rooms of the McSween compound. According to Otero, Dolan himself sets fire to the house, hoping to "burn them out like rats" (54). After the fire is set and shooting recommences, "Colonel Dudley established his camp in the street between the McSween and Murphy stores, placing his cannon in a depression in the road between the opposing factions. He announced that he would turn his guns loose on the clan which fired the first shot over the heads of his troops. Yet though the firing went on the big guns remained silent" (55). In essence, Colonel Dudley gives the Murphy-Dolan-Riley faction the upper hand. In the end, the McSween home continues to burn into the night. Despite personal pleas from Mrs. McSween to Colonel Dudley, several defenders die, including McSween, but Billy the Kid and a handful of others manage to escape in a mad dash from the flames and the shooting, over the dead bodies of many a comrade.

Although its relatively easy to get lost in the revenge-filled plot of this part of Otero's text and be seduced to ask what happens to Billy the Kid next, I would restrain us from doing that and instead return us to that odd mental picture that Otero paints when he asks the reader to visualize the Ninth Cavalry, its Gatling gun and cannon position between the McSween and Murphy stores, with the nearby McSween compound in flames. The geometric triangulation Otero draws between all the principal actors in this event also dovetails racially when you unpack and identify the participants. You have the Anglo-dominant Murphy-Dolan-Riley faction on one side, the McSween side overwhelmingly composed of Nuevo Mexicanos, and finally, in the middle, the Ninth U.S. Cavalry, which is composed exclusively of African American soldiers, soldiers who were specifically commissioned to aid and abet in the U.S. government policy of removal, containment, and eradication of indigenous people in the West or in South Texas, and to deal with both indigenous people and Mexicans from south of the border. When viewed again, this scene of hostility at Lincoln straddles other narratives of hostility. It is an event just begging to be analyzed. I do not know of another historical instance where such a rich confluence of racial narratives occurs in such a dizzying array of possibilities.

Later in the text, Otero offers his readers a second look, if you will, at the Ninth Cavalry that amplifies and deepens why we might want to think of the Battle of Lincoln in racialized terms.[23] After narrating the events that lead to Billy the Kid's death at the hands of Pat Garret, Otero transcribes a series of interviews he had with firsthand informants and Lincoln County War participants still alive in the 1930s. One of them, George Coe, described an incident that threatened to undermine the town's relationship with the soldiers at Fort Stanton:

> Murphy and his associates were not looking for honest men; they preferred men like themselves-with a lust for theft and murder. They always worked through men of this type and kept themselves in the background. They did the planning for the men, who in turn carried out their orders dutifully and cold-bloodedly.
>
> At about this time, a man by the name of Frank Freeman had come to Lincoln from Alabama. He was intensely southern in his feelings and made no secret of the fact that he hated a negro. Fort Stanton was garrisoned by the Ninth Cavalry, which was a negro regiment. Consequently negro soldiers were frequently in Lincoln. One day while Freeman was having breakfast, a negro soldier entered the restaurant and seated himself at Freeman's table. Freeman became indignant

and ordered the negro to move. The negro replied insolently that the country was free and declared that he intended to stay where he was. Freeman whipped out his pistol and shot the negro in the forehead, killing him instantly. Much excitement followed this killing. Freeman had to leave Lincoln on a fast horse in order to save his life. The other negro soldiers were naturally desirous of avenging the death of one of their number.

Major William Brady was sheriff of Lincoln County and under control of Murphy, Dolan and Riley. They always sought good favor with the officers and soldiers at Fort Stanton. It was not long until they instructed Brady to capture Freeman so that they could prove their good-will toward the soldiers at Fort Stanton. Brady went after Freeman energetically. Freeman had fled from Lincoln by the short way over the mountains and had taken refuge at the home of Doc Scurlock, near where I was living. By the time Brady reached that part of the country, Freeman had taken to the hills for greater security. . . .

But I must return to Frank Freeman. He did not get out of the country while he had the chance, and in the end was captured by the negro soldiers, who lynched him without any sort of a trial. (102–3)

Given the scant sources here, it is hard to know what went through the minds of the African American soldiers who participated in the Freeman incident or the Battle of Lincoln.[24] To whom did they give their allegiance? The United States government? Their commanding officer? The good citizens of Lincoln? Their comrades in arms? And if all of the above, could they really have supported the Murphy-Dolan-Riley faction that had hired Freeman in the first place? By contrast, was the McSween gang, despite its support among Nuevo Mexicanos, any better at race politics when it came to the African American soldiers at Fort Stanton? Even Otero's transcription of George Coe's testimony must come under scrutiny. Is Coe's almost genteel tone with regards to the Ninth Cavalry his or that of Otero, who was once a public official and is writing in the middle of Franklin D. Roosevelt's New Deal?

Altogether these questions point to the fact that more attention needs to be given to the intersections of raced communities in the United States.

The Lincoln County War is not the only recorded instance where people of African descent appear in the Southwest. As referenced at the beginning of this chapter, people of African descent were part of Coronado's expedition in 1540, including the well-known figure Estevanico.[25] Much later African American soldiers play a decisive role in the Hispanic Southwest. In fact, Otero's attention on the Ninth Cavalry inadvertently reminds us that by the end of the nineteenth century, during the Spanish-American War of 1898, African American soldiers and Nuevomexicano volunteers, some of whom rode with Teddy Roosevelt's Rough Riders, would come together clearly on the same side, on behalf the United States' armed conflict with Spain. Less clear though is the idea on the one hand of Hispano fighting Hispano in a hemispheric colonial war and on the other African American soldiers fighting Afro-mestizo Cubans, when otherwise hemispheric racism against people of African descent would have made them allies of one another.[26]

In the end, Miguel Antonio Otero Jr. makes it clear that he was a friend of and ally to Billy the Kid. After practically renarrating all his informants' stories, Otero finally tells about his meeting with Billy the Kid in late December 1880. Jailed in his town, Las Vegas, New Mexico, Otero met him as he was being escorted to Santa Fé. He and his brother traveled on the train to Santa Fé with Billy the Kid and other outlaws, and once in Santa Fé, they went about providing the Kid with "cigarette papers, tobacco, chewing gum, candy, pies, and nuts" (133). It's on the train ride that Otero connects with the Kid's reputation: "I was just one month older than Billy. I like the Kid very much, and long before we even reached Santa Fé, nothing would have pleased me more than to have witnessed his escape. He had his share of good qualities and was very pleasant. He had a reputation for being considerate of the old, the young and the poor; he was loyal to his friends and above all, loved his mother devotedly. He was unfortunate in starting life, and became a victim of circumstances." Whatever his faults, Otero seems to be saying, he recognized himself in Billy the Kid. Billy the Kid was a mirror version of himself, except for those circumstances that made him a victim. Throughout his text, Otero strives to portray events outside of some linear method more traditional in historical narratives. Rather, he privileges the perspectives of his informants to get at the truth:

"My purpose from the beginning has been to seek the recollection and impressions of these events from personal contact with the participants" (129). Aware that accounts might conflict with one another, especially after the lapse of fifty years, Otero's larger purpose is to trust those who lived through "one of the most remarkable outbreaks of lawlessness the United States has ever witnessed."

Hidden here beneath Otero's words of praise for the Kid is his own history with the Santa Fé Ring, and that period of lawlessness, and the steps he took to deal with the Ring. But he chooses not to delve into his own personal history; instead, he turns in the concluding chapter once more to the manner in which the Kid died. Otero again points to Pat Garrett's flimsy story of bravery. Against Garrett's own concluding testimony (136–44), the reader has in mind the details of the Kid's death from several informants, including an elderly Indian woman, Deluvina, who was very fond of the Kid and referred to him as "my little boy" (116): "'He [Garrett] was afraid to go back to the room to make sure of whom he had shot!' she exclaimed. 'I went in and was the first to discover that they had killed my little boy. I hated those men and am glad that I have lived long enough to see them all dead and buried'" (116). Given this indigenous woman's passion for the wrongful death of Billy the Kid, it's hard not to wonder what other wrongful deaths and injustices ride on her words. Her satisfaction with the deaths of the Kid's enemies reminds us of Geronimo's talk of going on the warpath against Old Mexico.

So if on matters of race, it is now becoming common to teach and conduct research on the Afro-mestizo of Latin America or U.S. Latinx communities or to take up the topic of anti-Blackness in our fields, there are still too few instances when we are asked to think of raced communities in connection with each other. Like many others, I feel the segregationist policies and discourses of the twentieth century continue to haunt us today in 2022, even in academia. Desegregating our respective archives remains one means of continuing the ideals of the civil rights movement, and within a global context furthering the efforts of many to decolonize the social and economic structures of feeling that often prevent one community of blood, kin, and culture from making common cause with another community of blood, kin, and culture. I say this mindful that it is only because of the newly expanded archive that we can recommit to desegregating not only our neighborhoods and barrios, schools, and workplaces but also, importantly, our minds. It is because of this archive and the continued commitment of scholars in all fields of recovery that we will be able to forward our commitment to future generations and together with our respective archives help meet the challenges that are sure to come.

4 Me Llaman Mexicana

Gender and Choice under Coloniality

UN INCIDENTE FEO
No quería entrar el jardín; sin ver a nadie, me
sentía humillada; pero de todos modos, Carlota
la criada, oyo el timbre y abrió el portón.

Mi abuela me recibió con un vaso de leche helada,
y unos bizcocho recién hechos. Al verme, mi
abuela dejó el libro que leía, y vino a mi lado.

Pero Nena, qué tienes! Qué te pasa?" Mira
no más que cara traes parece—parece que
te pico un panal de abejas.

Al oir estas palabras me puse a llorar más y
más. "Niña, niña, ¿que te pasa, que te pasa?
Y entre más me hablaba más lloraba. Por
Dios nena ¡habla, habla!

"Es que las muchachas americanas no
quieran jugar con nosotros Me llaman
Mexicana y dicen que soy mala, y debo irme
para Mexico

Yo arreglaré todo; iré a ver a la madre
superiora; a mí nieta no se le insulta.
Ni se le humilde.
—Jovita González (circa 1925)

Precisely because of the nation-state urgencies of the United States and Mexico after 1848, identifying, quantifying, and stabilizing what was meant by *Mexican*—as opposed to the identity of *Indian*—had a multitude of political and economic ramifications in the nineteenth century, most of which survived intact into the early twentieth century. Nowhere are these ramifications more deeply and sharply felt than along gender lines. As the epigraph make clear, Jovita González had ample memory of how, when, and where her Mexicanness was drawn into question, a schoolyard incident, among other Catholic-raised girls probably, where the American girls (read Anglo) refuse to play with "nosotros" (read with us girls of Mexican descent).[1] And why? Because to be "Mexicana" is to be "mala," bad. The presence of the family servant, Carlota, also serves notice that under the growing dominance of Anglo-Americans in South Texas class privilege is no protection against Anglo-Texan nationalism and racism. Despite her attempt to hold her tears back, the young Jovita releases her hurt feelings once under the protective aura of her grandmother, whose voice and kindness solicits what is wrong and who just as quickly forms a plan to see the mother superior the next day because no one insults or embarrasses her granddaughter.

This ugly incident of racial loyalty, "Un incidente feo," a childhood memory she sketches in her early twenties, frames a contest over identity—a kind of psychic battle all too familiar for children of Mexican descent since 1848, and especially in Texas—where there had not been one before, at least not one pitted against the superiority of Anglo whiteness and Anglo femininity. Marissa López considers such psychic battles as emblematic of the divestments of authority, wealth, and privilege that become all too frequent after 1848. Accompanying such moments of divestments, argues López, are these replacement "Mexican feelings" that are assigned racially to the Mexican body and conjure "a public image of Mexicans as diseased, dirty, and displaced" ("Feeling Mexican," 170). Although this is an isolated incident, I argue, it is the kind of racism that will come to mark a trend in González's published and unpublished works around the need to negotiate this ugliness between Mexicanos and Anglos. The difficulty in negotiating this ugliness will end up characterizing many of her life choices, whether as a woman, as an intellectual, or as a writer.

For González's generation, the term *Mexican* in the context of citizenship, especially with regard to immigration, oscillates, and had oscillated for decades, as something of a synecdoche to represent either an individual or a community of Mexican descent or as an individual or a community representative of the country of Mexico. And while this usage of *Mexican* was quite common in popular discourse at the time (and sadly even today), it was also quite common to read or hear the term *Mexican* used as a metonymy, where *Mexican* stands in for something else, like a Spanish speaker, a working-class laborer, an undocumented immigrant, or an uneducated, poor person of color. The interplay between the term's articulation as either a synecdoche or metonymy has had profound consequences for people of Mexican descent in the United States, but also for other Hispanic communities of non-Mexican origins as well.

I treat *Mexican* in this chapter as an important keyword, a portal, an index for understanding settler belonging, but within the broader historical framework of competing settler colonialisms, where the term *Mexican* became a potent marker for race, racism, nation-building in pre- and post-1848 North America.[2] Part of the necessary critical unpacking focuses on the presence and representation of the "Mexican" as a figure in Anglo-American and Mexican American cultural productions, political history, and political discourse. *Mexican* is in fact a very potent and particular instance of a modernity of subtraction. Besides its racialized connotations over time, the burdens of this subtraction are keenly situated along gendered lines. Historicizing the deployment of this term is therefore central to understanding the affective and political dimensions of being of Mexican descent in the United States at any given time. In this context, to claim a Mexican heritage, to claim one's Mexicanness, is to enter the space of colonial difference willingly.

All of this leads me to argue that the term *Mexican*, although conceived in an era of nineteenth-century nation-building and arising from the engines of colonialism, Spanish and then Mexican, is and has been, at least since 1848, a term that also derives its identity from the very same political and cultural terrain that seeks to limit if not deny its political efficacy in the first place. In short, *Mexican* is a product not just of the republic of Los Estados

Unidos de México but also of the United States of America. Given the rise of modernity out of coloniality, the ongoing manifestations of coloniality of power through nationalism and the refiguring of national boundaries because of military conflict on the border, including the Mexican Revolution, where the social construction of *Mexican* begins and ends is a very good question, but clearly it is not only south of the border.

Despite the ubiquity of the term *Mexican* in Chicanx studies and U.S. West studies, there has been very little critical pressure on it—nor on *Mexican American* for that matter. Critics' interests typically have leaned more toward *borderlands*. Treating *Mexican* as a keyword thus makes visible how the term has evolved in important tensions with, first, regional understandings (the Texas War of Independence in 1836 remapped multiple borders) and, second, national understandings (the Mexican-American War in 1848 added massive territory). It makes visible, moreover, that *Mexican* has been implicated across major transformations of identities, ideologies, territorial holdings, and politics. While the origins of the term belong to the Republic of Mexico, simultaneously, *Mexican* must be de-linked from exclusive ties to those national origins in order to recognize its construction, and the reasons for that construction, in the United States. The murky terrain between *Mexican* and *Mexican American* notwithstanding, it is clear that the former is deployed as a disqualifier for the latter, rendering the binational term practically unsuitable to denote U.S. citizenship.[3]

As a keyword, *Mexican* functions as an underestimated index for comprehending competing Spanish/Mexican/Anglo settler colonialisms in pre- and post-1836 Texas. It is also one of the more sly markers for race, racism, and white nation-building. In a place like Texas, for example, where Anglo-Texan nationalism is typified by a monument such as the Alamo or an institution such as the Texas Rangers, the circulation of the term *Mexican* ironically holds down the ground for an Anglo settler-colonial identity that continues a coloniality of power into the present. *Mexican* is coopted even when rhetorically absent—build a wall on the border for "national security" purposes instead of declaring a desire to "keep Mexicans out"—so as to forward a particular ideological and racialized political class as the true inheritors of the Texas state.[4]

Why is *Mexican* so malleable, prone to manipulation and distortion? Why is this term simultaneously such an inescapable feature of Mexican American social life in the United States? The heart of the matter lies with the history of the Treaty of Guadalupe Hidalgo on questions of citizenship.[5] Mexican Americans are not conventionally understood to be a stateless people. But in the immediate aftermath of the Mexican-American War, the U.S. Senate, in treaty revisions, eliminated the provision that granted citizenship after one year to those Mexicans who elected to remain in the newly conquered territories of the United States. At the moment of invention of the possible status of the Mexican American, the Senate disallowed the category. Disregarding the agreements made by the Treaty of Guadalupe Hidalgo, the Senate instead wrested power back to itself. Only Congress had the authority to render decisions about how, when, and where people of Mexican descent could claim citizenship. It is precisely in relation to embattled questions of citizenship that the term *Mexican*, in U.S. legal history, was initially constituted. By withholding a recognized status under U.S. law, *Mexican* could only articulate a status of statelessness.

Until the civil rights period beginning in earnest in the 1950s, in practice, all people of Mexican descent, even U.S. born, were thought of as *Mexicans*. Jim Crow laws were erected to obstruct or completely prevent people of Mexican descent from voting or performing other civic duties, such as being a member of a jury. At other times, de facto means of power segregated social spaces: no dogs or Mexicans allowed. Whether under a legal framework or de facto racial codes, the term *Mexican* could be relied upon to nullify claims on citizenship, or civil rights, or, even more broadly, human rights. If *Mexican* is a term of national belonging outside the borders of the United States, within its borders the term has evolved to signify statelessness and powerlessness. Despite and against the tremendous demographic growth of people of Mexican descent in the United States by the 1930s, the Senate's original dismantling of a path toward citizenship created a contradictory presence of millions of effectively stateless people inside U.S. borders. In short, the Senate's dismissal of citizenship for people of Mexican descent created stateless arenas where the term *Mexican* became a placeholder for *non-citizen, not American*.

In related but also distinct formulations against Indianization as discussed in the previous chapter, *Mexican* evidences a tension from its more regional connotations (old Californio missions, Mexican cuisine, nostalgia for Old Mexico) to perceived threats to the broader U.S. nation (represented over time by Mexican bandidos, pachucos, zoot suits, and so on). *Mexican*, like its cousin term the *West*, often slides from one register to another. The slippage is especially evident at the level of culture where borders are ambiguous. So just as *West* often stands in for *nation*, so too does *Mexican* stand in for *nation*, albeit the one that exists across the proverbial tracks, el otro lado.

This chapter explores how Jovita González as a folklorist comes to champion a regional Mexicanness as a birthright in the United States while simultaneously charting the limits of that birthright for women. Here I follow the feminist lead that María Lugones has established so well in expanding Aníbal Quijano's linking of coloniality with modernity so that gender and gendered systems are not stepchildren to the deconstruction of race, labor, and capital in the colonized Américas. To this end, I focus primarily on "Shades of the Tenth Muse," a short story by González, specifically because it so clearly calls attention to the intersection of coloniality of power and gendered creativity and labor. Throughout her work, one can see González's consistent effort to understand the burdens of coloniality and modernity for Mexican American women as a dilemma not just about choices to be made but also about region and regional identification. Hers is a critical regionalism that forwards neither an overwhelming desire for or against Mexicanness or Americanness but instead a value for social and political location. Local histories, traditions, languages matter, but so does change and exchange with those peoples and processes that threaten to undermine and erase one's heritage.

Shades of the Tenth Muse, Revisited

As María Cotera has argued, González was part of a generational impulse that sought accommodation through a political pluralism, but her pluralism sought more than mere mutuality; it always longed for a more fundamental reckoning with patriarchy, a topic that was consistently overlooked because of the racialized oppression of people of Mexican descent. All the same, long before the Chicana/o Movement, González was willing to critique Mexicanness for the sake of civil rights for everyone. For her own era, González defined a politic that was deeply personal, and perhaps for that very reason not always linear or "rational." Cotera "propose[s] a different kind of reading of Jovita's work, one that does not center on her position as a colonized intellectual trapped in the 'prison house' of colonial discourse" ("Engendering," 238). Keenly aware of the power of racialized strife to drown out issues of gender, González's writings enact what Lugones sees as a feminist imperative: "to make visible the instrumentality of the colonial/modern gender system in subjugating us—both women and men of color—in all domains of existence" ("The Coloniality of Gender," 1). Further, I link "Shades of the Tenth Muse" with Gonzalez's literary translation of South Texas folklore. I do that for two reasons: 1) to emphasize her long-term commitment to issues of gender, which is so pronounced that it actually demonstrates what Lugones means by a "gender system," and 2) to argue that because "Shades of the Tenth Muse" was not published during her life, and perhaps never intended for publication, it points to a personal drama/dilemma—itself an excess moment, uncontainable, of the pressure of being a "modern" woman of Mexican descent, raised Catholic, on the eve of marriage—that she felt could only be represented in a literary form that mimics what she learned in recovering and preserving Native, Spanish, and Mexican folklore for an English-reading audience. And what she learned from her work in folklore is that oral culture, precisely because it is unofficial knowledge, is better able to record how people survive and overcome the limits and oppressions that stem from the modernity/coloniality world system, but also how folklore can advance a critique of those forces while simultaneously charting strategies around those limits, and consequently communicating those strategies undetected by the authorities of official knowledge. Elena V. Valdez calls attention to such strategies as the folkloric difference that accompanies unofficial forms of knowledge production where folklore is "a persistent site of decolonial thinking for people of Mexican descent in the United States."[6]

Long before Américo Paredes published *With His Pistol in His Hand* (1958), a work until fairly recently often singularly linked as synonymous with South Texas of the early twentieth century, Jovita González had been writing, teaching, and organizing for a better future for Mexican Americans in Texas for decades. González was a fairly well-known figure in San Antonio, where she was raised, received her bachelor's degree at Our Lady of the Lake, taught Spanish at Saint Mary's Hall, and was routinely cited in the Spanish-speaking press of *La Prensa* as a folklorist in the 1930s. In fact, it is not overstatement to observe that *La Prensa*, as directed by its founder and editor, Ignacio Lozano, showed avid interest in her evolution as a writer and intellectual, as well as interest in the cohort of young women González associated with. Perhaps, unimaginable today except for Hollywood personalities, *La Prensa* frequently depicted her comings and goings, conferences, awards, and even personal events like news of her successful appendectomy and the kindness of her many friends who visited her in the hospital ("Fue operada la Srita. Jovita González," March 24, 1931, p. 5).

To be sure, *La Prensa* took notice of a number of young and talented people of Mexican descent such as Jovita González, but rarely did someone show up in the news quite like her. Her academic and intellectual accomplishments gave her a stature that few women from South Texas enjoyed. In addition, her social and academic connections, especially those in Austin, Texas, with the likes of J. Frank Dobie and Carlos Castañeda, often intimated a much wider influence and a cultural capital that was not always immediately noticeable within the aura of female propriety *La Prensa* enjoyed validating. Just as important, I would argue, are González's networks of female friendships that were deep and long-standing, especially among women and in the Catholic church. Before and after the newspaper's notice of her academic success, González's name often shows up in the society column, noting her participation in a number of groups such as Tipica del Club de Jóvenes Católicas de San Fernando or Club de Jóvenes Católicas Mexicanas. In the former, the young Catholic women have organized a lecture by Nemesio Garcia Naranjo, who will lecture on "El Problema Político de México" on November 4, 1927, in the auditorium of the Main Avenue High School. The members of this club include "Argentina Blanco, Marianita Umscheid, Sara Ortíz, Lupita y Cristina Icazbalceta, Elodia McClellan, Lupita Martínez, María Luisa Blanco, Refugio Rodríguez, Jovita González, Genoveva Hesse y Germain y Andrea Segard" (advertisement, Nov. 3, 1927, p. 10). Later that same month, there's a notice that the Club de Jóvenes Católicas Mexicanas organized and hosted a successful "Bunco Party" as a fundraiser to buy gifts for the elderly and orphans during Christmas and New Year ("'Bunco Party' del Club Jóvenes Católicos," Nov. 23, 1927, p. 7). The short article seems to delight in reporting the top four winners of the game, including Jovita González, who came in fourth. Further, the article also takes pains to list the leadership of this club and their duties; they include Ernestina Cabello, Refugio Rodríguez, Berta Padilla, Elena Benavides, Cristina Icazbalceta, María Luisa Blanco, Guadalupe Martínez, Consuelo García Garza, Carmen Perry, and Sara Ortíz. Interestingly, Perry is in charge of reporting to the English-language press and Ortíz to the Spanish-language press. Although memberships overlap in the two clubs, there are also differences. In addition, the presence of non-Spanish surnames, such as Umscheid, McClellan, Hesse y Germain, Segard, and Perry, suggests that some kind of Anglo-Mexican interaction as Catholics is afoot, on Mexican topics like border politics or in embodying the identity of Mexicanas when serving the needy.

The bonds of these young women for one another are also displayed in the press. In one instance Jovita González and Lupita Ochoa are the instigators of a "despedida" for María de Lourdes Mayo, who is about to return to San Luis Potosí with her mother. This farewell party was replete with dinner in Brackenridge Park, from 6 to 9 p.m. ("Cena de despedida a una señorita," June 5, 1929, p. 7). Later that same year, González is the object of the "despedida." Lupita Ochoa, Carmen Perry, and Amparo Lozano organized the event at Brackenridge Park on the eve of González's return to Austin to commence her postgraduate studies. Besides a treasure hunt, all the attendees enjoy "una merienda Mexicana de tamales, café, leche y exquisitos dulces" ("Despedida de la Srita. Profesora Jovita Gonzalez," Sept. 19, 1929, p. 7). As evidenced in the pages of *La Prensa*, this type of friendship with other women seems to have provided a deep level of support for González, especially as her studies and research often took her away from family and friends.

It is in this period of high intellectual production and social prominence that González decides to marry. María Cotera, one of the original recoverers of her work, frames the context of understanding this period of her life from a short story González wrote but never published:

> In the spring of 1935, a few months before her marriage to educational activist Edmundo Mireles (July 31, 1935), folklorist Jovita González stole a few moments for herself and penned a short story. Jovita had been awarded a Rockefeller grant to study ranching communities on the Texas-Mexican border the year before and was putting together a manuscript compiled from her fieldwork notes as the guest of a prominent Rio Grande City family. In spite of the "family's efforts to have [her] work in the house," Jovita opted to stay by herself in a "garage room," which she decorated with "relics" gathered from her "quest for stories of the ranch folk." The short story, titled "Shades of the Tenth Muse," is set in this "room of her own," and narrated in the form of a dialogue between the spirits of Sor Juana Inés de la Cruz and Anne Bradstreet, two preeminent poets of colonial America. "Shades of the Tenth Muse" bears analysis as both an example of an entirely unique narrative departure in Jovita's oeuvre and as a remarkable document that testifies to the complex positionality of early Chicana feminists. Contemporary Chicana writers can well imagine the pressures that Jovita must have felt on that spring afternoon of 1935 when she took a break from her university work and her wedding plans to write what could only have been a farewell letter to a "room of one's own" and the comforts it represented. (237)

Analyzing the short story from the vantage point of Chicana feminism, Cotera deftly unpacks the symbolic registers of a staged encounter between the Tenth Muse of New England, Anne Bradstreet, and the Tenth Muse of New Spain, Sor Juana de la Cruz. She focuses on the foundational status of each poet in their respective literary canons, their relationship to patriarchy, their shared compromised creative potential, and finally González's own attempt to narrate the hemispheric range of her identity as a Mexican American woman writer, intellectual, and social activist vis-à-vis this pair of foremothers. Given how the dialogue between the Tenth Muses develops into a mutual respect and curiosity about each other's poetry, Cotera reads González's not-so-subtle projection of her impending marriage into a story as a transition from the private, protected realm of limited independence in the figure of Sor Juana as a Catholic nun to the socially acceptable status as married Puritan woman and the compromised security it provides for Anne Bradstreet: "At the moment of separation from her life as an institutional intellectual (with all its contradictions), and on the eve of her final political commitment to the work of her husband in the arena of Mexican American politics, the dialogue serves as a fictional testament to Jovita's difficult passage from the world of Sor Juana to that of Anne Bradstreet" (245).

While Cotera takes as evidence of this transition the undeniable fact of her marriage to Mireles on July 31, 1935, two details at the end of the story (as we shall see) complicate whether her marriage should be seen as a choice between following Sor Juana's example to remain unmarried or that of Anne Bradstreet's to enjoy the domestic realm of husband and family. That is, it's not clear that she follows either a northern or southern trajectory, but rather some emergent third choice. In addition, it should be noted that the dilemma of a gendered choice González stages here is decidedly different from the gendered choice a character such as Lola Medina negotiates when confronted with the specter of colonial sexual violence at the hands of the Reverend Hackwell in Ruiz de Burton's novel *Who Would Have Thought It?* (1872). González's staged choice is closer to, but in the end different too, from those that María Cristina Mena often stages in her short stories. In "The Gold Vanity Set" (1913), the indigenous woman, Petra, for example, thinks of herself as dramatically transformed by the Anglo-American cosmetic technologies of Miss Young's vanity set. Urged by her father-in-law to return it to Miss Young, but contradictorily encouraged by Miss Young to keep it, Petra decides against either option and instead converts the vanity set into a sacred offering to the Virgen de Guadalupe, out of devotion and gratitude for having rescued her husband from alcoholism and her from his acts of domestic violence. Although González's staged third choice also involves violence, but perhaps in a lesser form, a lower note, it nevertheless points to the violence of coloniality in shaping the structure of choices for women in the Américas, but unlike Petra, González's regional environment provides a secular option.

As readers, we can perceive the folkloric qualities of "Shades of the Tenth Muse" right from the start: from local plants and herbs to ranch culture artifacts to the image and figures of Saint Teresa and the Virgen de Guadalupe:

> The air in the room is close and smoky. I can still smell the rosemary and lavender leaves I have just burnt in an incense burner to drive out the mosquitoes that have driven me insane with their monotonous droning music. For, in spite of the family's efforts to have me work in the house, I prefer my garage room with its screenless windows and door, its dizzy floor, the planks of which act like the keys of an old piano, and walls, hung with relics which I like to gather as I go from ranch to ranch in my quest for stories of the ranch folk. A faded Saint Teresa, in more faded niche smiles her welcome every morning and a Virgin of Guadalupe remind me daily that I am a descendant of a proud stoic race.... It is late, too dark to write, the smell of Rosemary and Lavender is soothing and I fall, can I say asleep; or am I transported three centuries back? ("Shades," 249)

So even before the Muses appear, there's already an ongoing regionalist dialogue, if only subliminal, in her room above the garage. Saint Teresa and the Virgin of Guadalupe are feminine figures who appear in the historical record as effecting changes in their respective male-identified environments; one rewrites the mission of her Carmelite order and the other contravenes on the patriarchal stubbornness of the local bishop. Under the unspoken tutelage of Saint Teresa and the Virgin of Guadalupe, the Tenth Muses emerge from the shadows to recite their own respective geopolitical colonial identities in the New World. Ironically, and unbeknownst to the speaking Muses, their fictional dialogue mirrors their "folkloric" status found in the nation-states that have evolved from the settler colonialisms they each hailed from. In the end, even Jovita Gonzalez's own fictional personality becomes part of the "folkloric" environment represented in the story.

Coloniality of Gender

Before we can proceed further, this issue of environment returns us to an essential question: What does an archive of early Mexican American literature look like when it comes to questions of coloniality and gender? And what does a modernity of subtraction explain? To get to the visibility of a coloniality of gendered choices that I believe Jovita González was aiming for in "Shades of the Tenth Muse," it might be useful to recollect the dominant context of her time for understanding the trials and tribulations of gender along the border. Specifically, it behooves us to look at a text that is self-consciously written as a bildungsroman and, more precisely, written in response to James Joyce's *A Portrait of the Artist as a Young Man* (1916). But from beginning to end, this comparison to Joyce and Stephen Dedalus serves more as a foil than a mirror. In Américo Paredes's *George Washington Gómez*, drafted by 1940 but not published until 1990, the protagonist, George Washington Gómez, is expected to become a leader of his people and a "great man among the Gringos" (16). Having fled Mexico and the Mexican Revolution, his father names him after George Washington to signal the hope that his son's future has a peaceful democratic outcome. Unfortunately for the son, his father underestimated the racialized and segregated nature of the democracy George Washington helped to found.

It is in the context of a U.S. education, classroom racism, and Texas nationalism that the son comes to experience the limits of his father's optimism:

> Consciously he considered himself a Mexican. He was ashamed of the name his dead father had given him, George Washington Gómez. He was grateful to his Uncle Feliciano for having registered him in school as "Guálinto" and having said that it was an Indian name. He spoke Spanish, literally as his mother tongue; it was the only language his mother would allow him to use when he spoke to her. The Mexican flag made him feel sentimental, and a rousing Mexican song would make him feel like yelling.... But there was also George Washington Gómez, the American. He was secretly proud of his name his more conscious twin, Guálinto, was ashamed to avow publicly. George Washington

> Gómez secretly desired to be a full-fledged, complete American without the shameful encumberment of his Mexican race. He was the product of his Anglo teachers and the books he read in school, which were all in English. He felt a pleasant warmth when he heard "The Star-Spangled Banner." ... But he also heard from the lips of his elders songs and stories that were the history of his people, the Mexican people. And he also fought the Spaniards with Hidalgo, the French with Juárez and Zaragosa, and the Gringos with Blas María de la Garza Falcón and Juan Nepomuceno Cortina in his childish fancies. (147–48)

This passage dramatizes the everyday and symbolic effects of a modernity of subtraction, the emptying of social capital on either side of the border, especially in relationship to citizenship. The passage represents a psychological drama all too familiar to readers of Mexican American literature. The school, the classroom, the playground, instead of sites for conferring civic legitimacy and confidence, become venues for embarrassment, shame, and confusion over national belonging, language, and gendered identity. Alternating models of colonial history and modernity present themselves to Guálinto as if all he has to do but choose, but these choices are themselves already structured for those few whose subtractive experiences are compensated by mastering the modes of colonial mimicry available to them.

In Guálinto's case, because his phenotype allows him to pass as "white," because his male privileges at home buttress his public vulnerabilities, and because of his uncle's sacrifices that provide economic security for the family during the Great Depression, he eventually becomes educated at Austin, becomes a lawyer, and changes his name legally to George G. Goméz. He drops the "Washington" only to become an officer in military intelligence. Even before the United States enters World War II, Guálinto, now George, has been ordered to provide "border security," to report on questionable elements south of the border like "German and Japanese agents," and also to keep an eye on so-called progressive groups that agitate in favor of civil rights for Mexican Americans.

The novel ends full of inevitable pathos and complicated layers of betrayals: At one end, there is George, with his sublimated guilt for having betrayed his parents' wish that he lead his "people," for having betrayed, from his Uncle Feliciano's point of view, his Mexicanness, and for having betrayed his childhood mestizo friends who become those progressives of questionable leanings. This all fuses together to produce nightmarish fantasies of heroism in which he single-handedly, and with the aid of modern weapons of warfare, beats back and defeats Sam Houston at the Battle of San Jacinto. On the other end, the reader, who expects and desires a Mexican Stephen Dedalus, feels betrayed because George is neither artist nor revolutionary but instead a "spy" to his uncle and to anyone else who remembers Guálinto as a "Cabrón! . . . Venido sanavavbiche!" (294).

In many ways, *George Washington Gómez* exemplifies the early Mexican American literary text that unmasks the "coloniality of power" of U.S. imperialism that was waged against Mexican American communities, but it also conceals when and where other forms of coloniality of power are secured to retain the status quo, especially when it comes to patriarchy and gendered relations. This type of coloniality of power expresses itself in a variety of ways throughout the novel, but it begins intensely with the patriarchal naming of the firstborn male son. For María Josefina Saldaña-Portillo, "the character of George G./Guálinto Gómez embodies, in literary form, the psychic split enacted by the Treaty of Guadalupe Hidalgo in the racial construction of Chicanos" ("Wavering," 158). As Saldaña-Portillo observes, despite the binational context of his birth, the child's naming overrides more local possibilities, like the fictional revolutionary in the novel, Anacleto de la Peña, or the actual historical person of Venustiano Carranza, a major figure in the Mexican Revolution at the time of Guálinto's birth (151–55). The overt naming of the son as George Washington makes visible the hemispheric power of the United States. He is named to emulate the political and economic stature of the United States in the hemisphere. Even from a broad Latin American context, a name like Simón de Bolívar, El Libertador, is displaced in order to curry favor with the real and imagined culture of the United States, the Colossus of the North.

Equally significant is the gendered nature of this naming. Although it was conceivable, however contradictory, to bestow a symbolic nationalist name on the male firstborn, the same was never an option for Gualínto's two older sisters, Maruca and Carmen. In fact, the text here enacts the kind of "indifference" to gender that, Lugones argues, racialized colonized men have been structured and conditioned to assume as unassailable (1). It never would have occurred to either fictional or real parents to name their daughters to reflect their desires for a national modernity by way of symbolic heroic names. There are no Mexican Martha Washingtons or Mexican Abigail Adamses pointing northward. Southward, there is no naming in honor of the thousands of the soldaderas, women soldiers who accompanied the men as revolutionaries in their own right. Women soldiers, like those immortalized through the corrido, La Adelita, were revered as a group of heroes of the Mexican Revolution but rarely singled out as individuals, and never elevated to the status of enduring national symbols. Figures such as Pancho Villa and Emiliano Zapata achieved over time national and international recognition, whereas women revolutionaries such as Dolores Jiménez y Muro and Hermila Galindo did not, nor did the heroic efforts of a Texas-Mexico border figure, writer, and educator Leonor Villegas de Magnón. So, with regard to the burdens of modernity and coloniality, who or what makes the case for Mexican American women? Where and how can we begin to understand modernity for Mexican American women? And what's the role of Mexicanness for those women who did engage in the more permissible public spheres of the United States?

Descendant of a Proud Stoic Race

In studying González's pre-1935 folkloric production, Díana Noreen Rivera encourages scholars to "remember that González, as a subversive linguistic performer, is an academic artisan. [She was capable of performing] multiple discourses for different rhetorical situations along with double entendres and other speech acts to confront her Anglo oppressors."[7] Along these lines, Rivera demonstrates how one must wait as a reader for her more private affiliations to reveal her truer self and truer politics. Unlike the clashes against Anglo-Texan repression—real and symbolic—in *George Washington Gómez*, the dialogue between the Tenth Muses is cordial, witty, and representative of their personas found in their respective works. Even when their colonial identities and experiences are at odds with each other, these differences do not override their growing fondness for each other:

"Who are you? Your words and attitude dismay and yet surprise me."

"Who am I? I am Sister Joan of the Cross. I serve the Lord, and I also write when my duties permit me. People call me the Tenth Muse of New Spain."

"They call you that? What a coincidence! I am also called the Tenth Muse, but of New England."

"Then we should be friends, and know more of each other. Where are you from? Where do you live?"

"I live in Massachusetts, the governor of the colony is my husband, but I was born in England, dear England," Anne Bradstreet, for she is no other, replied sighing again, a tear rolling down her cheek.

"Why do you weep?"

"For England, for my lovely home, for the friends I left there."

"Don't you like this new place where you live?"

"How can I like it? How can I like the savages, the discomforts of a new country? The ways are so strange! But I am convinced now that it is the way of God and to it I must submit. Do you like your country?"

"Do I like it?" answered the nun with the shining eyes. "You've never seen anything like the greenness of its valleys, and the blueness of the sky. The air is warm and soft, and the first thing my eyes see at dawn are two volcanoes in the distance covered with perpetual snow! I was born there just twelve leagues from the city of palaces, that's what we call Mexico, and there I would be now had it not been that my thirst for knowledge brought me to the city."

"Oh you like knowing too?"

"Yes, I was but three when I learned to read and write, and when I was thirteen my parents presented me to the viceroy who had heard of my learning."

"And when I was seven," answered Anne, "I had as many as eight tutors in languages, dances, and music."

"Strange isn't it that we should like the same things! I love music too." (251)

What is most striking about this fictional dialogue is González's attentiveness to the colonial structures of power and epistemology that underwrite these poets' lives in the Américas. Each has a solid foothold in their respective colonial enterprise; each enjoys a measure of cultural power because of powerful men; each exercises their own version of coloniality of power, Bradstreet over "savages," Sor Juana over "servants"; each produces poetry that in the end is meant to reflect well of their colonial presence in the Américas. One also finds a myth of exceptionalism at work in their autobiographies. Their possession of a unique intellect is meant to both explain their precocious aptitude for the arts but also quietly imply that the masses of women are not like them, Tenth Muses. Instead, the masses of women are unnoticed and unwritten. In the text, they are the "hens," "ladies," and "servants" of their respective gendered worlds. We are left to ruminate on this thought further when Anne Bradstreet and Sor Juana agree to move on from their disagreement on the relative stature of men to women, and vice versa. Sor Juana argues for the possibility of woman's superiority to man, whereas Anne Bradstreet insists on the possibility of essential difference but also equality. Although the argument here is sharp, González disallows any real antagonism. Instead, she moves them toward a quick but deep recognition of their poetic works. Again, differences in their personas arise: Sor Juana's willingness to explore potentially disruptive emotions in language and Anne Bradstreet's to conform herself and poetics to Puritan theology. But again these differences seem only to deepen their regard for each other. Pledges are made to meet again, and as they depart, each Tenth Muse comments on a framed prayer written by González's friend and fellow folklorist Frost Woodhull: "'Oh God, our cows are dying; we are not crying. Our tears are dry much like our land. It's rained on every other land'" (250). Bradstreet finds its familiar and jocular tone with God offensive, even if the content, praying for rain for the ranches experiencing a drought in northern Mexico, might seem reasonable. By contrast, Woodhull's mischievous turn of phrase appeals to Sor Juana's own penchant for disruptive language. Leaving after Bradstreet, Sor Juana "stood up, yawned, looked at me with what I thought was a wink, and following her companion, disappeared in the dimness of space" (255). González responds with her own wink by exiting the story with the short phrase, "Apt and Just."

Having written herself into the story from the beginning as a Guadalupana (an adherent of the Virgen de Guadalupe, patron saint of the Américas), a descendant of ranchers, and her family's keeper of unrequited dreams, González's choice of closure goes against the grain of our presentist temptation to want González to behave as a proto-Chicana, to choose Sor Juana over Anne Bradstreet. So there's an implicit disappointment in knowing that González, having penned her story in April of 1935, nonetheless marries Mireles at the end of July 1935. As Cotera argues, she did not continue in the vein of Sor Juana but married, like Bradstreet. But two things (as promised) should temper our presentist desire for a rebellious proto-Chicana in González, and these two things actually return us to Cotera's larger argument about González: that she should be understood as part of that generation of Mexican American intellectuals, like Carlos E. Castañeda, who sought to articulate a "pluralist vision of American culture that recognized the important historical, cultural, and linguistic contribution of 'Spanish America' in the development of American society" (246). First, Woodhull's prayer, as Cotera quotes in a footnote (255), is dedicated to his friends Helen and Max Michaelis, owners in 1935 of El Fortín Ranch in Coahuila, Mexico. González's admiration for Woodhull lies in his praying "not for himself, but for his friends in the ranches of Northern Mexico" (249). Woodhull's prayer is a miniature dialogue in its own right. The dialogue here is between ranchers of different ethnic and nationalist origins. Anglo and Tejano ranches had been the object of González's research for almost a decade by this point, but the indirect reference to Helen and Max Michaelis points to a rich ethnic and international set of relationships through ranching that overlaps economically the Texas-Mexico border. Like the poetry that connects the women of two different colonial projects, ranching is an activity and a culture that connects South Texas with northern Mexico, while also maintaining key differences. Here drought affects and harms everyone. Woodhull's prayer, and its place of prominence in González's story, points to a ranching space conditioned by competing colonialities of power but also provides a space where Mexican and non-Mexican ranchers can coexist.

Second, unlike in *George Washington Gómez*, the colonial conflict in "Shades of the Tenth Muse" does not depend or devolve into heightened displays of masculine anger, nor does the conflict require either a repression of memory in deference to the hegemonic power of the United States or a psychological sublimation of ethnic anger turned internalized racism against one's own people. Instead the conflict between Sor Juana and Bradstreet is always a measure of the differences between their colonial experiences. Otherwise, they are equally the Tenth Muse. Indeed, González's fictional dialogue reveals her acute awareness of the colonial gender system for each Tenth Muse and how each enabled and disabled her life as a woman and a poet. The real but muted conflict happens off the stage in the figure of the sleeping or transported persona of the writer. Caught between the voices of Bradstreet the settler on the one hand and Sor Juana the criolla on the other, González's voice is read, not heard, with the possible exception of "Apt and Just."

All the same, this unheard voice is itself lodged in the very space of her living accommodations:

> Back of the desk, a collection of ranch spits is witness of my ranching heritage, an old, crude treasure chest holds my only possession, a manuscript which will sometime be sold, if I am among the fortunate. Hanging from a nail above is a home-spun hand-woven coin bag, the very same which my grandfather was given by his mother on his wedding day with the admonition, "my son, may you and all who ever own it keep it filled with gold coins." It hangs there empty, for the descendant of that Don has never seen a gold coin, much less owned one. (249)

Long before Gloria Anzaldúa began writing about the border and borderlands, one can argue that Jovita González was also actively thinking about these two terms. She simultaneously is a "descendant of a proud stoic race" ("Shades," 249) but exists materially at the border of respectability.

She has a room of her own, as Cotera notes, but it exists at the margins of a larger world. All the same, Rivera argues that it is in these more quieted moments that "González's private discourse counters her racial academic persona in which she plays up her 'pure' Spanish heritage" ("Reconsidering," 68). González's affiliation as a Guadalupana confirms for Rivera that "she racially and culturally aligns herself with the progeny of Juan Diego, neophytes, and Mexican mestizos of indigenous and Spanish ancestry." Still, the material comforts of her inner world, rosemary and lavender leaves, old relics, and stories of ranch folk, fade without explanation when Sor Juana and Bradstreet appear out of nowhere. Once they arrive, instead of occupying her thoughts further with her own writing, González's private persona becomes a witness to the Tenth Muses' dialogue. Neither one acknowledges González's presence. Neither one has anything to say that particularly speaks to González's material life. Neither Tenth Muse actually speaks to González's stoic race. There's a Spanish colonial connection to Sor Juana, but the story, like the dialogue, is written in English, so one wonders how deeply one should view the connection. The writer's connection to Bradstreet should be tenuous but for her rediscovery by academia in the 1920s and 1930s in works by Samuel Eliot Morrison and Perry Miller. Like other Puritan figures, Anne Bradstreet was being cited as important to the evolution of American literature itself. As a university scholar, González would have been aware of Bradstreet's curricular and nationalist reintroduction. Strikingly, except for that parting wink of Sor Juana's, there is little or nothing to actually connect the writer to the dialogue. What then is "Apt and Just"? What is appropriate and fair? Accurate and balanced?

Modernity in South Texas

Despite González's deep-seated interest in studying how gender is implicated in folklore, it is not clear that "Shades of a Tenth Muse" is some kind of specific lamentation on her upcoming marriage. Instead, I see it as González's attempt to theorize her colonial condition in Texas, to see her colonial, gendered condition as related to but ultimately separate from the model of feminine creativity provided by the Tenth Muse of either New England or New Spain. Like Rivera, Karen R. Roybal understands

González as always conscious of negotiating the opportunities and limits her subject position afforded:

> Based on her historical and cultural knowledge and the family history that connects her to earliest descendants of the Texas/Mexico borderlands, we can assume that González was no stranger to the intersections of race, class, and domination that prevailed at this significant point in her life. Added to that history and experience were the consequences of being a woman—a gendered subject—who was attempting to insert herself into the social circles she hoped would propel her work into a broader and public sphere, one that would influence a (re)visioning of the sociohistorical reality of *her* Texas. (*Archives of Dispossession*, 70–71)

What neither Muse can speak to, because this was not their experience, is the effect of a racially charged modernity in South Texas. González might be a daughter of the Enlightenment, whether charted through England or Spain, but in Texas before the Chicana/o Movement such allegiances offer very little status or protection or solace. All the same, modernity presents to González what seems like a gendered choice: to choose as a Mexican woman because Mexican women are the designated guarantors of culture, tradition, and language, to choose one mother figure over the other, but she cannot because she hails and resides from a borderlands region whose traditional inhabitants are under economic, cultural, and legal assault. González is a member, as Cotera notes, of "a community struggling to negotiate the brutal political and economic imperatives that accompanied the [capitalist] modernization of what was once an isolated region of Texas" (*Native Speakers*, 104). To get a clearer picture of what modernity and its burdens mean to her and how they relate to her "stories of ranch folk" and her self-identification as "a descendant of a proud stoic race" ("Shades," 249), we need to turn to González's scholarship in her master's thesis in history for the University of Texas, "Social Life in Cameron, Starr, and Zapata Counties," from 1930. Written and defended five years before "Shades of the Tenth Muse," in this document we see an emergent third borderlands strategy that straddles the same divide dramatized by Sor Juana and Anne Bradstreet, a region that lies betwixt and between New England and New Spain.

María Cotera writes in her brilliant introduction to the publication of this thesis that we should treat this document as nothing less than a courageous challenge to Anglo-Texan historiography of the state.[8] According to Cotera, what González submitted to her thesis advisor, Eugene C. Barker, a historian and champion of the Texas Revolution, "was a counter-history, a narrative that offered a Mexican perspective on the history of Texas and contested negative representation of *Mexicano* culture" (17). Further, writes Cotera, "In [her] introductory statement, González neatly reverses the racialist discourse that had come to dominate both popular and scholarly representations of Texas history and culture, reminding her readers that not all Mexicans are immigrants, and that most Anglo-Americans come from immigrant stock themselves" (18). And yet González's notion of a counternarrative is not limited to contesting Anglos alone, nor is her sense of colonialism one-dimensional. As Cotera notes, González's thesis offers "a more complex and multidimensional vision of historical events in which 'heroism' and 'villainy' are not the sole property of any one nation or race" (19). In recounting the history of colonization of South Texas, González observes the obvious in chapter 1, that the violent displacement of the indigenous populations preceded settlement by Spanish and later Mexican colonists.

There is also no absence of gender analysis in her thesis. Unlike Paredes's seminal work on the corrido and the male-dominated horse culture in *With His Pistol in His Hand*, González's patriarchal critiques, as Cotera notes, reconstruct "the social spaces and gendered practices in which the often invisible expressions of women's work and women's thinking are found" in rancho culture (23). These reconstructions of traditional women's work come into hard contrast with the changing mores brought about by the promise of freedom offered by American culture. Setting it up as a generational divide, González is careful to document how Anglo modernity on the border affects the daughters of this region. She quotes an informant: "'I am told that becoming Americanized means being progressive,' said a leading Rio Grande City citizen, 'but if that means that my daughter will bob her hair, disobey her parents, chew gum, smoke, drink, and be out with boys until late at night, and finally elope, and get a divorce at the end of one or two years [of] married life, I do not want progress. That is just what American civilization means to us. Our customs may be of the old world, they suited our parents, they suit us now'" (*Life*, 115). Implicit in the words of this speaker from Rio Grande City is the willingness to reject not only "American civilization" but the daughter who chooses progress over the "old world." Although not voiced or represented, I would argue that this generational threat is also present in González's story about the Tenth Muses. She might have suspended choosing one over the other as a female writer, but as a woman of Mexican descent in South Texas she ends up choosing to marry a Mexican national in Mireles. Nevertheless, whether in public or private life, González consistently chose the "outward signifiers of a 'proper woman'" (Cotera, *Native Speakers*, 115). All the same, she also chose to be alternatively outspoken about the troubles in South Texas at times and to be hopeful at other times.

González concludes her master's thesis with thoughts about how the rapid influx of Anglo settlers into South Texas had altered a way of life that had evolved since the early days of the Escandon settlement of Nuevo Santander but that despite the wars, the conflicts, the racial discrimination, and displacement of families from their homes and ranchos, the generation just after hers nonetheless feels hopeful. González writes:

> Young Texas-Mexicans are being educated. Behind them lies a store of traditions of another race, customs of past ages, an innate and inherited love and reverence for another country. Ahead of them lies a struggle of which they are to be the champions. It is a struggle for equality and justice before the law, for the just demands of full-fledged American citizens. They bring with them a broader view, a clearer understanding of the good and bad qualities of both races. They are the converging element of two antagonistic civilizations; they have the blood of one and have acquired the ideals of the other. They, let it be hoped, will bring to an end the racial feuds that have existed in the border for nearly a century. (116)

For Cotera, the work as a whole rendered "the border [as] clearly something more complex than a simple geopolitical dividing line between two nations and cultures, [as] a contact zone where multiple cultures, languages, and histories—Indian, Spanish, Mexican, Anglo—had collided and recombined, forming a distinctive and categorically different kind of regional identity, a borderlands identity" (30). Perhaps for this reason, five years later, the best González could do, the most her social environment would allow her, is to stage the inner drama of what living in this particular contact zone as an educated woman of Mexican descent and U.S. nationality demands. Otherwise, as folklorist, educator, and civil rights activist, she could continue to document and narrate the struggle, educate the young, and hope for better times.

Indeed, her published folklore writing in the early 1930s showcase characters whose lives embody a philosophical response to the social, cultural, and legal pressures of their times, especially because and through their Mexicanness. Even global events such as the assassination of Archduke Franz Ferdinand of the Austro-Hungarian empire in Sarajevo on June 28, 1914, find their way into South Texas and make an impression. Take, for example, the short story "The Philosopher of the Brush Country," developed from Jovita González's fieldwork in folklore that began in the late 1920s but was published in 1935, the year of her marriage:

> Tío Pancho was a philosopher, and like all philosophers, he was at outs with the world.... The World War found Tío Pancho Malo with six husky, strapping boys, all physically fit and of age for service. However, he did not want them to serve in the army. "Why should they fight," he argued, "for a country that is not ours? First, the *Americanos* get this land from us, but that might have been our fault though; we could not defend it like men and now we weep for it like women. However, why should we worry when we have enough troubles at home; the drought, the sand storms, and the need of grass for the goats and sheep? Besides, why should they fight some poor Christians who have done us no harm? No, my sons will not be in the army." And to prevent this, he and his sons started trekking back to the old town of Mier. (in *The Woman Who Lost Her Soul*, 56–58)

As in much of her folklore, Jovita González is supremely aware of the geographic nuances of South Texas. What folklorist wouldn't be, right? And yet, given the political dimensions of Mexican American life in South Texas, these nuances take on more than just "local color." Geography is instead the subtext rendering not only the familiar, but in the hands of the minority writer, also framing the unfamiliar geopolitically. As we see, the archduke enters the geopolitical space of South Texas precisely because the more dominant Anglo-American culture refuses to see, acknowledge, or accede to Mexican Americans' prior privileged claim on place and region.

In "The Philosopher of the Brush Country," Jovita González reconstructs the region's own "organic intellectual," a figure that combats the very Anglo-American forces that seem bent on disrupting the structures of feelings that had dominated the area until only relatively recently, and specifically targeting one's ability to choose how to be a person in the world:

> The peaceful muddy Bravo, like a thread of quicksilver, was already visible, and the party was within an hour from safety when the Rangers came upon them.
>
> "You keep your mouth shut," said Tío Pancho Malo to his sons, "I shall talk to them and convince them that I am right." On being asked where they were going and why, Tío Pancho answered in the high flown way that characterized him:
>
> "Most esteemable gentleman, you inquire of me my destination and why I am traveling in this direction. Your ears shall be regaled by my narrative. Most worthy gentlemen," he continued with a bow, "I am taking these, my sons, to the birthplace of their ancestors, Mier, the heroic city that defeated at one time a band of Americans [the Mier Expedition, 1842]. No offense intended, *señores*; I am taking them there because I do not want them to fight, for your government. My sons are not cowards; they can, and will fight, but only when they have received an offense. How can they fight against people who have never wronged them and who they have never seen? We are sorry for the King that was killed and if you think it fitting and proper we can even write a letter of condolence to his widow, but as to fighting, that is another matter. I prefer my sons should not get involved in a fight that is not theirs."

"Do you know who you are talking to?" asked one of the Rangers.
"Most esteemable *señor*, yes; you are a Ranger."
"Don't you know I have power to arrest you and your sons also?"
"Most certainly, we know that."
"Then why have you not tried to evade my questions?"
"My father, may he be in a choir of Angels now, did not teach me to lie, *señor*."
Only the youngest remained with him; the others were drafted and after the necessary training went to fight their unknown foes, never to return. (59)

As many have noted, for Jovita González, South Texas was part of neither the United States nor Mexico. Though Américo Paredes comes to argue this point almost thirty years later, González, in the 1930s, already portrayed a region that is its own province. It is a region we have come to identify as the "borderlands," and it is this region and its more local histories, cultures, and folk stories that fuel Tío Pancho's ability to traverse this artificial border separating Mexico from the United States. And further, it is Tío Pancho's connection to place, "his native Mier," that legitimizes his opposition to the Texas Rangers. Tío Pancho understands perfectly well the logic of U.S. foreign policy that requires drafting his sons and the sons of the borderlands. In the borderlands, what counts as a pretext to war is direct hostile aggression. You hit me. I hit you. You invade my land. I defend our land to the bitter end. Tío Pancho's opposition harkens back to nineteenth-century notions of warfare based clearly on territorial conquest, not some more abstract notion of a country's "vital interests" abroad. Tío Pancho clearly understands that not contesting a U.S. foreign policy that would obligate people to fight will lead to dire consequences for his borderland community.

Powerless against the police arm of the nation-state, though, Tío Pancho's sons are drafted against their father's will and they inevitably die. Still, González's folklore preserves this minority community's registered opposition to drafting Mexican Americans to fight in foreign wars for a geopolitical logic that further alienates them from their own homeland interests: "The youngest died of small pox. Tío Pancho was left alone, and he went up and down the river from ranch to ranch expounding his theories and his queer philosophy. He would not touch one cent of the insurance due him. 'This money is the price of the innocent blood spilled in a useless war. If I accepted it I would feel like the butcher of my boys,' he contended" (59–60). Tempted here by yet another form of abstract nationalist thinking, in this case over the value of human life lost in war, Tío Pancho is faced with a choice: accept the insurance money and accept the capitalist logic of fighting someone else's war, or refuse the money, refuse the very idea that a life can be quantified and insured against unwanted outcomes. So when we think of World War I, we might think of many things, but unless you have been schooled differently, Anglo-European epistemological traditions and ontological philosophies would never encourage you to think about, much less ask, if people of Mexican descent cared about this war, or if they were ever drawn to participate in it. More poignantly, there is not one iota of consideration in dominant Anglo and European circles that Mexican Americans might have had some opinion in the matter.

On the other hand, regionally, an alternative knowledge system, what Walter Mignolo calls border gnosis, is at play. It is a "bordering thinking" that emerges from "moments in which the imaginary of the modern world system cracks" and local histories reveal themselves ("On Gnosis," 23). Without a doubt, this European conflict is being thoroughly digested on its own terms in the Spanish-language press of the Southwest and West but also in dialogue with the ongoing Mexican Revolution. In *George Washington Gómez*, Américo Paredes, who had worked in his youth for the bilingual newspaper *El Heraldo de Brownsville / The Brownsville Herald*, makes this precise link early on:

> Feliciano reached into the Model T and brought out a handful of papers. He shuffled them angrily. "You went and bought Gringo newspapers again!" he said. "Why didn't you bring some reading matter in a Christian language?"
>
> Gumersindo smiled. "I've got to practice," he answered.
>
> "Well then," said Feliciano, "practice now and tell me at least what the big letters say. Austria, Austria, it says there. What about Austria?"

Gumersindo pored over the headlines. "I can't make them all out," he confessed. "But it's something about the duke of Austria getting shot. Sara Jevo. No, that sounds like a women's name."

"A duke?" said Feliciano. "That's fine. They ought to kill all those sons-of-bitches. Look farther down the page and see what it says about Carranza." (13–14)

Elsewhere, we know at least of one eyewitness account of that War World I through the eyes of José de la Luz Saenz, who entitled his wartime diary *Los méxico-americanos y la gran guerra y su contingente en pro de la democracia, la humanidad y la justicia* (1933, 2014). According to Emilio Zamora, the recoverer of this text, Saenz appropriates "the wartime rhetoric of democracy and the sacrifice of the Mexican soldier to craft an argument of his own" (215). Saenz brought home what was essentially a global argument for democracy. His text, though a singular example, reflects what Zamora observes as "part of a general discourse on minority rights emanating from Mexican communities throughout the southwestern part of the United States" (215). In short, World War I was a significant event for many Mexican American communities.

In this context, it is not surprising that the first global war appears some fifteen and twenty years later in Jovita González's folklore and in Americo Paredes's first novel. But of course, in light of Mexican American history being routinely displace to the bitter margins of official history, it does come to late twentieth- and early twenty-first-century readers as somewhat of a curiosity. Because of this culturally enforced amnesia around the history of Mexican Americans, recovered texts have this uncanny effect on us readers to reorient our historical regard and respect of the Mexican American community. These moments indeed decolonize our very habit of reading and understanding the Mexican American within just the local and away from the national and global.

Published in 1935, the same year she wrote "Shades of the Tenth Muse" and the same year of her marriage to Mireles, one has to wonder whether González was juxtaposing Tío Pancho's "I prefer my sons should not get involved in a fight that is not theirs" (59) against the growing threats in

Europe: Franco, Mussolini, and Hitler. Regardless, Tío Pancho's preference seems prophetic given the tragic repetition of Mexican Americans and wars later in the twentieth century, including, of course, the most recent wars in Iraq and Afghanistan. Thus, one can see how important it might be to read Recovery texts as always already existing in the world. By extension, these texts allow us to appreciate the Mexican American as a historical figure, not just a member of a subordinated minority community, but as a member of the world community. Finally, we must ask ourselves what might have happened had González's literary and scholarly work not been forgotten? What might have been the cultural work of Tío Pancho during the Vietnam War had he been available during the Chicana/o Movement? Obviously, the Chicana/o Movement came up with its own means of opposing the war, but it did so in the absence of this literature and this writer's critical thinking. Fortunately, unfortunately, Tío Pancho may yet serve us in the near future given current global circumstances. To be a Mexican American in the world is a challenge, but certainly not any more of a challenge, not any safer, than not being accorded a place in the world.

La Profesora de Español

Given the tension between local history and global coloniality, one can only imagine the challenges and obstacles the institution of marriage foisted on the shoulders of Jovita González. Even so, her actual marriage was a celebrated event in the social pages of *La Prensa*. A Sunday, August 4, 1935, article presents a community that totally embraces the marriage, beginning with a picture of the bride and her matrons of honor, all well-known figures in the elite circles of Mexican and Mexican American communities at the time.[9] Hers was a Wednesday morning wedding that was preceded by three days of prenuptial festivities, including a dinner hosted by Frost Woodhull and his spouse. Following the custom of the times, the article lists the wedding gifts the couple received, peppered with names of Anglo Texans as well. The article ends following another custom of the times, listing the telegraphed well-wishes received by the couple. Last mentioned, but surely noted, is a telegram from Mr. Frank Dobie. After the wedding in the three-hundred-year-old Misión de la Purisima Concepción, the couple left to honeymoon in Mexico by way of Laredo, Monterrey, and Saltillo. Regrettably, their journey was cut short by the unexpected death of the new husband's father, Sóstenes Mireles.

With her marriage, González's reputation as a folklorist and writer expands with her growing role as an educator. She becomes an educator to those same young Texas Mexicans she hoped will bring an end to the racial feuds of the border when she wrote her master's thesis. With the exception of coauthoring the manuscript of *Caballero* (1939), a novel depicting the local dimensions of the Mexican-American War that directly links the futility and waste of war as a feature of colonial hypermasculinity gone mad and fascistic, González's future writings lie concentrated in a series of instructional textbooks to teach Spanish at the elementary level. Cowritten with her fellow educator spouse, Edmundo Mireles, and premised on years of work in the schools of Corpus Christi, Texas, the six-volume series El Español Elemental enacts a vision of a Texas borderlands balancing English speakers with Spanish speakers, Anglo-Texas history with a Spanish Mexican colonial past, and finally the state of Texas with Latin America, a politically correct term of the period that actually meant Mexico. The authors explain, "The Spanish Program in our Public Schools has definite objectives. Primarily, it is to give the child the ability to speak and read a language which he hears daily on our farms and in our cities; secondly, to make him better acquainted with the Latin American [read Mexican] history and culture, conditions, and customs which we of the Southwest share; and, finally, to create a sympathetic attitude toward other peoples and their ways, so that a better understanding of human relationships may be established" (ii). Learning Spanish here is both local and intimately tied to the post–World War II world order that ensues.

Elsewhere, but also in South Texas, the struggle over civil rights is gaining momentum, especially with friends like civil rights lawyer Alonso S. Perales. Although Mireles and González have no children of their own, there is no doubt that they lay down an educational foundation for the latter half of the twentieth century, and part of that foundation is the resistance to make, however difficult, that either/or choice, choosing neither the United States nor Mexico, but forging a middle ground and insisting on mutuality and communication as the basis for better regional and international relations while also insisting on the region's Mexicanness as something valuable for all to share, as a hedge against the worst expressions of coloniality, be it U.S., Mexican, Texan, or all three.

In the context of her work to bring Spanish into the classroom as a mature and credentialed writer, intellectual, and society person, one cannot help but remember González's poem "Un incidente feo" and wonder once again about its impact on a lifetime of choices, including how she ends up problematizing choice as gendered and racialized and nationalist, as well as conditioned by two competing settler-colonial linguistic registers. "Un incidente feo" encourages us to also wonder about the role that experience must have played. There's the active refusal of the Anglo schoolgirls to play with her because she's Mexican. Where did they learn to think like that, much less say that? Then there's the young Jovita's experience of shame, betrayal, and anger as manifested by her tears, and, most important, the momentary loss of words. Hers is the novel experience of feeling out the new grammar set in motion by the clause: "Me llaman / Mexicana y dicen que soy mala." Followed by the depiction of her grandmother's agency, the experience of an agency that will categorically intervene on behalf of the granddaughter's tears and set things right by talking, if not reminding, the mother superior of the grandmother's still potent social position in the community. Intervention here, one imagines, was direct, unapologetic, and unwavering. But then what happened? What was the next day like, and the week after, and the years after that for the granddaughter, especially when there was no longer a grandmother who could intercede on her behalf?

Up to now, Chicanx studies has focused, and for good reason, on Jovita González's intellectual and literary production as a scholar, folklorist, and novelist. But I would like to offer a parallel critical genealogy that has been noted but underappreciated, one that might shed further light on "Un incidente feo" and on her role as a profesora de español. For sure, teaching Spanish will become a means of earning a livelihood and supporting her research and writing, but in the pages of *La Prensa*, and its constructed readership, this role as profesora de español also becomes valued for its potential to mediate and intervene on the social and political issues of the day. As Cotera notes, when González entered the University of Texas in the mid-1920s, she took courses in Spanish and was mentored by Lilia Casis. Interestingly, her mentor was the first tenured woman professor at the University of Texas. It is Casis who introduces González to J. Frank Dobie (Cotera, introduction to Gonzalez's *Life*, 11). And very likely, it was Casis who taught, trained, and mentored Edmundo Mireles when he entered the University of Texas. Although it is tantalizing to speculate that Casis introduced González and Mireles to each other at some point, the real story lies in Casis and her role in inspiring both of these pupils to take up the instruction of Spanish as a lifelong social and political pursuit. Indeed, even as early as April 22, 1916, *La Prensa* took notice of Lilia Casis's university work in Spanish as a social good for the broader Spanish-speaking communities of Texas (2). Casis was probably involved in getting González inducted into the National Honorary Spanish Fraternity in 1927.

Again, *La Prensa* is there to celebrate this honor and to emphasize its Hispanist significance: "Dicha Fraternidad se encuentra en todas las grandes Universidades de los Estados Unidos y es miembro honorario de las Universidades de Madrid, México y Chile" (Feb. 9, 1927, p. 7). This same article also notes that the induction ceremony was hosted by the Women's Faculty Club of the University of Texas. Thus, over time, as much as her relationships with male mentors like Dobie and Castañeda deepen, so too are her professional female associations a critical base of advancement for González. From here on, one can see how her training and status, as *La Prensa* frames it, "bien conocida en nuestra colonia y que actualmente se halla en la Universidad del Estado de Texas como profesora de historia y de español," are united in one person. That is to say, her folklore research and writings are perceived and celebrated as intimately related to her work as a professor of Spanish; they are inseparable from one another.

From *La Prensa*'s vantage point, we can and should appreciate better how González's career takes her to these social moments that speak directly to the politics of pluralism that Cotera has historicized. Her choices in this period lay the foundations for her critical work in the 1930s and well beyond. So when we see the front page news of Ignacio Lozano as the subject of an article in *La Prensa*, reporting on his being honored by the distinguished alumni of the department of Spanish and the faculty of the University of Texas on the anniversary of the Fraternidad Honoraria Sigma Delta Pi ("Conferencia del Sr. Ignacio Lozano," March 17, 1931, p. 1), we are simultaneously asked to absorb all the cultural registers of an event held at the Pan-American room of the Driskill Hotel in Austin. Attendees were greeted by Lillian Wester, followed by a Professor Glascock, who welcomed everyone on behalf of the University of Texas. Then there was a public ovation for R. May, the founder of Sigma Delta Pi. Right afterward, one reads that Carlos E. Castañeda introduced the keynote speaker, Lozano, whose twenty-five-minute lecture was entitled "Las dos civilizaciones del continente americano." Honored guests included Lozano's wife, Alicia E. de Lozano, and "los Profesores Charles W. Hackett y E. R. Simms y las profesoras señoritas Lilia Casis, Jovita González y señora M. Kress" (2). We can only speculate the actual content of the talk, but there's ample evidence in *La Prensa* of its institutional desire to foster cross-cultural and bilingual exchanges between the United States and Mexico, not unlike what we see in "Shades of the Tenth Muse." This can also be said of the University of Texas in this period.

Soon after this event, *La Prensa* reports that Jovita González is traveling to Mexico City to study at the Universidad Autónoma for the summer ("Sale para México la Srita. Jovita González," June 28, 1931, p. 5). The article explains that her travel coincides with that of her professor E. R. Sims, chair of the Department of Spanish at the University of Texas. Further, she's teaching a class at the Universidad Nacional de México and assisting in an annual seminar that meets in Mexico City. Of course, her return from Mexico is also reported on ("Regresó la Srta. Jovita González," Sept. 12, 1931, p. 5). During her time there, we are told, González was well received by "el Secretario de Relaciones Exteriores, Genaro Estrada." With Estrada, González was able to talk about the educational system of the United States, as well as expound on her Mexican folklore research. As secretary of foreign relations, Estrada would have dealt with many aspects of U.S.-Mexican relations, including the ill treatment of Mexican immigrants and their children.

A later article establishes that beside her degrees at Our Lady of the Lake and the University of Texas, González also studied at Derecho Internacional en Universidad National de México ("Profesora," Sept. 11, 1932, p. 13). Her studies in "international rights" establish her credentials to teach an evening civics class on government at Sydney Lanier in San Antonio, beginning that September in 1932. It is not clear whether the class was for high school credit, but it was part of a program that had been implemented a year before by Edmundo E. Mireles and Alonso S. Perales to expand and improve educational opportunities for "la colonia mexicana" ("Habra clases nocturnas en la 'Lanier,'" Sept. 7, 1932). By 1932 González's role as profesora was also expanding, and with a deepening political character.

As such, there was another dimension to her role as profesora, the one that directly navigated the Mexican-Anglo divide in San Antonio by putting into practice a pedagogy she was hopeful for in her master's thesis. *La Prensa* captures this pedagogy at work for her readers:

> La señorita Jovita González, profesora de la Universidad de Texas y del colegio católico de San Antonio, "St. Mary Hall", visitó ayer las oficinas de este diario en compañia de varias estudiantes americanas de ese colegio que pertenecen al club "Margil", de estudiantes de español. Entre las visitantes figuraron las señoritas Mary Adams Maverick, Amelia Maverick y Jean Lapham, pertenecientes a distinguidas y prominentes familias de la sociedad de San Antonio y quienes quisieron visitar el periódico La Prensa que ellas leen durante sus clases de español, bajo la dirección de la profesora señorita Jovita Gonzalez. ("Estudiantes que visitan," Oct. 21, 1932, p. 6)

Although it is easy enough to notice the upper-class markers that make this visit of González's Spanish class to the office of *La Prensa* possible, what is less obvious is the important fact that her Anglo Catholic students read *La Prensa* as part of their formal instruction, which meant they were absorbing and mediating what the press was presenting to its intended Spanish readers. What sense her Anglo students made of *La Prensa* we may never know, but again and again in the public sphere we see Jovita González literally in the middle of things. And there are times we have to think that she is selectively shaping her own public persona, selectively feeding *La Prensa* information about herself. For example, her studies in Mexico—how could

La Prensa have reported on the details if she had not offered them in the first place? If true, this degree of self-fashioning was not in itself unusual in the Spanish-language press, nor should it undermine our appreciation of her political and cultural astuteness. On the contrary, it should alert us to her intensity and commitment of her poetics and politics, as well as her courage and bravado as a Texas-Mexican woman of the border to move the needle on improving social relations without forgoing or apologizing for her Mexican heritage.

Three years after defending her master's thesis and two years before the publication of "Shades of the Tenth Muse" and her marriage to Edmundo Mireles, *La Prensa* publishes, on December 12, 1933, Jovita González's bold own version of the story of the Virgin Mary's apparition to Juan Diego on the slopes of Tepeyac. Her sketch of la Virgen María and Juan Diego is not unlike her folkloric work elsewhere. It intriguingly anticipates her speculative visit with the Tenth Muses later. Yet it is her only publication in Spanish that I have found to date in *La Prensa*, or any Spanish-language press for that matter. I end here with the final sentence of the sketch, where she offers her own gloss on the legend, one that I believe stands as a testament to her corpus of work, teaching, politics, and with her standing as a Mexican member of the community: "Y desde entonces Nuestra Virgen María de Guadalupe, la Virgen Morena del Tepeyac es la Patrona de los mexicanos" ("La Inmaculada del Tepeyac," Dec. 12, 1933, p. 4). As a Guadalupana, González's faith in la Virgen Morena, as the patron saint for all Mexicans, marks her own commitment to her people in the rapidly changing, increasingly Anglo-dominated South Texas. She chooses to identify, as Rivera notes of González's rhetorical strategies in "Shades of the Tenth Muse," with "a brown, Mexican virgin rather than a Madonna of Spain" ("Reconsidering," 68). And yet unlike her dreaming persona in that sketch, she inscribes herself here, as mexicana, publicly and without any ambivalence in the pages of *La Prensa* for all to read.

5 Barrio Modernity

Speaking Pocho,
Being Chicana/o

Scene: The Parley between the U.S. Cavalry and the Apache.

SGT. BEAUFORT: Tengo el honor, ilustre jefe, de presentarle el distinguido Comandante de regimento—El Colonel Thursday, Capitán Collingwood, el Capitán York, y Señor Meacham que usted ya conoce.
Gentleman, this Alkesay, Head of the White Mountain Apaches, Satanta of the Mescaleros, and the Chiricahua Medicine Man, named Jerome in our language, but in Spanish, Geronimo.

COL. THURSDAY: Well, time to get on with it Beaufort.

SGT. BEAUFORT: El Colonel le invita hablar.

COCHISE: Los Apaches son una gran raza, orgullosos y no hemos nacido para vivir esclavizados. Su nación nos hizo la guerra, y no nos derroto.

COL. THURSDAY: What's he saying?

SGT. BEAUFORT: That the Apache are a great race, sir. They've never been conquered.

COCHISE: Pero una nación no debe estar siempre en guerra.

SGT. BEAUFORT: But it is not well that a nation be always at war.

COCHISE: Los jóvenes mueren.

SGT. BEAUFORT: The young men die.

COCHISE: Las mujeres entonan canciones tristes.

SGT. BEAUFORT: The women sing sad songs.

COCHISE: Y los viejos pasan hambres en el invierno.

SGT. BEAUFORT: And the old ones are hungry in the winter.

(*Fort Apache*, directed by John Ford, RKO Radio Pictures, 1948)

In *Fort Apache,* John Ford explores a critical moment in how the U.S. army deals with indigenous insurgence in the Arizona territory. This film offers two competing post–Civil War white male protagonists: Captain York as played by John Wayne, the firm but experienced border-crosser in the territory who sees the Apache people as a much maligned and mistreated people, and Colonel Thursday as played by Henry Fonda, a more rigid and decidedly more Yankee version of Captain York, who carries the superiority of New England on his sleeves and cares little for the regional claims of the Apache. The nemesis to both is Silas Meacham, Indian agent of the reservation, played by Grant Withers, who represents and embodies the corrupt and corrupting bureaucracy of the Bureau of Indian Affairs. Throughout the film, Colonel Thursday demands uncompromising loyalty to the army and to himself, loyalty beyond question. But Thursday's brand of loyalty comes to a head toward the end of the film, when he has to decide whether or not to force the Apaches, led by Cochise, back onto the reservation, despite ample evidence that the true source of the problem is Meacham, the Indian agent.

At the end of a pivotal parley between the U.S. army and the Apaches, Colonel Thursday's insistence on loyalty reveals itself to be really about loyalty to race. Given the choice to accept the terms of peace offered by Cochise, Colonel Thursday instead sides with Meacham, a figure that everyone agrees is corrupt, greedy, and a murderer. And although Captain York, John Wayne's character, stands up to Colonel Thursday's ill-conceived plan to go after the Apaches—who vastly outnumber the regiment—he is demoted on the spot for insubordination and remanded to the rear to help protect the supply wagons. What follows next is a foolhardy charge into a canyon where the Apaches lie ready to ambush the cavalry in a deadly crossfire. This scene and its overwrought bravery on behalf of the uniform easily calls to mind Alfred, Lord Tennyson's 1854 "The Charge of the Light Brigade." In this fictional encounter with Cochise and his warriors, Colonel Thursday commits himself and his men to a suicidal outcome, and every member of his command knows it.

Minutes after the charge, Colonel Thursday's remaining forces are pinned down, surrounded by enemy fire. Captain York risks his own life to rescue

Colonel Thursday, and when he reaches him, Colonel Thursday insists on staying with his men, ordering York to take the surviving members of the regiment back to the fort. A year later, York, now in command of the fort, is asked by a journalist to comment on a painting depicting the now-celebrated bravery of Colonel Thursday. When asked whether it captured the bravery of Colonel Thursday, York decides not to answer with the true circumstances that led to the massacre but instead to honor the men, including Thursday, who died on the field. Despite Thursday's considerable flaws, York chooses racial loyalty over truth and against his considerable appreciation for the Apaches; otherwise, the truth would have documented the battle not as a massacre but as a victory for the self-determination of the Apaches who refused to be unfairly and murderously treated by the U.S. government. The film ends with the splendor of military regalia fully displayed, with the Apaches well out of the visual frame, an absence that reinscribes the logic of Manifest Destiny for the region. Significantly, the cavalry's parading exit is the final visual cue for how the audience—at least the Anglo-American intended audience—is meant to align its own racial loyalty.

Reminiscent of the racial dynamics explored in chapter 3, the film's staging of racial loyalty is often more complicated than at first glance. The film's stark patriotic insistence of loyalty to the memory of Colonel Thursday and his men is inconsistent with the plot of the film. Couched within the broader sympathetic portrayal of how the Irish became American through military service, the viewer is largely encouraged to view the Apaches sympathetically and their grievances as legitimate. The film's official account of the battle and its jingoistic interplay with the press, the so-called massacre of the regiment, actually forces a suspension of that sympathy. Read through the lens of the coloniality of being, this suspension of sympathy for indigenous people makes sense: coloniality and coloniality of power demand that the film reinscribe the logic of white, male, European superiority. And while this is an intriguing reading of the film, what makes this reading all the more interesting, if not fascinating, is the staging of racial loyalty itself in the pivotal scene where Colonel Thursday is presented with the means to choose peace over war.

It is good to remember here Nelson Maldonado-Torres's thesis that the imposition of racial hierarchies through colonization could only be sustained by artificially constructing the specter of the Other and by maintaining the logic of this Other through the constant threat of warfare. This constant threat of warfare and violence is what gives urgency and primacy to racial loyalty. So when Cochise proposes, "pero una nación no debe estar siempre en guerra," that logic falls on deaf ears on the military representative of Manifest Destiny; Colonel Thursday and his regiment are precisely constructed to adhere to the unspoken credo that racial superiority, as part of coloniality, must be secured at all costs. Thus, when Cochise offers his terms of peace, which mainly target the removal of Meacham as Indian agent, Colonel Thursday cannot help but react defiantly, as if gravely insulted that an Apache would even dare dictate terms of peace. Peace is not an option in the colonial handbook. But in terms of decoloniality, peace, the end of violence, is in fact what might unravel the stranglehold that racial loyalty has in perpetuating racial violence as a method of social control.

In apparent attempt to appear historical, despite being a work of fiction—the events in this film never happened—Ford allows an impassioned and dignified Cochise to make his case to Colonel Thursday during the parley that preceded the battle.[1] But Cochise makes his case all in Spanish, which is historically correct given how under Spanish and then Mexican rule, indigenous people in this region were forced to learn Spanish. But Colonel Thursday does not speak Spanish, despite the fact that a majority of West Point officers who participated in the Civil War, on both sides, had their first experience with Spanish and territorial expansion during the Mexican-American War. Colonel Thursday therefore asks Sergeant Beaufort, a reintegrated Southerner played by Mexican actor, Pedro Amendáriz, to be their translator. In turn, Cochise, who is played by another Mexican actor, Miguel Inclán, relies on Sergeant Beaufort for an accurate translation of his people's grievances but also his terms for peace.

Ford provides for a dramatic presentation of all interested parties: present for the parley is Cochise, Alkesay, Satanta, and Geronimo for the Apaches, and Colonel Thursday, Captains York and Collingwood, and Meacham for the U.S. government. Visually Ford creates a bifurcated tableau, reminiscent of many nineteenth-century portraits depicting the first "encounter" between indigenous people and Anglo-Europeans. Thus, we have the indigenous on one side, Anglo-Americans on the other, and thinly veiled Mexican actors occupying the middle. Depending on a viewer's racial identity and racial loyalty in 1948, one had at least two options for choosing a racial side if one was Anglo or Native. But for the Mexican or Mexican American in the theater, Cochise's spoken Spanish presents an unsettling choice. Because Ford provides no film subtitles to translate Cochise's speech in Spanish, translation duties fall to the character Sergeant Beaufort. Beyond Hollywood in 1948, Pedro Amendáriz and Miguel Inclán were well-known actors in Mexican cinema. So in essence, the well-informed Mexican and Mexican American viewer would have recognized that a Mexican actor provided Cochise with a deep Mexican Spanish, only to be translated by another Mexican actor portraying a displaced Southerner in the West. (There seems to be a joke here somewhere.) Regardless of this potential confused set of alliances and connections, Cochise's grievances are persuasive in either Spanish or English, but only Spanish speakers truly know how eloquent Cochise delivers his words. Sergeant Beaufort's translation hardly comes close.

Given Inclán's elegant delivery of Cochise's grievances, one should speculate how those grievances might have overlapped with the grievances of those Mexicans and Mexican Americans living in the United States at that time. In terms of postwar racial loyalties, while the Anglo viewer is meant to side with Colonel Thursday's decision, no matter how distasteful, what about the Native viewer or the Mexican or Mexican American viewer? Does the Mexican American viewer side with the Anglos despite grievances since 1848? Or does the Mexican American side with Cochise, who is after all played by a Mexican actor, or because of a connection through a broadly understood mestizo heritage? If the Mexican hesitates to choose, is it because there's an older colonial memory of fighting and displacing indigenous people on the frontera? Or is there a hesitation because of a cultural imaginary produced by a settler-colonial casta system that in 1948 still operates and places "indios" below "creoles" and "mestizos," but above "negros"?

And what are we to do with how Ford frames the close-up of the actors portraying the Apache leaders at the beginning of this scene, especially the close-up of Geronimo? Ford invokes a sentimentality that is powerfully present but also visually tinged as if to foreshadow Geronimo's future struggle with the U.S. army. It is as if Ford constantly teases his audience with multiple paths to choose racial loyalties, with Monument Valley, Utah, as the silent but towering backdrop to this drama of settler expansion. And of course, we would do well to remember that the movie theater of the 1940s sold tickets to other moviegoers, from African American to Asian American viewers to women and children to straight and queer viewers alike.

Ford's much-revered 1948 cavalry film, *Fort Apache*, stands out in my mind as an example of the conundrum that the burdens of modernity posed for Mexican Americans in the immediate aftermath of World War II. Although much celebrated for their service, heroism, and patriotism during the war, the Mexican American men and women who served were almost immediately disappointed by the lack of respect, and outright hostility, that the country demonstrated toward them and the barrios where their families, friends, and neighbors strove to be worthy of citizenship and belonging. *Fort Apache* is illustrative of a myriad of ideologies. While some were re-produced and packaged by Hollywood to greet audiences eager for promises to be kept after defeating fascism, the parley scene is especially curious for how it depends on spoken Spanish. This scene is pivotal to the plot of the film, pivotal to its complicated but sympathetic portrayal of Native Americans, and even pivotal to understanding the unyielding logics of a renewed Manifest Destiny about to confront the exigencies of the Cold War. And yet all this depends on Spanish speakers, who since 1848 had been all but marginalized, demeaned, and held under suspicion as unworthy of any civil rights. The privileged role that Spanish plays in this scene is in dark contrast with the actual lives of those who spoke and dreamed in Spanish daily, still one hundred years after the Treaty of Guadalupe Hidalgo.

This chapter continues to examine the places of modernity for Mexican Americans, but through spoken Spanish, and how this colonizing language evolved linguistically to represent their burdens and identities by the mid-twentieth century. For Luis Valdez, growing up in the postwar years, language and identity were determined foremost by place: "The barrio came into being with the birth of the first mestizo. Before we imitated the gringo, we imitated the hacendado; before the hacendado, the gachupin. Before we lived in the Westside, Chinatown, the Flats, Dogtown, Sal Si Puedes, and El Hoyo, we lived in Carmargo, Reynosa, Guamuchil, Cuautla, Tepozlán. Before the Southwest, there was México; before México, Nueva España. The barrio goes all the way back to 1521, and the Conquest" ("La Plebe," 1972). In Valdez's rendering of what has shaped the Mexican American experience, he offers what we would now call a territorial map of the structure of modernity and coloniality that had come to underwrite the general idea of what is a Chicana, a Chicano, a person of Mexican heritage but residing in the United States. Vital to his vision of Chicanidad is Valdez's linkage of place and ethnic formation through colonization of the New World. Born in 1940 in Delano, California, Valdez conceives of the barrio as the site and symbol of the birthplace of mestizaje but also the semiotic arena where the clash of Native versus European cultures had its most powerful engagements. Although the barrio was not necessarily the same for everyone who claimed the identity as Chicana or Chicano during the movement, nor was the barrio the only way to identify historic living places for people of Mexican descent, it was a way to visualize a map of Chicana/o experience.

For this final chapter, the barrios mentioned above constitute the most important network of sites for colonial difference prior to the Chicana/o Movement. As visualized by Valdez with their roots in coloniality, these barrios shared many characteristics, from economics to social life to life expectancies to cultural productions. But most important, I would argue, the barrio in the United States is where people of Mexican descent spoke Spanish, and variations of it, with impunity. The relationship of that impunity with Spanish, including its coloniality, and its role in the construction of Mexican American ethnic identities that are related but separate from Mexicanness, such as pocha/o and chicana/o, is the subject of this final chapter. This chapter focuses on how speaking Spanish as pochas and pochos and becoming American as chicanas and chicanos begin the long-term redirection of modernities of subtraction, however imperfectly, toward a more decolonial future.[2]

¿Hablas Español?

Some years ago I had the privilege of meeting one of the most charismatic, controversial, but also effective political figures of the Chicana/o Movement, José Ángel Gutiérrez.[3] As the founder and leader of the La Raza Unida Party, Gutiérrez not only helped to politicize Mexican Americans, but he and his compatriots devised a political mechanism, an infrastructure, for demanding civil rights through the electoral process, first in Crystal City, Texas, then regionally, and then nationally. La Raza Unida Party was nothing less than an amazing political machine of its era, and nothing has come close to it since its demise. In short, here I was meeting the man, a mero mero, an important figure, and who, by the way, had gone on to earn a PhD, became a professor and a prominent one at that at the University of Texas, Arlington. Of the many memories that remain of that meeting, one is the most vivid. He asked me, "¿Hablas español?" He basically went on to describe how Spanish, Mexican Spanish, barrio Spanish, and other versions were the language of Chicanas/os. In other words, it was the means of determining if someone was a member of la raza, the people. I had heard this before and experienced it in more subtle ways around older Chicanas and Chicanos; the default language of communication was Spanish, with English whenever it was more practical. But being asked by Gutiérrez, I was struck by his directness. Was I member of la raza? And the question has lingered with me, personally and professionally. Was (is) membership in la raza fundamentally a question about language, and if so, why? And was this the reason so much of early Chicana/o literature was written and performed in Spanish?

Many years later, I had an opportunity to investigate these questions with my graduate students in a directed reading.[4] I made it our task to study what it would mean to teach a Mexican American literature with texts written in Spanish through our English department. How would our pedagogy need to change to accommodate for the linguistic demands of the texts? How would we navigate the inevitable divide that comes with the popular understanding of a national literature as written in a national language, in this case English? But of course, the United States as of yet has not proclaimed any language as its national language, and yet the working presumption for most is that English is the country's national language. So what would we do with students who did not read Spanish, much less converse in it? Since this would not be a class to improve one's Spanish, what role would English play? Could the class be bilingual? What about exams and written assignments? And finally, what does a body of literature in Spanish by U.S. writers tell us about Chicana/o literature in particular and American literature in general that we do not already know?

Outside of the occasional Chicana/o literature course taught in a department of Spanish, where the texts are in Spanish, these same texts are rarely if ever taught in departments of English, where one finds most Chicanx literature positions. In addition, with the exception of fewer than a handful of publishers, such as Arte Público Press or Editorial Bilingüe, where one still finds published texts in Spanish, most Mexican American writers since the late 1970s have sought out mainstream presses to publish works in English. The combination of these forces, coupled with graduate education in Chicanx literary studies that invariably needs to train students to publish in English-language journals and university presses, has marginalized a body of work that actually was the foundation of the whole critical field. Although the irony here is a kind of open secret among Chicanx critics, the one-to-one relationship of English to the study of American literature has been practically impenetrable.

Nevertheless, there have been conspicuous attempts to deal with the political economy of such an entrenched monolingualism in the broader study of American literature. The well-publicized efforts of the Longfellow Institute at Harvard University, founded by Marc Shell and Werner Sollors in 1994, are a case in point:

> The Longfellow Institute was designed to support the study of non-English writings in what is now the United States and to reexamine the English-language tradition in the context of American multilingualism. Named after Henry Wadsworth Longfellow, the polyglot nineteenth-century poet who, in his translations and academic work, helped to

develop literary study across linguistic boundaries, the Institute has set itself the task to identify, and to bring back as the subject of study, the multitudes of culturally fascinating, historically important, or aesthetically outstanding American texts that were written in many languages, ranging, for example, from works in indigenous Amerindian languages, Portuguese, Spanish, Italian, French, Dutch, German, Norwegian, Swedish, Russian, Polish, Yiddish, Hungarian, Chinese, and Japanese, to Arabic and French texts by African Americans.[5]

In its essential mission, the Longfellow Institute is not unlike the Recovery Project, which began in 1991.[6] Both projects began by promoting the idea that the study of American literature needed to include texts written in languages other than English that had emerged from locales that are now part of the United States. A quick glance at either website for the Longfellow Institute or the Recovery Project would verify the critical depth of recovering literatures in languages other than English. How to make use of these recovered writers, texts, and histories within the everyday structure of the English department has been the ongoing challenge.

The consequences for the inclusion of such texts, and its ramifications for the field of American literary studies and the basic organizing structure of the English department, was brilliantly explored and exposed in Annette Kolodny's 1992 essay "Letting Go of Our Grand Obsessions." What Kolodny proscribed in 1992 continues to be the most challenging but ethical case as to why and how we should be Americanists. Nevertheless, her blueprint for American literary studies in the twenty-first century was controversial. The controversy was not so much what she had outlined as a method for the future of Americanist literary studies, that it be about multiplicity and historicity, linguistically nuanced, and interdisciplinary, all the while eschewing furiously the coloniality of power inherent in any nationalist myths of origins. No, this was not the controversy; her vision has just been difficult to implement given the economics of most English departments in the United States. It could only be hoped to be resolved through commitment, hard work, creativity, and a bit of luck along the way. Kolodny lays out the controversy this way:

> Too little of what I have outlined here can come to fruition, however, as long as American literary specialists remain trapped within Departments of *English*. For if we are ever to have what Andrew Wiget calls "a new literary history that is both just and useful," then American literary specialists must move beyond the training that prepares us to analyze only texts written in English or to recognize only European (or "Western") antecedents.... American literary scholars must begin to create their own frontiers, openly declaring their agenda as radically comparativist, demandingly interdisciplinary, and exuberantly multilingual. (15)

Central to Kolodny's radical comparativism is the need to also work in languages other than English, to restructure our course offerings so as to encourage these other languages, to restructure our graduate programs so as to encourage students to use archives in other languages, to resist the hegemonic pull to always see the study of American literature as an offshoot of British literature or of some other European tradition. While in the last thirty years such comparativism has increasingly gained creditability, renovating the field along the way, as in hemispheric studies, Kolodny's vision for comparativism continues to lag far behind in the classroom, especially at the undergraduate level.

With Kolodny's radical comparativism in mind and Mignolo's map for understanding how coloniality and modernity are both the conditions for oppression but also the vehicles for liberatory contestation and expression, I asked my graduate students not just to think of the predominance of Spanish in early Chicanx literature as a protest language within the context of the civil rights movement, but to think of its textual presence as emblematic of a communally lived experienced since 1848. Not only was Spanish a colonizing language in North America since 1492, but it, and its speakers, also became colonized after 1848. In this context, my graduate students and I conducted a review of the secondary literature on the study of Spanish as used in the United States. The idea here was to have a better appreciation of the historic conditions of Spanish-speaking communities of Mexican descent, whose versions of Spanish would one day become the lingua franca of the Chicana/o Movement.

To our surprise, we found that linguistic and sociological interest in the Spanish spoken by people of Mexican descent in the United States coincided in earnest with the later years of the Great Depression and the early years of War World II. This whole period has been of great interest to Chicana/o historians not just for the ways it laid down the means for the rise of a Mexican American middle class but also for the entrenched pejorative views mainstream society would come to have of Mexican Americans, stereotypes that fed into legal and de facto negative consequences even after the Chicana/o Movement.[7] This period is marked by massive deportations of both undocumented Mexicans and Mexican Americans during the Great Depression, the unprecedented drafting and enlistment of men of Mexican descent into War World II, and the national institutionalization of Mexican migrant agricultural and industrial labor, setting up patterns of Mexican immigration, both documented and undocumented, that went virtually unchanged until the late 1960s.[8]

In addition, events like the Zoot Suit Riots in California created a national awareness of a community of people, especially its youth, who spoke a language that was neither Castilian nor English, and not even something in between, but something entirely else. It is in the context of the delinquent youth who come to be identified as pachucos and pachucas that researchers find a sociolinguistic phenomenon that has little or no documentation but that is demographically increasing in prominence throughout the Southwest and West.[9] In these various assessments and evaluations, we found yet another demonstration of what Ana Margarita Cervantes-Rodríguez and Amy Lutz have identified as the "English-Spanish asymmetry": "We argue that coloniality of power informs power relations and regimes designed to regulate behavior, including language-regulating mechanisms that have shaped the English-Spanish asymmetry in the United States through global and national projects (e.g., nation-building, educational, and media projects) entangled in translocal histories" (523). Overall Cervantes-Rodríguez and Lutz argue that there's an ironic but ultimately oppressive relationship between the rise of Spanish speakers in the United States since the early twentieth century and the various state and socially produced means of regulating Spanish-speaking communities despite their economic importance to nation, and despite their constitutional rights. Indeed, one gets a sense of this regulation almost immediately from the social science literature of this earlier period.

For example, one is immediately impressed with the transnational dimensions of this field's disciplinary interests, especially as regulatory steps are taken to understand and control this language of the pachucos. William E. Wilson writes in his "Author's Summary" in 1946, "The fact that U.S. Border Patrol Trainees are expected to learn many *pocho* expressions is a reflection of the widespread usage of this hybrid language in the Southwest. Despite opposition on the part of Mexican intellectuals, it is slowly but surely being accepted by even the most conservative Mexican newspapers" (345). Wilson goes on to offer what becomes the standard definition of pochismo: "derived from *pocho*, an adjective which originally meant discolored, has now come to mean a type of popular slang in Mexico. In the ever-growing list of *pocho* expressions are many hybrid words, artificial combinations of English and Spanish" (345). While Wilson vaguely locates the popularity of pochismo in Mexico, like others he cannot help but also notice its usage along the border between the United States and Mexico. It is precisely because it is a border language that Williams cites the 1940 El Paso Border Patrol publication "Supplementary Vocabulary and Practice Manuel in Spanish for Border Patrol Trainees": "Indicative of its spread is the inclusion of many words of this type in a Spanish vocabulary list prepared from U.S. Border Patrol Trainees, with the remark that 'those words underlined are colloquialisms but are often used on the Mexican border and the officer will get better results if he understand them'" (345). Williams does not elaborate on what those better results might be, but, given the tense international politics of the 1940s, we can imagine a range of things related to the growing global warfare.

By the early 1950s, studies of pochismo dovetail neatly with observations and assessments of its speakers, the pachucos, as in the eye-opening exploration in *American Me* (1948) by Beatrice Griffiths. Researchers too become increasingly aware of the territorial spread of pochismo as well as its regional differences. Jacob Ornstein refers to a "Border Spanish belt [that stretches] roughly from Corpus Christi, Texas, in the east to San

Diego, California, in the west" (138). Ornstein cites John Sharp, who calls the "Border Spanish" in West Texas a "'linguistic no man's land'" (139). This broad mapping of pochismo, coupled with Sharp's vague, negative attribution of the language's statelessness or lawlessness or both, underwrites attempts to define pachucos: "One of the strongest influences during the past ten years upon the spoken language of New Mexico and indeed the whole of the Southwest has been that of the *Pachucos*. A product of semi-assimilation, the *Pachucos* in southwestern cities are a fairly recent group distinguished by an aversion to steady work, outlandish grooming and dress, as well as the use of a special and picturesque vocabulary meant to serve as a secret language" (Ornstein, 139). If Ornstein refrains from calling pachucos delinquents, the popular print press does not. From the Zoot Suit Riots on, pachucos become synonymous with Mexican American gangs, criminal activity, drugs, and their covert means of communication.

Although not without advocates, such as Beatrice Griffiths and Carey McWilliams, pachucos or their pocho language are rarely found to have any redeeming qualities. Criticism and suspicion of the pachucos and their language is also found south of the border in Mexico, and even in the Spanish-language press in the United States. In its section "Miscellany," the journal *American Speech* (1945) summarizes a couple of reports, one from the *Tribune* of Albuquerque, New Mexico, on February 21, 1945, and the other from an article entitled "Gringo Lingo," found in *Newsweek* on August 14, 1944. Together the articles portray a backlash among Mexican intellectuals who are appalled by the corruption of Spanish because of the increasing usage of English: "A group of Mexicans in the northern border state of Nuevo Leon is campaigning against 'a barbaric invasion of the mother tongue'—*pochismo*—Mexican slang for 'a rapidly increasing vocabulary of bastardized words which are neither Spanish nor Yanqui'" (235). Of course, this bastardization of Spanish preceded the appearance of the pachuco by decades. In fact, the appearance of English in what becomes the Southwest and West was due to early trappers, traders, merchants, and adventurers who traveled to the older Spanish/Mexican settler communities; some even married into Spanish/Mexican families.[10] Before 1848 it was they who struggled to learn the lingua franca of the times, Spanish.

But after 1848, with the increased immigration of Anglo-American settlers and related commercial interests in the territories first held by Spain and later Mexico, the cultural and legal capital of speaking Spanish began to reflect the political demotion of its speakers (as also noted in chapter 1).

In his *A Life Crossing Borders*, subtitled a *Memoir of a Mexican-American Confederate*, Santiago Tafolla remembers the moment his life changes forever when he is invited to join a wagon train that just departed Santa Fé and is headed for Independence, Missouri. The year is 1848: "When my cousin Plácido and I saw the wagon train, we stood paralyzed with fear. We didn't know what to do until a man in one of the carts, said in very poor Spanish: 'Machacho, ¿quiero vamos Estados Unidos?' I answered him, 'Sí, yo quiero'" (11). Despite getting *muchacho* wrong, as well as conjugating the verbs wrong, this Anglo-American makes himself understood because of the nature of their happenstance meeting and Santiago Tafolla's desperate need at that moment to make an economic choice about his future livelihood. It is in the context of growing Anglo-American economic and political power in the region that the "English-Spanish asymmetry" first appears and widens along those same colonizing economic circuits, establishing deep changes along the way. Cervantes-Rodríguez and Lutz observe, "Eventually the global rise of the Anglo-Saxon/Protestant hegemony would transform the Spanish language into a racial marker employed to described and identify colonial subjects first, and a subaltern group or 'minority' later (Mignolo 2000). Like its ascendance, the displacement of Castilian from a hegemonic position to a marginal one was not an isolated phenomenon. It was part of a great world-systemic transformation, already consummated by the early 1800s" (525). Consequently, it is from this new marginalized position that Spanish becomes yet another commodity, albeit a cultural one, in the service of newly evolving imperial contexts (Cervantes-Rodríguez and Lutz, 525).

It is in the wake of such a language-power asymmetry, based on asymmetrical modernities, that a newspaper reporter for the *San Francisco Morning Call* finds Guadalupe Vallejo living in Oakland and teaching Spanish to support herself and her mother. According to F. Arturo Rosales in "'Fantasy Heritage' Reexamined," the *Call's* reporter sought her out, curious to interview her after the publication of her essay in *Century Magazine* (as explored in chapter 1). He finds her, "'a daughter of one of the oldest and proudest Spanish families,'" living with a sign out front advertising "Spanish Taught" (95). Unlike her more careful presentation in the essay for *Century Magazine*, Rosales notices Vallejo's lack of attempt "to ingratiate herself" with the reporter or portray "Anglos in a favorable light" (95). Instead, in her interview, she admits to having been frightened as a child by the "'terrible Americans'" who came to her father's house and jailed her uncle Mariano Guadalupe Vallejo during the Bear Flag Revolt (1846). According to Rosales, "The reporter found it highly ironic that she was supporting herself and her aging Mother through 'teaching her mother tongue to the invading Americans'" (95). In short, Vallejo had to sacrifice one kind of mother in order to care for her other mother. Such are the subtractive bargains under modernity.

From 1848 on, these kinds of interactions between English and Spanish speakers become registers for a whole range of colonial power relations between Anglos and people of Mexican descent. Conflicts that arise through miscommunication and/or mistranslation are legion, none more infamous than the case of Gregorio Cortez. As recorded in the corrido of Gregorio Cortez, if it had not been for the sheriff's overreliance on his faulty Anglo interpreter during the questioning about a stolen horse, Cortez might not have shot the sheriff in self-defense; there would have been no man-hunt, no eluding of the Texas Rangers, no subsequent prolonged trial, and no heartache for the family. Yet, as provocative as these entanglements over language were, an equally compelling realm of interaction between English and Spanish was also establishing ethnic points of differentiation among Spanish speakers of Mexican descent, north and south of the newly established border. As already seen in the 1882 poem "Un tipo," published in *El Eco de la Patria*, a Los Angeles newspaper whose title roughly translates to "an echo of the fatherland," there was an early concerted effort to dramatize the negative effects on spoken Spanish in areas that once belonged to Mexico, and before Spanish rule:

Mas como estaba educada
En la americana escuela,

Inglesaba alguna frases
Que olían á gringo á la legua. (417)

Here the young woman under scrutiny is ridiculed for her vulnerability to the allure of English, and for corrupting Spanish with the odor of English. Maintaining the integrity of Castilian Spanish was akin to celebrating Mexican nationality, and therefore a linguistic means of projecting critique at U.S. culture. Efforts to deploy the newspaper as a vehicle for improving the correct usage of Spanish only intensifies during and immediately after the Mexican Revolution, when more than one hundred thousand refugees take up residence in the United States and are subsequently exposed to the corrupting linguistic influences of the United States; these linguistic influences are seen as the vehicles for even more corrupting Anglo values that challenge everything from traditional gender roles, like women working at home not in public employment, to proper family etiquette, like not smoking cigarettes in front of your elders.

Despite these cultural challenges, by the mid-twentieth century, it is U.S. popular culture and the popularity of baseball throughout Latin America that is ushering in a new phase of English-language influence, which in some Mexican circles allows for the acceptance of pochismo: "Opposed to the purists, said Newsweek, August 14, 1944, p. 76, are 'the nonintellectuals, comprising the majority of Mexicans, café society which uses pochismo to smart up its chitchat, slapstick actors, like Tin Tan (Herman Valdes) who get comic effects with pocho patter, and the Mexican bobby-sox crowd which dotes on English'" ("Miscellany," 235). Yet other Mexican intellectuals, such as Octavio Paz, saw something else beyond the chitchat and slapstick. Luis Leal calls attention to Paz's treatment of the pachuco in his 1959 *The Labyrinth of Solitude*. While it is clear that Paz also identifies them as part of gangs, Leal focuses on how he theorizes the social conditions that have produced in the pachuco a negative character, a nexus of contradictions, and a public bravado of resistance; in essence the pachuco is, for Paz, one of the extremes of the Mexican character. But for Leal the social conditioning occurred not just in the United States: "What Paz does not say in his essay is that the Pachuco was not only rejected in American society, but also by Mexico. If the Pachuco did not want to become a Mexican again or blend into life of North America it was because he could not do either" (117). As with John Sharp's comment about a "no man's land" (Orenstein, 139) over and over again there is a sense that Mexican American youth in particular—but all generations, really—experience neither a here nor there to Mexican American life in the United States; it is a border life even if they are hundreds of miles away from the border. While speaking Spanish could or should offer some broad transnational connection to Mexico, it does not provide that in a satisfying manner, a manner that connotes belonging and respect.[11]

All the same, in a response to Ornstein's assessment of pachuco speech in 1951, one finds in Daniel Wogan's 1951 "Discussion" a genuine curiosity about this "picturesque argot" (142). Comparing this argot to the "*lunfardo,* the *caló* of the *compadrito*" in Argentina, Wogan believes one is seeing the beginnings of a literary tradition: "As yet, however, the *pachuco*, less fortunate than the *compadrito*, has inspired no writer of genius to dramatize his restless existence and immortalize his colorful idiom. But the day when the *pachuco* will find his Florencio Sánchez may not be far off" (142). The Chicanas and Chicanos of the movement period would prove Wogan right, but the seeds of that literature lay in a language that was as picturesque as it was embattled; it was part of a Spanish-speaking experience in the United States whose burdens of modernity could not then rise above the subtractions of that modernity. It would take some other historic force or combination of forces to move beyond the collective memory and understanding of Spanish and its variations as colonized speech and to move its speakers beyond the coloniality that bound them to the discursive and regional spaces where they could speak without impunity.

Do You Speak Pocho?

For at least twenty years before Anglo-American social scientists became interested, the Spanish-language press was deeply involved in reporting, discussing, and largely lamenting the phenomenal rise of pocho speech by Mexican Americans and Mexican immigrants throughout the Southwest and West. Well-known columnist and humorist Jorge Ulica writes on

October 11, 1924, for the newspaper *Hispano-America*: "El pocho se está extendiendo de una manera alarmante. Me refiero al dialecto que hablan muchos de los 'spanish' que vienen a California y que es un revoltijo, cada día más enredado, de palabras españolas, vocablos ingleses, expresiones populares y terrible 'slang'" ("La Semana en Solfa, Do You Speak Pocho?," 2). In tongue-in-cheek prose, Ulica worries out loud that if this alarming trend of pocho speech continues, "una Academia" will have to publish an "español-pocho" dictionary. Even before Anglo linguists start publishing lists of pocho words and phrases, one finds those same lists directed at the readers of the Spanish-language press in the United States. In "Pochos y Pochismos," V. Salado Alvarez asks, "¿Quiénes son los 'pochos' y que cosa es el 'pochismo'?" (*La Prensa*, Aug. 14, 1928, 3), and in due course, he offers his own list of words, including "agarrar fon—de 'Have fun,' divertirse"; "Baqueria. Viene de 'Bakery,' panaderia o tahona"; "Bato. No es un anglicismo sino un arcaísmo. 'Bato' equivals a hombre tanto rustico de pocos alcances"; "Chutabaco.—Tabaco de mascar. (De 'chewing tobbaco')" (3). The imperfect speech of pochos, neither wholly Castilian nor wholly English, was treated as the outward most recognizable social characteristic of a group of speakers who were poor, non-skilled laborers, undereducated, often illiterate in Spanish and English, and deemed unfit for citizenship both in the United States and in Mexico. Their pocho speech was held in contrast to the middle-class or upper-class speech of people of Mexican descent who could speak either Castilian or English correctly and who were therefore deemed proper candidates for citizenship in either the United States or Mexico or both.

Such is the concern for this ever-growing demographic of pocho speakers that by the mid-1940s a columnist such as Alfredo G. Vazquez can propose that the problem is one of national identification: "Lo que hace real una nacionalidad no es una vaga noción cargada de emotividad. Son las cosas reales como el ambiente, el clima, la educación, las experiencias, las costumbres, las actitudes de un determinado conglomerado. Un individuo expuesto a estos elementos en México es y será un mexicano ejemplar. Otro expuesto a las mismas condiciones en EE.UU., sea cual fuere su sangre o el color de su cutis, es y será exponente de la civilización americana"

("Discriminacion ¿Culpa Nuestra?" *La Prensa*, May 30, 1944, 3). Vazquez argues that national identity originates not from emotion, but rather from the lived experience of a country's climate, social environment, education, shared customs, and shared social attitudes, and such identity does not depend on the color of one's skin or bloodline.

But for the individual who does not, cannot, or will not evidence such a national identity, the experience of discrimination becomes an active fact in one's life: "Pero el que a medias se ha expuesto a los dos ambientes y ha recibido de ellos sólo imperfectas influencias no es ni de la una ni de la otra nacionalidad; ni agua ni pescado. Y la dura realidad nos ha enseñado que ni la sociedad puramente mexicana lo recibe, ni la estrictamente americana lo acepta. Lo que aquí es 'descriminación racial' allá es 'discriminación social.'" In an astute observation that presages worsening conditions right up to and during the Chicana/o Movement, Vasquez correlates the imperfect absorption of national influences with the discrimination experienced by those who manifest "la imperfección del lenguaje es manifestación exterior de la insuficiencia de espíritu." Unable to demonstrate a national identity, such speakers are victims of racial discrimination in the United States and social discrimination in Mexico. Despite being inheritors of two great cultures, Vasquez writes, "son tristes víctimas *de condiciones adversas y actitudes erróneas.*"

While sympathetic to their adverse conditions and the wrong attitudes they have to deal with, Vasquez ultimately locates the solution in a better education that leads to a more fundamental assimilation in the United States, but with one ambiguous caveat: "hemos de recoger real, inteligente y decididamente cual de las culturas hará mas feliz a nuestros hijos que han de formar sus hogares, labrar sus destinos y enterrar sus huesos en esta tierra ¿la latina o la americana?" While arguing throughout the column that current and future Mexican immigrants must do their best to adapt to their new country, to become knowledgeable of its language, customs, and laws, Vasquez also argues that national identity is in the end about a place-based sense of belonging. Yet he ends by suggesting that on behalf of their children it might be possible to choose one culture over the other, either Latin American or American, where they can shape their lives, homes, and destinies more concretely. And so with this choice it might be possible to determine where to bury happily one's bones. Taking Vasquez at his word, how does one make sense of such ambivalence?

Vasquez's ambivalence is not his alone. It is a broad feature of the print culture of this period. On the one hand, there is a diverse range of writers from Texas to California calling attention to a varied and rich Spanish Mexican heritage prior to 1848, from Adina de Zavala and Jovita González in Texas, to Miguel Antonio Otero Jr. and Fabiola Cabeza de Baca in New Mexico, to the Vallejo family in Northern California and Leo Carrillo and Ana Bégué de Packman in Southern California. But on the other hand, the Spanish-language press is actively trying to attend to the presentist needs of its readers, a readership that dramatically changes over the course of the Mexican Revolution (1910–21) and its more than one hundred thousand refugees to the United States. But this readership also changes because of the equally dramatic labor needs of agribusiness, mining, railroad, steel mills, and construction in the United States; all industries that require a consistent and available migrant labor pool. Because of the influx and flux of this newer but vastly larger segment of the Mexican heritage population in the United States, intellectual, political, ethical, and moral positions change with some frequency, as do the terms that identify these Mexican nationals who are comprised of immigrants, refugees, and exiles. The terms used to identify living in the United States also vary. One can read everything from José Vasconcelos's "el México de afuera" to "México extranjero" to "México pequeño" to "el otro lado." Decades later, Américo Paredes will sweep up all these terms and combine them to promote a "Greater Mexico" in an attempt to unify all the terms, pre- and post-1848, into a more inclusive geographic concept that allayed most of the obvious contradictions and exceptions. But until then, and until the rise of Chicanx studies, the Spanish-language press in the United States offered and performed a cultural pedagogy, for better and worse, that existed nowhere else. In short, despite their best intentions, the press reflected the ambivalences of their readers when it came to strategizing what was best for la raza in the United States. No one really knew, because no one really had the power—economic, political, and moral—to effect change in a nation that was still invested in seeing everyone as Mexicans and definitely not as citizens of the United States.

Pos Les Decimos "Pochos" a los Muchachos Mexicanos Que Nacen Gringos

This vague cultural indeterminacy of civic belonging frames how to understand the Spanish-language press's many discourses on the figure of the pocho or pocha and their status in the United States and Mexico. It is these discourses that are, in fact, present in José Villarreal's groundbreaking novel *Pocho* (1959), written in English, which is generally regarded in Chicanx literary studies as the first Chicano novel. All the same, it is decidedly not the first novelistic attempt to portray el pocho. That distinction, for the moment, belongs to Mexican writer Jorge Ainslie, who wrote *Los pochos*, a serialized novel with illustrations by Enrique de la Peña, for the Lozano family newspapers in the United States, and which first appeared in *La Prensa* of San Antonio, Texas, on April 22, 1934.[12] Like Villarreal, Ainslie writes a story that begins in Mexico during the Revolution, focused on a male protagonist that must flee to the United States in order to secure a better life. But unlike the Villista revolutionary Juan Manuel Rubio, Ainslie's Féderico Godínez aspires to a middle-class life as a government bureaucrat or manager of some business. His departure to the United States is hastened by the imminent arrival of Villa's troops in the town of Santa Rosalia, Chihuahua. Like Rubio, though, Godínez commits a crime that also hastens his departure. He steals from the cashbox of his employer, the timber company, afraid that he will lose everything once the Villistas take control of the town. Once he crosses into El Paso, he's not alone like Rubio, who crossed the border because he gunned down someone who had disrespected him. In fact, Godínez travels with his pregnant wife, María, and it is in El Paso that she gives birth to a daughter.

Although *Los pochos* is in actuality about many things affecting the lives of Mexican nationals living in the United States in the 1930s, making the case repeatedly about the need for the Godínez family to return to Mexico; it is the birth of the children in the United States, first the daughter, Virginia, and later her brother, José, that anchors this novel as an anti–U.S. immigration text based on the idea that U.S.-born children of Mexican parents have no better recourse than to be repatriated to Mexico. As an anti-immigration text, *Los pochos* has much in common with Daniel Venegas's novel *Las aventuras de Don Chipote, o Cuando los pericos mamen* (1928). As in *Las aventuras de Don Chipote*, Ainslie's protagonist's, Godínez's, immediate experiences of "en el otro lado" are in El Paso. But unlike with Don Chipote, who is motivated by his extreme poverty and his family's hunger to cross the border for work, Ainslie spends no time detailing the rigors of the actual border crossing, nor does he portray the humiliation of having one's body disinfected by U.S. border officials. Instead, because Godínez stole money, over thirty-two thousand pesos, we come to learn, he is able to purchase train tickets and food during his journey across the border. While *Las aventuras de Don Chipote* is a parodic text, comically portraying Don Chipote as a latter-day, bumbling Don Quixote, with a stray dog as his Sancho Panza, written for a middle-class readership, *Los pochos* is also clearly geared to the middle-class readership of *La Prensa* of the early 1930s. But its more dramatic "novel of manners" style allows for a more complex, and ultimately uneven, reckoning of ethical and moral accountability. When Venegas encourages his readers to excuse Don Chipote's greenhorn tribulations because of his country bumpkin ways and lack of education, it is easy enough to understand it as Venegas's class solidarity with the poor. By contrast, Godínez's education and penchant for rationalizing his mistakes, especially when, as a greenhorn in the United States, he is duped out of his money after several failed business ventures, might lead the reader to despise this character. But Ainslie disallows this outcome. Instead, Ainslie challenges the reader to have a sentimental fondness for an otherwise foolish character.

Don Chipote and Godínez deep down are the same foolish characters, but from very different class backgrounds, with different economic goals. Don Chipote heard that the streets of the United States are paved with bricks of gold; he wants to live the elite's life of leisure. Godínez feels he must flee the political uncertainty of Mexico in order to continue to aspire to a middle-class life of the well-educated intelligentsia. There is leisure in Godínez's aspirations, but it has to do with the expectation of security from violence that a higher social status promises. In this respect, Godínez has much in common with Américo Paredes's Gumersindo Gomez in *George Washington Gomez* (1990), who also flees from the violence of the Revolution, if only to fall victim to the violence of the Texas Rangers. Nonetheless, although held to a promise he made to a dying Gumersindo, Feliciano, his brother-in-law, believes him to be a foolish man, unschooled in the ways of the border. While Villarreal's Juan Rubio is decidedly written not to appear foolish like Godínez or Don Chipote—here he has much in common with Feliciano—he nonetheless becomes foolish the longer he remains in the United States as a reluctant immigrant. The more his patriarchal authority is questioned and undermined, the more Rubio becomes rigid, authoritarian, and violent, not unlike Jovita González and Eve Raleigh's Don Santiago de Mendoza y Soria in *Caballero* (1939, 1996). Like Rubio, who is pushed out by his family well before the end of the novel, Godínez and his wife, María, are also reluctant immigrants. Making matters worse, they are unable to assert their combined patriarchal and matriarchal authorities over their children due to their Mexican nationality and heritage. Once they come of age and earn money, the children do not push out or abandon their parents, but neither do they let themselves be ruled by them. It is here, in this family power struggle over filial values, national belonging, and gender norms, that the title of the novel, *Los pochos*, promises to connect with its readers.

Like Venegas before him and Villarreal in the future, Ainslie's narration captures the social and economic conditions that forced thousands of Mexican nationals to leave for the United States. He also carefully charts how these immigrants consciously attempt to retain their ties to Mexico and Mexican heritage while simultaneously isolated, if not reviled, by mainstream American society:

> Conociéndose despreciados por los hijos del país, que han creído siempre superiores, se aislaron voluntariamente formando para vivir, un barrio aparte, donde por su afinidad de ideas y costumbres hacían la misma vida llevaran en su tierra natal.
>
> Sin excepción, los habitantes de aquel barrio eran descendientes de la clase más humilde de su país. Habían emigrado en busca de trabajo para mejorar su situación, siempre con la idea de regresar más tarde a la patria, cargados de oro. Poco a poco, sin sentirlo, olvidaron sus propósitos y se establecieron para siempre en un país donde encon-

traban más fácil y cómoda la vida; restándole con esto a la patria, un contingente muy numeroso de brazos fuertes y hombres útiles, tan necesario para el engrandecimiento de un pueblo. (chapter 4, 22)

While admitting to, and seemingly sympathetic of, the vast majority of Mexican immigrants who are humble and of the lower classes, Ainslie's narrator also vaguely charges them for abandoning the rebuilding of Mexico, presumably in the wake of the Revolution, and lending their skilled hands instead to a life of ease and comfort in the United States. This life of ease and comfort is understood within the class terms of the working poor all the same: "El barrio a que nos referimos, situado a espaldas de la Misión, estaba formado por un hacinamiento de casas y jacales de madera despintados y pobrísimos, que pregonaban la idiosincrasia de nuestro pueblo y su desprecio por todo lo que era progreso y adelanto" (chapter 4, 22). Again, seemingly sympathetic to these immigrants' humble lives, the narrator nevertheless calls attention to the ramshackle and discolored condition of their homes. Literarily in the shadows of a dilapidated Californio mission, Ainslie's narrator projects an embarrassment of how this barrio might be read by Anglo-Americans as indicative of the idiosyncratic, antimodern, antiprogressive whole of Mexico. Yet despite this embarrassment, Ainslie carefully represents the migrant farm labor that anchors such a barrio. He evidences a fundamental understanding of the political economy of a majority bachelor society that works from Monday to Friday for cash, whose earnings go to paying off debts made during the week and drinking on the weekends, only to start the cycle all over again on Monday. It is here, in this kind of barrio, that the Godínez family arrives for a brotherly reunion between Féderico and his older brother, Raymundo, who had left to make his fortune in the United States years before. The Godínez family also includes María's longtime loyal servant, Julián Gutiérrez, former mayordomo of María's sister's rancho.

Ainslie has set up the reader to witness Godínez's middle-class aspirations, and his perceived sacrifice of leaving Mexico, clashing with the lower-class culture of Mexican immigrants in the United States. Within minutes of their arrival in the barrio of San Fernando, California, Féderico and María are scheming for the quickest escape possible from Raymundo's offer of hospitality. Godínez cannot believe how far his brother has fallen: "Cuando recibió su carta en El Paso, se lo imaginó buenazo y sencillote, pero nunca supuso que hubiera descendido hasta el grado de adquirir los modales y el lenguaje de la gente más humilde. Sus padres fueron pobres, y él también se había criado bajo un ambiente de miseria. Pero lo que les faltaba en recursos, lo tenían en educación y maneras" (chapter 4, 13). Although he could understand how Raymundo might live in poverty—after all they grew up miserably poor with their own parents—what he could not countenance was his adoption of his humble neighbors' speech and ill manners. Raymundo should know better, given his education. By speech, Ainslie means not just the lower-class-inflected language that Godínez is accustomed to hearing in Mexico but also linguistic elements and social cues that reflect a reshuffling of values that made sense of race, class, gender, and nationalism in one national context but not another. Even when Raymundo reveals his actual wealth—he runs a successful general store in the barrio—Féderico cannot overcome his own class prejudices, nor his fascination with the appearance of class markers of wealth, power, and security.

In this same chapter, in which Ainslie stages the meeting of brothers within this barrio, he introduces the word and concept of *el pocho*. First, he does so in the rough and tumble language of Doña Librada García, owner of la fonda, the local restaurant where she feeds the migrant labor community and acts as their unofficial banker. Around eighty years old, Doña Librada is so beloved by all that she's affectionately referred to as the barrio's abuelita. Full of generosity, Abuelita also knows how to pilfer profits on the sly here and there and how to talk to men of all ages. She's also a renowned storyteller. When asked to tell one of her stories, she replies in a teasing manner:

>—A todos ustedes los he visto nacer, "Pochos" arrastrados, —les decía bromeando— Y a tu padre y a tu madre también, —les decía a dos o tres señalándolos con el dedo.
>
>—Cuántas desveladas y sustos me han dado ustedes malditos ... y luego pa qué, pa que ni me lo agradezcan siquiera! (chapter 4, 22)

By playing the reluctant storyteller, Abuelita indirectly reifies her importance in the barrio. She has in truth, she claims, helped birth many in her audience as a local midwife. She calls them wretched pochos, because for her a pocho is someone of Mexican parents born in the United States. Of course, their shared wretchedness is also tied to living in the United States. It is with this definition in mind that Abuelita greets Féderico and María's Virginia:

> ... ¡Pero qué requetebonita! —prosiguió destapándole la carita—. Se parece a usté. ¿Dónde nació? ... ¿en México?
> —No, —contestó Godínez,— en El Paso.
> —¡Ah! ... Entonces es pochita.
> —¿Pochita? ¿Y qué es eso?
> —Pos les decimos "pochos" a los muchachos mexicanos que nacen gringos.
> Río el matrimonio de la fraseología que usaba la anciana y del apodo con que llamaba a su hija. (chapter 4, 15)

Although the parents laugh at the strange phrasing used by Abuelita and her term *pochita* for Virginia, Féderico and María do not understand how contradictory terms of identification, to be Mexican and gringo at the same time, will nonetheless come to dominate how they make sense of their children's lives in the United States and their own lives by extension. Unable to return to Mexico for fear of being arrested for the stolen company money, Godínez proceeds to Los Angeles with all his misconceptions intact, and overtime becoming poorer than his brother, Raymundo. The hope of returning to Mexico fades with each passing year. He becomes a member of a community he condemned and ran away from in San Fernando.

Unlike the bildungsroman structure found in *George Washington Gomez* and *Pocho*, the structure of *Los pochos* finds a resolution for its family's conflicts through a marriage plot, as in *The Squatter and the Don* and *Caballero*. But in this case the groom-to-be is Mexican, and the bride-to-be is Virginia, la pochita, but before any marriage can be officiated, the narrative obliges the Godínez family to come to terms with their pocho way of life. The appearance of Rafael, the son of María's sister, the ranch owner, precipitates a series of events that culminate in the eventual departure of the Godínez family. Tall, dark, handsome, and loaded with money, Rafael, without any preconceived notion of what this trip would entail for him except to meet his extended family, who had not seen him in seventeen years, and to be a tourist in Los Angeles, comes to symbolize the healthy and robust recovery of Mexico from the ruins of the Revolution. Within hours of his arrival, the family's future is penned on his broad Mexican shoulders, starting with Virginia.

As usual in such anti-immigrant texts, Virginia's and José's adoption of American customs is the topic of much criticism for the ways that Anglo values disrupt gender and filial norms in traditional Mexican culture. Right before Rafael's arrival, the narration makes it clear that while the children's ability to earn a living relieves economic hardship, it comes with a price:

> A los pocos meses de empezar a trabajar y dar dinero para el gasto de la casa, se volvieron libertinos y malcriados, exigiendo de la madre servicios de criada y contestando con groserías los reproches del padre.
>
> En una ocasión que José llegó borracho a la casa. Godínez quiso castigarlo con la mano.
>
> —Si me pegas me largo de la casa. Aquí no estamos en México donde los hijos son esclavos de la casa.
>
> Doña María quiso intervenir, pero Virginia se opuso:
>
> —No te metas en lo que no te importa. José tiene razón. Pues no faltaba más que no pudiéramos hacer lo que nos dé la gana, cuando nosotros pagamos por la comida.
>
> La pobre madre se contentó con retirarse a su cuarto llorando.
>
> Godínez acabó por acostumbrarse a las groserías de sus hijos y optó por hacerse el desentendido. (chapter 5, 22)

Although this is a common enough scene of what we would call now teenage rebellion in any immigrant family, Ainslie paints a picture of troubled domestic life that anticipates not only the teenage angst and rebellion found in *Pocho* but also later in much of Chicanx literature, from Tomás Rivera's *... Y no se lo tragó la tierra* (1971) to Sandra Cisneros's *The House on Mango Street* (1984). Speaking from the parents' perspective, the narrator labels

Virginia and José as libertines, ill mannered in their speech and disrespectful in behavior toward their parents. By contrast, when José expresses his frustration over being held to Mexican values that condone a child's servitude to a parent's wishes, rational or not, he threatens to leave home for good if Godínez attempts to discipline him with physical force. While Godínez refrains from hitting his son, María leaves for her room crying, having been rebuffed by her daughter, who defended José by arguing that since they pay for their family's food, they can now do what they want. In the face of such obstinance, Godínez decides to look the other way whenever he witnesses their boorish behavior.

This stalemate of filial rupture and parental disempowerment, explains Godínez to María, is all his fault for having raised the children in United States: "Es inútil tartar de corregirlos. Yo tengo la culpa para haberlos criado en este ambiente. Pero tan luego como volvamos a México, ya verás cómo cambian. Los malos ejemplos los ha pervertido" (chapter 5, 22). It's useless to try to correct their behavior. In Godínez's reckoning, their behavior is related to national belonging. Since they do not belong in Los Angeles, all the children have is bad examples to follow. It is these bad examples that have corrupted their children and spoiled their family life. In the face of such disappointment, when and how to return to Mexico becomes Féderico's and María's mid-life crisis:

—¿Y cuándo volveremos?
—Ahora sí que muy pronto. Nos vamos con Rafael. En un tren de repatriados o como se pueda; pero nos vamos. ¡Eso sí te lo aseguro yo!
—Cuántas familias han sufrido como nosotros los rigores del destierro sin embargo, no se van, ni quieren volverse, —dijo doña María, suspirando.
—Ya volverán . . . cuando se convenzan de que es más sabrosa una tortilla comida entre amigos, que una tajada de jamón entre enemigos . . . o cuando los echen, como han estado haciendo con otros! (chapter 5, 15)

In response to María's desperate desire to leave for Mexico, Féderico insists that they will get to leave with Rafael, even if it is by one of those trains used by the government to repatriate Mexican citizens during the Great Depression. Such is María's frustration with her family's well-being that she cannot help but wonder out loud about the many families that share their misery of living in exile. Féderico predicts that families will leave when they come to realize that it is better to eat a tortilla among friends than to have a slice of ham among enemies, or when they get kicked out forcibly on these repatriation trains.

From here on, Ainslie dramatizes how the "groserías" and acts of "malcriados" of Virginia and José have come to dominate family life in Los Angeles. With Féderico and María as virtual hostages to their children's interpretation of life in Los Angeles, it is only with Rafael's appearance that the family stalemate begins to waver. Excited with the prospect of Rafael's visit, María finds a way to engage her children through their shared cultural value for extending hospitality to family members:

> Cuando los muchachos regresaron a casa se encontraron con la nueva, y con las súplicas de la madre que les rogaba por lo que más quisieran en el mundo, se portaran como gentes aunque fuera en su presencia, pues qué diría la tía si se enteraba de la clase de muchachos con que vivía su hijo.
> —Ha de ser un ranchero mugroso, —dijo Virginia.
> —¡Qué te importa lo de la mugre si trae muchos dólares! Yo me encargo de que se bañe y de que los gaste, —se apresuró a decir José.
> —You said it! Ya te veo gorreándolo y llevándolo con tus "bolillas" para que lo exploten.
> —¿Y tú qué eres? Una pocha infeliz que ni a "bolilla" llegas!
> —¡Niños! Hagan el favor de callarse la boca! —interrumpió doña María.
> —Pues que se calle ella primero y no me insulte a mi novia! (chapter 5, 22)

Reacting to her mother's plea that she and José act like "proper people" during their cousin's visit for fear of what he might report back to their aunt, Virginia masks her feelings of being insulted by launching into an insult of her cousin, whom she has never met and who has not even arrived yet.

By calling Rafael a dirty rancher, Virginia triggers José to make his own disparaging remarks: he only cares to help his cousin spend his money no matter how dirty he is. From here on, the tension between the siblings boils over to unmask the deep-seated inequities of life for pochos in Los Angeles. Rafael's presumed coherent, masculine, and nationalist identity as Mexicano is a pretext for Virginia and José to expose the gendered rifts that exist between them as immigrant children of Mexican parents in the United States. While José is eager to get his hands at his cousin's money, Virginia seizes that idea as an opportunity to attack José for having an Anglo girlfriend. José rejects the idea that all bolillas want to exploit someone like Rafael for his money and counters that his sister's pochisma is the reason she cannot measure up to an Anglo woman's standards. Ironically, all this dialogue is comically delivered despite the serious nature of the insults being traded here. It ends with José pleading with his mother, like the younger sibling he is, to stop Virginia from insulting his girlfriend.

Once Rafael arrives in Los Angeles, the whole family, even the pocho children, cannot help but find him attractive, attentive, courteous, and, of course, rich. Despite Virginia being his first cousin, Rafael quickly finds himself enamored of her. Physically attracted to her because of her dark eyes and blond hair, which he admits to her in a semiplatonic way, he also quickly comes to find her un-Mexican ways attractive, if not exotic. As is common in this text, these differences are mostly noticed and communicated through language:

—Y dime, ¿dejaste novia en el pueblo? —preguntó, curiosa.

—No. ¿Y tú tienes novio? ¡Algún americano, con seguridad!

—No me gustan. Si yo me caso ha de ser con un chicano, que me lleve a México.

—¿Un qué?

—¡Un mexicano, hombre! (chapter 5, 15)

The most fascinating aspect about Ainslie's method of unpacking a marriage plot is how he insists on using the plot as a referendum on the ethnic and gender differences that Rafael encounters with the Godínez family. From Virginia's cagy exploration of Rafael's romantic availability by asking him if he has a girlfriend back home, Rafael's inevitable line of questioning Virginia takes a racial and nationalist turn. On the heels of denying he has a girlfriend, Rafael ventures that surely Virginia must have an American boyfriend, by which he means Anglo, presumably because Virginia's phenotype features mark her as neither a mestiza nor india. Whether because she feels slightly embarrassed or insulted or both, Virginia's response is equally laden with racial and national overtones. Not only does she admit to not liking Anglo-American men, Virginia claims to prefer marrying any chicano who would return her to Mexico. For Virginia, in answer to Rafael's question, a chicano is emphatically a Mexican man. But Rafael does not know the word; much less is he aware of it as a synonym for *Mexican*. Nor does he recognize the kind of woman Virginia embodies. Although he finds her ways curious, it takes him aback when she proposes that they "go Dutch" on the rollercoaster at the amusement park near the Ocean Park beach. Given his usual masculine swagger, he does not recognize himself when he declines to go on the rollercoaster again. By contrast, Virginia is clearly ready to challenge herself to the thrills of the ride once more. By using the term *chicano* here to signify a Mexican male when it does not mean that in Mexico, Ainslie consciously signals to his readers that making sense of the ethnic and gender differences that pochos embody requires a thorough understanding of the political economy that underwrites the existence of families like the Godínezes.

Ainslie cannot or will not bring the story to a close without using Rafael as foil to expose a different aspect of his critique of the Anglo-American treatment of Mexican immigrants. Rafael comes to learn that his aunt, María, out of pride and stoicism, never confides in Rafael's mother, her sister, Josefina, the depths of economic deprivation and social discrimination her family had endured over the years. It is only with the promise of return that the reader hears of María's and Féderico's gendered stories of hardship. When María first started working as a seamstress in a garment sweatshop, she tells Rafael, she started earning eighteen dollars a week, but now it's only fourteen dollars a week with more work. On the bright side for her, now that she's older, she does not mind the additional work for less pay given that the owner has stopped sexually harassing her: "Imagínate que el maldito sinvergüenza me estuvo haciendo proposiciones cochinas por mucho tiempo; como si yo fuera una cualquiera y me amenazaba con correrme si no le hacía caso. Hubo veces que estuve tentada de aventarle con la plancha y quebrarle la cabeza, pero las otras trabajadoras mexicanas eran muy buena conmigo y doña Mariquita no se despegaba de mí un momento y me recomendaba paciencia. 'Todas hemos pasado por eso', me decía" (chapter 6, 22). Despite the owner's threats to fire her, María rebuffed his advances, but after so many advances, she contemplated braining him with an iron to stop the harassment. Only the solidarity of her Mexican coworkers, their generosity, and the help of her neighbor, Doña Mariquita, who never left her side, prevented her from killing her boss. Doña Mariquita advised her to be patient: it had happened to all of them as well; with time the owner would lose interest. Ainslie's startling direct treatment of the gendered exploitive conditions for immigrant women is only matched by his representation of how such women cope through solidarity and manipulation of the very same economic environment that oppressed them. María does not lose her job, and she does not capitulate to her boss's advances.

Féderico tells his story only after María reveals to Rafael that she had kept secret her troubles with her boss because she feared that Féderico would only make things worse. Plus Féderico would periodically fall ill, during which times she was the only breadwinner in the family. Indeed, the novel carefully notes how Féderico's decline into the proletariat has severe health consequences for him. What the reader does not know until this very moment is the kind of hunger the family experiences or the kind of work that frequently made Féderico sick: "Nada más te diré —dijo Godínez— que aquí la he hecho de lavaplatos, he trabajado con el pico y la pala y tantas otras cosas que jamás me había imaginado que un hombre pudiera hacer para llevarse a la boca un pedazo de pan. El mejor puesto que he tenido, es el de velador, y en ese, por poca pierdo la vida" (chapter 6, 22). Féderico gives the kind of resumé common to all unskilled laborers, from washing dishes to manual labor using the pickax and shovel. But ironically it is the better job as night watchman that made him so sick with pneumonia he almost died.

Rafael comes to hear that even among the poor of color in Los Angeles, there's a racial hierarchy governing free health care that was available only on Sundays: "y allí nos hacían esperar horas enteras, pues como éramos mexicanos no nos hacían caso, y pasaban primero los negros y japoneses que eran ciudadanos, y luego nosotros" (chapter 6, 22). Thus, on top of their poverty, low-paying jobs, and job-related illness, their lack of citizenship, or denied citizenship, regulated them and families like them to last in line behind African Americans and Japanese Americans, who by contrast were recognized as citizens. Once again, Ainslie mirrors what his readers likely experienced and witnessed in terms of socially and culturally reinforced discrimination targeting people of Mexican descent. But Ainslie's writerly outrage at such treatment also comes with his own racist views, especially antisemitism. However subtle in *Los pochos*, these racisms also likely mirror his readers' views on race.

After hearing the misery the family has endured, and witnessing the conflict between parents and children, Rafael forces the issue to know why they haven't left. After years of fear of retribution, Féderico confesses his crime to Rafael only to learn in a kind of comedy of errors that indeed the Villistas did ransack the town of Santa Rosalia. Féderico's crime was never reported because it was assumed that the Villistas had stolen the company's money. Further, Rafael shocks everyone with the news that the government had issued a general amnesty to a whole range of crimes committed during the Revolution as a matter of survival (chapter 6, 22). Apparently, news of the amnesty policy had never reached the Godínez family. Quickly, now more than ever, since nothing obliges them to stay, they prepare to leave. Only the pocho status of Virginia and José remains to be resolved.

The narrative goes after José first, displaying an acute sociological intuition how ethnic subject formation is invariably a function of race, class, and gender, and with the Godínez children, and many others like them, about nationality as well. Unlike the fate of Paredes's Guánlinto Gomez or Villarreal's Richard Rubio, the fortunes of the family do not depend on José. Despite being the firstborn son, he has none of the projections of destiny that Guánlinto has to endure, nor does he seem to evidence the kind of guilt that Richard exhibits for the male privileges he enjoys while his mother and sisters do not. Indeed, this José, given his rebellious, taciturn nature, should be thought as manifesting characteristics that will harden and evolve into those associated with the pachucos of the 1940s and thereafter. Hardly living "la vida loca," José is nonetheless the outlier in the family, how much of an outlier becomes clearer when Rafael tries to coax his cousin to return to Mexico:

> —¿Y tú José, no te vas con nosotros? —preguntó Rafael.
> —¿Yo? ¡De tarugo!
> —¡Qué se va a ir ese pocho! ¡La novia lo tiene agarrado de una pata! —dijo Virginia.
> —Oh yeah? Yo no tengo más novia.
> —¿Te "peliaste" con ella?
> —Sure! El otro día que fuimos a un party quería que fuéramos a Tijuana a casarnos, y cuando le dije que no, me dijo . . .
> —Mexicano mantecoso, —interrumpió Virginia riendo.
> —Say! ¿Cómo lo sabes?
> —Porque así nos dicen cuando se enojan con nosotros.
> —¿Y tú qué le contestaste? —preguntó Rafael que se divertía oyendo la fraseologia usada por sus primos.
> —Le di un "guantada" y ella se fue al teléfon a llamar a la chota.
> (chapter 7, 22)

When José refers to himself as a "tarugo," he voices sarcastically the family's opinion of him that he is stubborn and simple-minded, so how could he possibly imagine returning to Mexico? Virginia seizes on José sarcasm as an opportunity to insult her brother further by calling him a pocho whose white girlfriend has him trapped by the foot. And so begins yet another series of near-comic exchanges whereby Ainslie means to reveal further the déclassé nature of pocho culture. All the same, there is poignancy in this scene as well, and it has to do with a sense of inferiority that José intimates with the word "tarugo." A decade later in *La Prensa*, Vazquez will actually identify José's behavior as part of an inferiority complex that has risen in part from Anglo-American society's belief and treatment of Mexican and Mexican Americans as a "minority" culture that could never come to represent the country: "La actitud de una minoría de mentalidad lugareña jamás podrá ser representativa del pensamiento de toda la Unión Americana. Pero lo que nos importa aquí es que la indoctrinación de esta teoría ponzoñosa hace a nuestros jóvenes desarrollarse con un complejo de inferioridad o con un espritu [sic] de arrogancia altanera cargado con rancor y odio que no son normales en el espritu [sic] humano" (May 30, 1944, 3). Within the context of Anglo America's white racial superiority, Vasquez argues that a kind of cultural indoctrination and theory has had a negative effect on the youth and their abilities to evolve. In general, Mexican and Mexican American youth either display an inferiority complex or alternatively an arrogance that carries with it a deep rancor and hatred; either outcome diminishes the human spirit in his view. Thus, when José admits that he has broken off his relationship with his Anglo girlfriend because he refused to drive to Tijuana to marry her, Virginia guesses correctly how the girlfriend responded because she too lives under the constant specter of Mexicanness as inferiority. She guessed right that the girlfriend called José a "greaser." Whether she guessed José's inevitable gendered response to that insult is not clear, but that deep-seated arrogance with rancor and hatred that Vasquez speaks about is in full display when he hits the girlfriend. Also in full display, much to Rafael's amusement, are pocho words from *guantada* to *telefón* to *la chota* that anchor the all-too-familiar circuit of violence in barrio life that ends with the chota, the police state. In the end, José leaves this scene and the family home bitterly without giving a clear answer to Rafael's original question, though he voices doubt whether his family can actually make it in Mexico.

With Féderico and María having made clear their willingness to leave José in Los Angeles, the narrative turns to Virginia. As with her birth in El Paso, her growing affections for Rafael set in motion not just a geographic return but an economic one as well. After a shopping spree that includes new clothes and a car, Virginia is happy to forgive amorous advances as long as he's serious about a relationship. So, like high school sweethearts after the prom, they look at each other as they drive down the road:

Comenzaron ambos a sonreír, y entre más se veían más sonreían.

—¿Sabes? —dijo él quitando una mano de volante y pasándola por sobre su hombro,— que hoy mismo le hablo a los tíos para que arreglen y nos vamos a México... ¿Quieres casarte conmigo? —prosiguió, atrayéndola un poco más hacia él.

Le miró riente y sorprendida...

—¡Qué pregunta! —exclamó, cogiéndole la mano y besándola con cariño. (chapter 7, 11)

Awkward but ultimately effective, Rafael literally offers his free hand from driving to Virginia in marriage, but only after reaffirming that he will talk to her parents about leaving for Mexico. In turn, Virginia literally accepts his proposal by taking his hand and showering it with loving kisses.

From there the novel quickens to an end. Even José softens his exterior bravado and agrees to return to the family. Packed and in the car, all that remains, declares María, is to pay their respect to Julián Gutierrez, the faithful charro friend of the family who served them until he died from exhaustion and a broken heart, unable to return to Mexico. With everyone in tears at the thought of his poor old bones in a country that did not want him, nor he it, first Féderico and then Rafael promise to repatriate Julián's remains to Mexico in the near future. And with that promise to leave no one behind to suffer any further poverty and indignities of living in the United States, Féderico offers María one final consolation: "No llores, —le dijo atrayéndola hacia sí—. Es cierto que dejamos enterrado a nuestro mejor amigo, pero en cambio, nos vamos de la tierra donde desperdiciamos lo mejor de nuestra vida, bastante afortunados somos con llevarnos a nuestros hijos!" (chapter 7, 15). Urging her not to cry any further for Julián, he asks her to appreciate that even though they have wasted their lives by leaving Mexico, nonetheless as parents they can feel fortunate in returning their children to their tierra, land of their birthright. And thus ends, in Féderico's mind, the pocho lives of their children.

Already Home

There is no doubt that Ainslie's ending is a romantic fantasy of sorts. Beyond thriftiness and their penny-pinching ways, Rafael does not really explain how his parents have built the wealth of their ranch since the end of the Revolution, and further, none of the characters actually question the cause and effect that has led to this wealth. Ainslie simply projects an inevitable aura of well-being around Rafael and his coherent masculine identity, which includes being well monied. But if Ainslie's narrative is a conservative one, ignoring the positive reasons why Mexican immigrants might decide to remain in the United States, other conservative voices in *La Prensa*, such as Catalina D'Erzel's, are willing to spell out the irony in anti-immigration discourses to the United States: Where are the jobs for these returning immigrants? In her article "Los sin patria," she identifies those without a country as individuals who are neither American nor Mexican: "Los compatriotas ausentes no son americanos ni mexicanos. Son 'Los sin patria' cuya existencia se deliza suspirante y amarga, porque su falta de adaptación al país que los hospeda es causa muchas veces de desorientación y aun de fracaso, especialmente en los centros de trabajo" (April 1, 1938, 3). Because they cannot adapt to the United States, such immigrants, full of sighs and bitterness, become disoriented, thereby affecting their employment possibilities. But those who do wish to return to Mexico encounter other obstacles just as grave: "Pero entonces también la realidad se impone. ¿Encontrarán trabajo en este México, empobrecido y sindicalizado? Cierto que vienen a fundirse en las masa del proletariado, pero, ¿permitirá el proletariado su ingreso al sindicato que defiende los derechos del pobre? En los sindicatos están tantos, que ya no caben más." Here D'Erzel aligns Mexico's deep poverty with its overabundance of unions, calling these twin conditions the reality that confronts returning immigrants. Questioning the integrity of the unions, she plays with the language of the proletariat, and their championing of workers' rights. She points out the unions' unwillingness to add more workers to their rolls. However partisan D'Erzel's choice of argumentation is, the root cause of immigration to the United States, and the lack of voluntary repatriation, boils down to the availability of jobs. In this regard, Ainslie's novel plays into the political cracks and fissures of a global economic crisis, with widespread unemployment, hunger, and massive displacement of families whether in the United States, Mexico, or elsewhere in the world. His narrative was for sure one of many fantasies in 1934.

If Kolodny's 1992 essay encouraged the larger field of American literary studies to let go of its obsession with English, we in Chicanx studies would do well to return to one of our old obsessions, Spanish. By doing so, we not only increase what we know and what we suspect are the influences transnationally on Mexico, Latin America, and the world, but transregionally, we might recover influences or processes or events that might turn out to be just as important to recover. It would do us all well to rethink the importance of the Spanish-language press in the Southwest and West, and in particular, the tremendous cultural influence that a newspaper chain like Ignacio E. Lozano's played from Brownsville to Los Angeles, especially in the fields of politics, history, literature, and criticism.[13] If we do so, we might be able to see how a writer like Jorge Ainslie, and the many others in the pages of *La Prensa* and other newspapers, might have influenced someone like Jovita González, who, as we have seen, was also featured in *La Prensa*.

It would also help us to see more dramatically the evolution of someone like Américo Paredes, who published his early poetry in newspapers like *La Prensa* and in his own way already provided an alternative ethnic response to writers like Ainslie by claiming his pocho identity rather than running away from it. In his love poem "Como el Nenufar," he clearly embraces it:

Como esa flor hermosa y perfumada
que los pochos llamamos "el lampazo",
que busca para abrir agua estancada
ya en potrero, en maizal o en llano raso. (August 8, 1938, 4)

In this poem, Paredes associates with his beloved the ability of a water lily to flourish wherever there might be stagnant water, be it on a pasture, a cornfield, or open flat plain. Paredes prefigures here what will not be fully comprehended for at least another thirty years: the soulful poetics of a pocho sensibility and a pocho language that locates its speaker as always, already home, somewhere between Mexico and the United States.[14]

By 1948, a full one hundred years after the Mexican-American War, pocho speech and chicana/o speakers were already flourishing. Long before Luis Valdez staged his play *Zoot Suit* (1978) on Broadway, depicting the events known as the Sleepy Lagoon Murder Trial of 1942, pocho speech would evolve from its pejorative portrayals in the Spanish-language press to quotidian representations of everyday life and poetic speech like Paredes's.

From time to time, this new speech, including code-switching and neologisms, would even appear in the hands of Mexican American women writers such as Gregoria Salinas. In her 1944 short story "Igual que hermanos," Salinas captures how pocho speech and the war effort at home combined to produce new social relations among women in the work force. Salinas even dramatizes how U.S. foreign policy with Latin America, and Mexico in particular, provided women with new modes of mobility between the two countries:

> Los "grandes" de América tienen su corazón puesto en un amor fraternal Inter Americano, los "chicos" nos esforzamos por convertir la santa idea en realidad. Por el momento, ya nos amamos un poco como . . . ¿buenos? . . . hermanos.
>
> Margarita y Annie suspenden la conversación y se lanzan hacia el aparato telefónico a un tiempo. Annie, llega la primera.
>
> —Army Tailorsssss —contesta con columpio, mientras acomoda el chicle en un rincón seguro de la mejilla derecha.
>
> —Oh! How are you, Sergeant? . . . Fine! I do not think so. Yes, she is here. Do you want to talk to her? . . . Alright, I'll let you talk to her.
>
> —Andale, Ana, presta, —impaciente, Margarita arranca el aparato de manos de Annie.
>
> —Hello, Jimmy! Yes . . . Next week . . . Annie Smith, Anna Marie Johnson, and myself . . . Monterrey, Mexico . . . I hope yo get younr furlough by then. Maybe yo can come with us . . . Is that so? . . . Well! . . . O.K. I'll be seeing you. Goodbye!
>
> —¿Vendrá con nosotros? —pregunta Annie.
>
> —Na seba . . .
>
> —Yo mejor quisiera que viniera él con nosotros y no Anna Marie. ¡Es tan bruta!
>
> —¡Ana Smith! En qué forma te expresas de tu prima hermana.
>
> —Pos si . . . Listen, she doesn't even speak Spanish.
>
> —Do you?
>
> —Un poquito. Ella no habla nada, nada . . .
>
> Y tal era el caso.

> Algo se habrá ya adivinado. Margarita es una mexicana. ¡Linda como una Virgen de Guadalupe! Tiene unos ojos negros que dan luz cuando miran y una sonrisa particularmente hermosa. Annie Smith es mexicana por su madre. Los ojos y el cabello son latinos, el resto, anglo-americano.
> Anna Marie Johnson es anglo-americana por todos lados. Los ojillos azules, el pelo castaño claro, la naricilla respingona y unas pecas muy graciosas sobre las mejillas y la nariz, la acusan. Su verdadero nombre es Mary Ann, pero como la influencia latina es tal, pues le "alatinaron" el nombre y le llaman Anna Marie.
> La 'Sastretía del Ejército' o 'Army Tailors' que es el verdadero nombre de la firma, empezó a conceder vavcaciones [sic] a sus empléados comenzando por las tres chicas ya conocidas, las que, en vista de la armonía inter-americana y la política del "Buen Vecino", arrastradas por la corriente de Buena Voluntad, decidieron cruzar la frontera de México y pasar dos semanas de vacaciones en Monterrey. (*La Prensa*, Jan. 30, 1944, p. 13)

As the omniscient narrator explains, the three young women, working as part of the war effort as army tailors, are excited about Roosevelt's New Neighbor Policy with Mexico because it has translated into a short vacation for them. The war effort in San Antonio has brought together Margarita, a Mexican national, Annie Smith, a Mexican American, and Anna Marie, an Anglo-American; theirs is an evolving friendship, where code-switching from Spanish to English and vice versa is a signature feature of their exchanges and of how they navigate their worlds, be it in San Antonio, Texas, or their vacation destination in Monterrey, Nuevo León, Mexico.

After the war, such representations of pocho speech and code-switching, including misspellings to denote dialect, in the Spanish-language press will eventually spill over to English publishing venues. It's no accident then that Tucson native and Navy veteran Mario Suárez's short stories of the chicanos and chicanas of El Hoyo find their way to publication in the *Arizona Quarterly* by 1948.[15] Between 1948 and 1968, many more publications would follow in both Spanish and English, each language reflecting the burdens of modernity that both the Cold War and the civil rights movement would invariably produce for succeeding generations to write about. Ironically, for all its collective vitriol of *pochos, pochas,* and other similar terms, it is the case that we partly owe the invention of Chicanas, Chicanos, and their literatures during the movement to presses like *La Prensa,* especially to the stubborn will of its publishers, editors, writers, and workers to survive even as their readerships changed and grew beyond their original missions.

Radio and television in English and in Spanish will play a role in the decline of the Spanish-language press, as well as changing class and social demographics in Mexican American communities. And yet its decline will be met with the rise of an identifiable Chicana/o print culture, including newspapers, journals, manifestos, magazines, newsletters, chapbooks, literary presses, and curricula. In truth, an uninterrupted print culture since 1848 has existed—a print culture that scholars and students can point to with ever-increasing degrees of sophistication. Without knowing, those early writers of Mexican America laid down a future only their children's children's children would get to read about. Given the print landscape we enjoy today, we owe them a debt of gratitude for daring to write. This book joins many others that write back to those previous generations. Perhaps now we can all move forward together.

Afterword

"For Modernity," Enrique Dussel wrote in *The Invention of the Americas*, "the barbarian is at fault for opposing the civilizing process, and modernity, ostensibly innocent, seems to be emancipating the fault of its own victims" (137). But this statement requires a caveat: any attempt to define modernity necessarily requires the concession that such an attempt is in fact a work in progress, under construction, provisional, to say the least. I wholeheartedly include this book as well. Throughout this study, my interest in the term *modernity* and its constant companion, *coloniality*, has been how to understand and better describe the social, political, and economic foundations that have underwritten what we call Mexican American literature in particular and the Mexican American experience in general. I have also been interested in this matrix called modernity/coloniality, like many scholars in many fields, in order to grasp better what might be the local and global stakes of decoloniality and thus how from that perspective we might collectively decolonize our respective fields. In short, to inquire about modernity is to inquire about power; it is about making visible a power that made itself manifest in 1492 and thereafter in a series of related events, institutions, documents, ideologies, politics, technologies, and economies to this day, each, as Walter Mignolo has written, immersed in its own local history, histories that are themselves riddled with global designs.

An ongoing meditation on the meaning of *modernity* is necessary in any attempt to do the heavy lift that will be required to decolonize Chicanx studies—a field of study that only lately has understood its formation as partly a consequence of the visible powers of coloniality and modernity that cohere with Europe, as well as the consequence of powers that resist visibility and therefore scrutiny, but which also cohere with Europe. Thinking about how Chicanx studies might be decolonized has been circulating for a while now, from Gloria Anzaldúa's borderlands to Emma Pérez's use of decolonial imaginaries as a method of perceiving historic ruptures to Chela Sandoval's focus on decolonial practices and oppositional consciousness. More recently, a growing body of work has emerged to challenge the boundaries between Chicanx studies and Native studies precisely over the definitions of indigeneity, but also transnational practices, networks, and politics. The work of Inés Hernández-Ávila, Maylei Blackwell, Sheila Contreras, María Josefina Saldaña-Portillo, Domino Perez, and Lourdes Alberto come to mind. My own inclination has been to follow in the footsteps of Martha Menchaca's work in the nineteenth century that unpacks the complicated and often contradictory legal, social, and political affiliations that resulted because of coloniality's hierarchal, often violent, constructions of race and race relations.

Although my research through the Recovery Project has been rewarding, I have found myself troubled by the very archive I have summoned to make the case for this book. Although less so in the literature of the Chicana/o Movement, early Mexican American literature, including folklore, periodicals, diaries, and recipe books, is at times deeply mired in the darker side of coloniality, especially around race and indigenous displacement. I have been troubled, as I said, by this archive, not because of the intellectual conclusions I have drawn but more because of the limits of knowing itself: the knowledge of coloniality as an inheritor of privilege is one thing, knowledge of coloniality as its object of possession or target of violence is quite another. I have to admit that I largely write from the position of the former. And even though I do my best to remember my own heritage as a second-generation immigrant, a mestizo Mexican American born in the barrio to working-class parents, and increasingly feeling more Mexican as I get older, I still drink Starbucks coffee every morning; I still insist on *The Walking Dead* every Sunday evening; Elvis Costello still speaks to me. The limits of my knowing are directly related to the privileges, including being a straight man, that I exercise every day.

Where does that leave the project of understanding modernity/coloniality, much less the project of decoloniality?

My answer of late has been that it is fundamentally a philosophical enterprise of shifting one's perspectives. Indeed, shifting one's perspective is perhaps the most difficult thing one can do to access a decolonial imaginary. For instance, I'm intrigued by Enrique Dussel's statement: "For Modernity, the barbarian is at fault for opposing the civilizing process, and modernity, ostensibly innocent, seems to be emancipating the fault of its own victims" (137). The first part seems easy to accept. The Native denies Christianity; she therefore refuses spiritual salvation. The Native denies European language; he therefore refuses literacy. The Native denies property; she therefore refuses the accumulation of individual wealth. Because of these self-perpetuated denials and refusals, the Native remains uncivilized and thus barbaric. But the second part of the statement, "and modernity, ostensibly innocent, seems to be emancipating the fault of its own victims," falls apart semantically. How can modernity present itself as a liberating force when it is the cause, the site of a disciplining power to control, to name, to victimize? Modernity can't. This statement is gibberish, unless one notices the modifier, "ostensibly innocent," and then one can apprehend the irony always present in modernity's offer of emancipation to its own victims. For it is modernity that makes the distinction of civilized versus barbaric; it is modernity that stipulates the logic of gente de razón versus gente sin razón. It is modernity that trades infected blankets for goodwill. Whose fault is it for failing to perceive the blankets as infected, poisoned? Better question, who is responsible for such false acts? Even better, who should we hold accountable? What Dussel, Quijano, Mignolo, Lugones, and Maldonado-Torres always seem to be pointing out philosophically is the preponderance of perspective that is required to move toward a decolonial imaginary in light of such questions. To that perspective I would add: there is a profound need to reflect on the historic archive as it is and, not, how we might want it to be.

Because Mexican Americans have occupied such a variety of locales between 1848 and 1948, there are theoretically just as many responses to the effects of modernity. The challenge of this study has been the scope of its field imaginary. In order to link the variety of responses found in this field imaginary, I have offered several ways to conceive how writers from different regions and periods—and different from each other because of race, sex, gender, education, and ties to Mexico—might nonetheless cohere in a study of modernity. I have argued that attention to place was one of the primary ways in which all these writers literally grounded their apprehension of the modern. Hence, place for this study—both the material and physical, like a Spanish/Mexican land grant, and socially constructed, like labeling somebody as Californio or Nuevo Mexicano—becomes a method for critically indexing the changing social and political terrains of Mexican America after 1848. Indeed, growing disaffection or alienation from one's native place—casa, hogar, país, tierra, and so forth—becomes a visible marker of modernity for Mexican Americans. No less visible are the markers made by those Mexicanos who immigrated into places that still retained residual traces of a Native-Spanish-Mexican past. Altogether, I have striven for a representation of modernity that is effectively at odds with the modernity offered by most Anglo-European models. Nevertheless, as evidenced by the literature left behind, the Mexican American community was earnestly interested in the modern. As Chicanx labor historians have noted, for a good part of the twentieth century, Mexican Americans strove to see themselves as evolving citizens of a U.S. modern polity. Yet theirs was also a search for a communal metanarrative that offered some refuge from the negative forces constraining the Mexican American experience itself, forces that were undermining a sense of place even as those forces affirmed a righteous place for some.

In this book I have argued that place, writ large or small, is a potent way to register how Mexican Americans dealt with the new Anglo-American order after the Mexican-American War. By reviewing the role that place plays in articulating the emergent status of Mexican America after 1848, this project sought to demonstrate how early Mexican American writing shows a slow but steady erosion of the efficacy of place to center a broadly defined, functional political imaginary for Mexican American identity. During the postbellum years, one can see in María Amparo Ruiz de Burton's writings how place still retains the trappings of a colonial structure of power, which enables her as person and writer to evidence a confidence about place. Place terms such as Californiana and her beloved Rancho Jamul empowered her travels, both real and imagined, whereas for someone like Gregorio Cortez, toward the end of the nineteenth century, there is already no place where he can find empowerment as a Mexican American. Especially under Anglo-Texan nationalism, Texas had been colonized by then away from its indigenous, Spanish, and Mexican Tejas antecedents. Cortez's agency in the ballad resides completely in his ability to evade and elude Anglo-Texan forms of colonization; his ability is all about moving about and being invisible in a recolonized space and not about occupying place. The corrido as a cultural form becomes symptomatic of increasing Mexican American estrangement from place under modernity.

There are several lessons in this study for reading modernity through place. One lies in the ability to resist the seduction that European mapping of the New World had over the settler and later the would-be traveler. With the ability to erase or confound a prior significance of place, such mapping had the effect of undoing or marginalizing existing relationships to place. To read modernity through place, through geography, invariably disrupts and questions the naturalizing effect of timelessness that each colonizing institution—by, for instance, using European place-names—has had over space. In this regard, reading geographically should be thought of as a decolonizing habit of reading that offers critique centered around an engagement with place through history, culture, politics, and narrative. The value of geographic readings of literature from colonized spaces is the ability to measure how the socioeconomic and political relationships of everyday place-making entered the imaginative trappings of narrative, be it oral or textual. Further, through the lens of place and place-making, one can theorize the cultural work that such narratives performed locally. Combined with all the advanced work on cultural geography, feminist geography, Native studies, Latinx studies, and settler-colonial criticism, reading geographically positions us to apply those tools toward a wide range of U.S.

texts that are derived not from a single Anglo-Puritan colonial history—a position that dominated most of twentieth-century U.S. literary studies—but rather a tradition that rests upon a conflicting set of multiple colonial histories, languages, cultures, and peoples.

In this study, it has been important to note when and how place in Mexican American culture does not work as it does or might in mainstream U.S. culture. Overall, this study does not find writers or texts that mirror a wholly transparent relationship to land—there are no Walt Whitmans in this archive, nor even a fictional transparency to land—no Mexican Dorothys ever return to Kansas. By contrast, Mexican American culture often spills over with a sense of insecurity, fraudulence, and impermanence with regards to landownership and collateral issues such as civic identity, labor, and language. Indeed, as this study has demonstrated, there is an anxiety over place that recalls the colonization of the Américas and the displacement of indigenous people from traditional lands. Moreover, recent findings from the fields of archeology, anthropology, and botany paint a surprising and more complex picture of pre-Columbian life in the Américas: where migration, alliances, and the trafficking of foodstuffs and goods are of such a hemispheric scale that even by European standards, it is impossible to imagine. In other words, the scale of indigenous displacement throughout the Américas looms larger than ever before considered possible.

Given the histories of settler colonialism in North America, place, much like modernity, has been a very confusing and contradictory site of identity for Mexican Americans. Even if fleeting, however, there was a historical moment and a cultural imaginary that supported a territorial basis for a settler Mexican identity. By 1846 this territorial imaginary stretched from the Yucatán in the south to the Great Plains in the north, from Nacogdoches in East Texas to Mission San Francisco in Alta California. In truth, it required a distinct political imaginary to sustain and contain such geographic distances and diverse peoples. The conclusion of the Mexican-American War in 1848 thus marks a very curious moment for Western-inspired colonialism: the subjugation of one "settler country" by another "settler country," in essence the deterritorialization of one colonial matrix in favor of a more dominant reterritorialization of the same geographic space. I believe early Mexican

American literature, as staged in the preceding chapters, provides us with ongoing opportunities to analyze this phenomenon and to forward place as a critical means to historicize modernity.

It is from this in-between continuum of location and dislocation, in which the United States has been reluctant to embrace Mexican Americans, that we can access the modernities captured through this production of literature. It is from a modernity of subtraction that we can appreciate those aspects of the archive that seem anomalous by comparison to modernist figures in the United States and Mexico, out of place, forever unfamiliar. The lack of connection among Mexican American writers such as María Amparo Ruiz de Burton, María Cristina Mena, Daniel Venegas, Jovita González, and Américo Paredes is a *symptom* of their modernity, not a comment on their lack of fitness to chronicle the world. A modernity of subtraction assists us in resisting hegemonic tendencies to discipline the archive into a narrow set of identities. Instead, we must embrace the messy, contradictory, volatile anarchy of the Mexican American archive.

To do the kind of work a modernity of subtraction requires, we have to accept what the historical record tells us about writers between 1848 and 1948. Pre–Chicana/o Movement authors did not appear under the banner of either American or Mexican literature; they did not appear in either their own lifetime, or with the generation before or after them, as part of some emergent literary tradition. Ultimately, neither were they hailed as part of some nation-building imaginary that Donald Pease might recognize, nor were they party to what Doris Sommer might identify as national foundational fiction. Although one finds regional conversations between figures such as Mariano Guadalupe Vallejo and M. A. Ruiz de Burton in California, and convergences between the literary and the scholarly in writers such as Jovita González and Américo Paredes in Texas, neither conversations nor convergences translated into a literary movement or a literary influence of any measurable sort. Although there are regional exceptions where the audience from the Spanish-reading press supported publications by immigrant groups from Mexico and Latin America, in cities like New York, Philadelphia, San Antonio, and Los Angeles, these moments did not outlast the historical specificities of their origins or their locales;

they faded just enough to be mostly forgotten by the early 1960s. These writers were individually at work and only occasionally associated with others who were also of Mexican descent and living and writing in the United States. To confront the modernities contained in their works is in the end also to confront the limits of their place in the world, their lack of communal ties with each other.

However sobering these Mexican American predecessors might be for the scholar in search of usable pasts, their limits are nonetheless ours to explore and interpret. We might still benefit from Ruiz de Burton's advice to eighteen-year-old Platón Vallejo, on a letter dated April 23, 1859. As Rosaura Sánchez and Beatrice Pita have noted, Ruiz de Burton became a fierce proponent of Californios' embracing their own regional culture and history as a way to demand their rights from their new Anglo-American masters whenever an injustice was committed, and there were many.[1] Notwithstanding, she holds her own paisanos, countrymen, accountable for equating patriotism with drawing "themselves into this shell of impotent discontent" (*Conflicts of Interest*, 157). Race should be understood, she tells Platón, very generously in the context of Anglo-Americans:

> But it should be cherished, my dear Platon, with liberality, that is, without the surliness, bitter and repelling, which some seem to think is the best proof of true patriotism; without the narrowness of view which will not see virtues in others or faults in ourselves; but with that judicious liberality, true magnanimity which will grant their due to others fully and willingly we can keep sacred that holy feeling; the love of own race. (157)

As was her practice with all her correspondents, especially men, Ruiz de Burton did not allow anyone to perceive her as politically naïve.

Soon after exhorting Platón to "liberality," Ruiz de Burton nevertheless reconfirms widespread Californio sentiment when she notes:

> It cannot be denied that the californios have reasons to complain. The Americans must feel it; their boasted liberty and equality of rights seems to stop when it meets a Californian and witness, the

Land Commission—and we are *a child's handful in their mighty grasp*; they can crush us with impunity, they know it and broke their faith so solemnly pledged at Guadalupe Hidalgo, broke it by stooping to a miserable stratagem too. How shameful this, in the conquering, the prosperous, the mighty nation! Better to crush us at once and not trick us out of our lands; to us it will be all the same in the end, die and pass away; poor, despised and unnoticed! (157)

Despite incontrovertible proof of the malaise effecting the fortunes and spirits of her paisanos, Ruiz de Burton refuses to concede to the totalizing status quo of the new political masters. She shakes away the gloom by articulating a mission that becomes her life story: "It is then, by the exertion of individuals that this evil must be somewhat remedied or neutralized and with this in mind, remember my consejo when you grow up" (157–58). Whether or not Platón Vallejo took her advice is not known. And yet he did travel east, as Ruiz de Burton encouraged, for his continued education. He became a surgeon during the Civil War, returning home to Sonoma to live out his days as the first Californio physician.

In hindsight, the efforts of a Ruiz de Burton or Platón Vallejo were not enough to stem the tide against the crushing effects of a modernity of subtraction, especially in becoming "despised and unnoticed." However, today they are no longer "despised and unnoticed." However unimaginable to them, it will take several generations of Chicanas, Chicanos, and now Chicanx, to turn that tide. Now the histories and writings left behind since 1848 have become our means of battling that evil that Ruiz de Burton wrote so passionately about. Like hers, our evils are many, and some are very different in 2022. Unlike her, though, we now have the opportunity to actualize, to merge better than ever the past with the present in anticipation of a fuller knowledge project for all Mexican Americans. This book is dedicated to that cause, however long it takes.

NOTES

INTRODUCTION

1. See Mignolo, "Coloniality: The Darker Side of Modernity." For more on Mignolo's framing of coloniality, see Mignolo's "Coloniality at Large." See also Alcoff, "Mignolo's Epistemology of Coloniality."
2. For more, see Aranda, "Recovering the U.S. Hispanic Literary Heritage."
3. For more on Seguín and similar figures of Mexican descent, see Olguín, "Sangre mexicana / corazón americano."
4. For more on authenticity and hybridity, see Bell, *Relating Indigenous and Settler Identities*.
5. For more on liberation philosophy, see Silva, "'The Americas Seek Not Enlightenment.'"
6. See Dussel, "World-System and 'Trans'-Modernity."
7. For more on liberalism, see Coronado, *A World Not to Come*.
8. See Craib, "A Nationalist Metaphysics," 35–36.
9. For more on the casta system, see O'Hara and Fisher, *Imperial Subjects*.
10. For more on assimilation, see Cutler, *Ends of Assimilation*.
11. For a classic rendering of such historic moments, see Acuña, *Occupied America*.
12. See Gaonkar, "On Alternative Modernities."
13. See Coronado, *A World Not to Come*.
14. See Leal, "Octavio Paz and the Chicano."
15. See Weber, *The Spanish Frontier*.
16. LeMenager, *Manifest and Other Destinies*.
17. See Williams, *Marxism and Literature*.
18. See Lazo and Alemán, eds., *The Latino Nineteenth Century*.
19. See Comer, "Taking Feminism and Regionalism."

20. See Comer, "Exceptionalism, Other Wests, Critical Regionalism."
21. See Limón, "Border Literary Histories, Globalization."

1. MODERNITY DEFERRED

1. Ninetta Eames was an important figure in San Francisco literary circles; her support of Jack London was instrumental. See Charmian London's prologue in *The Book of Jack London*.
2. See Eames, "Autumn Days in Ventura," 561–80.
3. For a classic treatment of the "decline" of Californios, see Pitt, *The Decline of the Californios*.
4. The five Californianas were Guadalupe Vallejo, Prudencia Higuera, María Antonio Castro, Brigida Briones, and Amalia Sibrian.
5. See "Topics of the Time."
6. See Thomas, *Our Centennial Memoir*.
7. For more on this kind of ideological work, see Gruesz, *Ambassadors of Culture*.
8. In his introduction, James H. Wilkins insists that Platón Vallejo is telling his own story, but it's a story arranged and framed at the beginning of each chapter by Wilkins's own narrative voice. This framing gives the impression that Wilkins might have transcribed a narration delivered orally by Vallejo; see Wilkins's introduction to Vallejo's *Memoir*, 1–2.

2. CALIFORNIO SETTLER HISTORY

1. Poem by M. G. Vallejo, trans. Francisca Vallejo McGettigan, in Lyman, "The First Native-Born Californian Physician," 289.
2. See Rosaldo, "Imperialist Nostalgia."
3. For a contemporaneous account of this period, see Revere, *A Tour of Duty*.
4. For more on the Land Commission of 1851, see Gates, "The California Land Act of 1851"; Bastian, "'I Heartily Regret That I Ever Touched a Title'"; Chanbonpin, "How the Border Crossed Us."
5. See McGettigan, Scripts for KYA radio series "Padres, Gringos and Gold." Transcriptions for this chapter are my own.
6. See Flores, "Adina de Zavala and the Politics of Restoration."
7. See Simpson, "The Ruse of Consent," 21; and for more on refusal, see also Simpson's *Mohawk Interruptus*.
8. See August Twenty-Ninth Movement, *Fan the Flames*, 6.
9. In this chapter, I have been inspired and guided by F. Arturo Rosales's treatment of the Bandini and Vallejo family archives: "All the Californios discussed here lamented the decline of their culture and in some cases were critical of Anglo oppression.

A more thorough recovery of manuscripts and forgotten publications written by Hispanic California writers will allow us to make the assessment with more precision, however. One that will hopefully refrain from a presentist scolding of dead historical figures" ("'Fantasy Heritage,'" 101).

10. One piece of music entitled "Paloma Mia," written for the play, might have been a version of Iradier's song or the very music she used for her radio program. But when the title of the song appears on the radio transcripts, it is clearly "La Paloma," not "Paloma Mia."
11. Elsewhere, she includes her married name of McGettigan, especially with publications.
12. For more on María Ygnacia López de Carrillo, see Roybal, "Hidden Histories."
13. For an insider view of this trade, see Higuera, "Gold Hunters of California."
14. For specific examples of their work, see Leo Carrillo, *The California I Love* (1961); Ana Bégué de Packman, *Early California Hospitality* (1938) and *Leather Dollars* (1932); Fabiola Cabeza de Baca, *The Good Life* (1949) and *We Fed Them Cactus* (1954), who also hosted a radio show on KVSF on homemaking; Adelina (Nina) Otero Warren, *Old Spain in Our Southwest* (1936), who was also an educator, politician, and entrepreneur; Cleofas Jaramillo, *The Genuine New Mexico Tasty Recipes / Potajes Sabrosos* (1939), also preservationist and businesswoman; Adina Emilia de Zavala, *The Story of the Siege and Fall of the Alamo* (1911) and *History and Legends of the Alamo* (1917), also preservationist; Jovita González, see chapter 4.

3. GAME OF MODERNITIES

1. See especially chapter 1, "Worlds Apart," in Weber, *The Spanish Frontier*, 14–17.
2. The actual text that Coronado used as the requerimiento is not among the surviving documents for his expedition. The one quoted here comes from an earlier expedition in 1514 or 1515. Alonso de Ojeda was given command of the Province of Tierra Firme, which was essentially the island and lands shaping the perimeters of the Caribbean Sea. He is credited with naming the region known as Venezuela. See appendix 4 of his requerimiento, in Flint and Flint, *Documents of the Coronado Expedition*, 617–18.
3. For the entire text, see O'Sullivan, "The Great Nation of Futurity."
4. For more, see Hutchins, "A Colorful Accompaniment."
5. See Pratt, "Arts of the Contact Zone."
6. See Maldonado-Torres, "On the Coloniality of Being."
7. Blackwell, Lopez, and Urrieta, "Introduction."
8. From *Geronimo, His Own Story*, 110.
9. For a good example of a thorough but U.S.-centric treatment of Geronimo, see Utley, *Geronimo*.

10. For more such narratives, see Robinson, *Apache Voices*.
11. For a more expanded treatment, see Hixson, "'They Promised to Take Our Land.'"
12. See Hutton, *The Apache Wars*.
13. For an expanded treatment, see Kuhn, *Chronicles of War*.
14. For more on the enslavement of indigenous people in what becomes known as the Southwest, see Brooks, *Captives and Cousins*.
15. This mention of a survey is probably a reference to the survey begun by the Boundary Survey Commission in 1849; it had been stipulated by the Treaty of Guadalupe Hidalgo, which ended the U.S.-Mexican War in 1848. For more on this survey, see St. John, *Line in the Sand*.
16. For more on the history of mesquite in Texas, see Pierce, "Marvelous, Maligned, and Misunderstood."
17. This entrenched, double-edged racism is fairly common in Mexican American communities until the 1960s, when the Chicana/o Movement centers much of its collective identity in a recuperation of an indigenous past. But this recuperation also reifies a settler-colonial heritage. For more on this recuperation, see Alberto, "Nations, Nationalisms, and Indígenas."
18. For more on such labor, see Roybal, "Hidden Histories."
19. Jovita González, unpublished poem, circa 1925, Benson Latin American Collection, University of Texas, Austin.
20. Portions of this section are found in a previous essay, Aranda, "The Recovery Project."
21. See Otero, *The Real Billy the Kid* (1998).
22. For more on Billy the Kid and the Lincoln County War, please consult Jacobsen, *Such Men as Billy the Kid*; Nolan, *The Billy the Kid Reader*; Tatum, *Inventing Billy the Kid*; Utley, *High Noon in Lincoln*.
23. For more on the Buffalo Soldiers and the Ninth Calvary, please consult Billington, *New Mexico's Buffalo Soldiers*; Glasrud and Searles, *Buffalo Soldiers in the West*; Kenner, *Buffalo Soldiers and Officers of the Ninth Cavalry*.
24. For corroboration on the Freeman incident, see Leckie and Leckie, *The Buffalo Soldiers*, 198–99.
25. For more on Estevanico, see Gordon, "Following Estevanico."
26. For an eyewitness account, see Steward, *Buffalo Soldiers*.

4. ME LLAMAN MEXICANA

1. Jovita González, unpublished sketch, ca. 1925, Benson Latin American Collection, University of Texas, Austin.
2. For more on *Mexican* as keyword, see Aranda, "Mexican."
3. For more on Mexican American citizenship, see Rodriguez, "More than Whiteness."

4. For more, see Montejano, *Anglos and Mexicans*.
5. For more, see Griswold del Castillo, *The Treaty of Guadalupe Hidalgo*; for temporal effects on literature, see Murrah-Mandril, *In the Mean Time*.
6. For more, see Valdez, "Chicana/o Literature and the Folkloric Difference," 1–2.
7. See Rivera, "Reconsidering Jovita González's Life," 74.
8. See Cotera, "Introduction."
9. See "El Matrimonio Mireles-González," *San Antonio La Prensa*, Aug. 4, 1935, p. 3.

5. BARRIO MODERNITY

1. The screenplay, written by Frank S. Nugent, was based on James Warner Bellah's short story "Massacre," published February 22, 1947, in the *Saturday Evening Post*.
2. In this chapter, I use the older form of *chicana* or *chicano* to reference subcultural terms that work in tandem with *pocha* and *pocho* to identity types among Mexican American youth. But when I reference the terms *Chicana* or *Chicano* as formal nouns, I do so in recognition of their usage during and after the Chicana/o Movement to denote a people of Mexican descent in the United States.
3. See Gutiérrez, *The Making of a Chicano Militant*.
4. I am forever grateful to the members of this directed reading, affectionately referred to as Café con Plática—Priscilla Ybarra, Lourdes Alberto, John Escobedo, and Cecilia Ballí—for the work they produced and inspired.
5. For more on the Longfellow Institute, see their website at http://www.fas.harvard.edu/~lowinus/.
6. For more on the Recovery Project, see Aranda, "Recovering the U.S. Hispanic Literary Heritage."
7. See Garcia, *Mexican Americans*; Sánchez, *Becoming Mexican American*; Guerin-Gonzáles, *Mexican Workers and American Dreams*; Gutiérrez, *Walls and Mirrors*.
8. See Balderrama and Rodriguez, *Decade of Betrayal*; and Deborah Cohen, *Braceros*.
9. See Ramirez, *The Women in the Zoot Suit*.
10. More on this, see Deena J. González, *Refusing the Favor*; and Moyna, "Back at the Rancho."
11. For more on the figure of the pocho in society and literature, see Hernández, "Las caraterísticas cómicas."
12. For more on Jorge Ainslie, see Aranda, "Critical Translation."
13. See Rodriguez, "Ignacio E. Lozano."
14. For more of Paredes's early poetry, see his volume *Cantos de adolescencia*.
15. See Suárez, *Chicano Sketches*.

AFTERWORD

1. See Sánchez and Pita, "Across the Line," 105–7.

BIBLIOGRAPHY

Acuña, Rodolfo F. *Occupied America: A History of Chicanos*. 7th ed. Upper Saddle River NJ: Pearson, 2010.

Ainslie, Jorge. *Los pochos, novela mexicana*. Serialized in *San Antonio La Prensa*, April 15, 1934–June 3, 1934. Readex, *Hispanic American Newspapers, 1808–1980*, https://infoweb-newsbank.

Alberto, Lourdes. "Nations, Nationalisms, and Indígenas: The 'Indian' in the Chicano Revolutionary Imaginary." *Critical Ethnic Studies* 2, no. 1 (Spring 2016): 107–27.

Alcoff, Linda Martín. "Mignolo's Epistemology of Coloniality." CR: *The New Centennial Review* 7, no. 3 (2007): 79–101.

Altrocchi, Julia Cooley. *The Spectacular San Franciscans*. New York: E. P. Dutton, 1949.

Aranda, José F., Jr. "Critical Translation: The Politics and Writings of Jorge Ainslie." In *Writing/Righting History: 25 Years of Recovering the U.S. Hispanic Literary Heritage*, edited by Antonia Castaneda and Clara Lomas, 441–67. Houston: Arte Público, 2019.

———. "Mexican." Special issue, "On the Occasion of the 50th Anniversary of the Western Literature Association," guest edited by Krista Comer and Susan Bernardin, *Western American Literature* 53, no. 1 (Spring 2018): 49–52.

———. "Recovering the U.S. Hispanic Literary Heritage." In *The Routledge Companion to Latino/a Literature*, edited by Suzanne Bost and Frances R. Aparicio, 476–84. New York: Routledge, 2012.

———. "The Recovery Project and the Role of History in Chicano/a Literary History." In *A History of Western American Literature*, edited by Susan Kollin, 31–46. New York: Cambridge University Press, 2015.

Atherton, Gertrude. *Before the Gringo Came*. New York: J. Selwin Tait & Sons, 1894.

The August Twenty-Ninth Movement. *Fan the Flames: Revolutionary Position on the Chicano National Question*. Los Angeles: ATM, 1976.

Balderrama, Francisco E., and Raymond Rodriguez. *Decade of Betrayal: Mexican Repatriation of the 1930s*. Albuquerque: University of New Mexico Press, 1995.

Bandini, Helen Elliott. "Our Spanish American Families." *Overland Monthly and Out West Magazine* 26, no. 151 (July 1895): 20.

Barr, Juliana. "Geographies of Power: Mapping Indian Borders in the 'Borderlands' of the Early Southwest." *William and Mary Quarterly* 68, no. 1 (Jan. 2011): 5–46.

Bastian, Beverly E. "'I Heartily Regret That I Ever Touched a Title in California': Henry Wager Halleck, the Californios, and the Clash of Legal Cultures." *California History* 72 (1993): 310–23.

Bégué de Packman, Ana. *Early California Hospitality: The Cookery Customs of Spanish California, with Authentic Recipes and Menus of the Period*. Glendale CA: Arthur H. Clarke, 1938.

———. *Leather Dollars: Short Stories of Pueblo Los Angeles*. Los Angeles: Times-Mirror Press, 1932.

Bell, Avril. *Relating Indigenous and Settler Identities: Beyond Domination*. New York: Palgrave Macmillan, 2014.

Bhabha, Homi. "Of Mimicry and Man: The Ambivalence of Colonial Discourse." In *The Location of Culture*, by Homi Bhabha. London: Routledge, 1994.

Billington, Monroe Lee. *New Mexico's Buffalo Soldiers, 1866–1900*. Niwot: University Press of Colorado, 1991.

Blackwell, Maylei, Floridalma Boj Lopez, and Luis Urrieta Jr. "Introduction" to special issue on "Critical Latinx Indigeneities," edited by Maylei Blackwell, Floridalma Boj Lopez, and Luis Urrieta Jr., *Latino Studies* 15, no. 2 (2017): 126–37.

Brooks, James F. *Captives and Cousins: Slavery, Kinship, and Community in the Southwest Borderlands*. Chapel Hill: Omohundro Institute and University of North Carolina Press, 2002.

Byrd, Jodi A. "Still Waiting for the 'Post' to Arrive: Elizabeth Cook-Lynn and the Imponderables of American Indian Postcoloniality." Special issue on "Essentializing Elizabeth Cook-Lynn," *Wičazo Ša Review* 31, no. 1 (Spring 2016): 75–89.

———. *The Transits of Empire: Indigenous Critiques of Colonialism*. Minneapolis: University of Minnesota Press, 2011.

Cabeza de Baca, Fabiola. *The Good Life*. Santa Fe: San Vicente Foundation, 1949.

———. *We Fed Them Cactus*. Albuquerque: University of New Mexico Press, 1954.

"California." *The American Review: A Whig Journal of Politics, Literature, and Science* 3 (1846): 82–99.

Carrillo, Leo. *The California I Love*. Englewood Cliffs NJ: Prentice-Hall, 1961.

Carson, James Taylor. "Ethnogeography and the Native American Past." *Ethnohistory* 49, no. 4 (Fall 2002): 767–88.

Castañeda, Antonia I. "Gender, Race, and Culture: Spanish-Mexican Women in the Historiography of Frontier California." *Frontiers: A Journal of Women's Studies* 11, no. 1 (1990): 8–20.

Cervantes, Lorna Dee. *Emplumada*. Pittsburgh: University of Pittsburgh Press, 1981.

Cervantes-Rodríguez, Ana Margarita, and Amy Lutz. "Coloniality of Power, Immigration, and the English-Spanish Asymmetry in the United States." *Nepantla: Views from South* 4, no. 3 (2003): 523–60.

Chanbonpin, Kim David. "How the Border Crossed Us: Filling the Gap between Plume v. Seward and the Dispossession of Mexican Landowners in California after 1848." *Cleveland State Law Review* 52 (2005): 297–319.

Cisneros, Sandra. *The House on Mango Street*. Houston: Arte Público, 1984.

Cohen, Deborah. *Braceros: Migrant Citizens and Transnational Subjects in the Postwar United States and Mexico*. Chapel Hill: University of North Carolina Press, 2011.

Cohen, Matt. *The Networked Wilderness: Communicating in Early New England*. Minneapolis: University of Minnesota Press, 2010.

Comer, Krista. "Exceptionalism, Other Wests, Critical Regionalism." *American Literary History* 23, no. 1 (Spring 2011): 159–73.

———. "Taking Feminism and Regionalism toward the Transnational Third Wave." In *A Companion to the Regional Literatures of America*, edited by Charles Crow, 111–28. New York: Blackwell, 2003.

Coronado, Raúl. *A World Not to Come: A History of Latino Writing and Print Culture*. Cambridge MA: Harvard University Press, 2013.

Cotera, María Eugenia. "Engendering a 'Dialectics of Our America': Jovita González's Pluralist Dialogue as Feminist Testimonio." In *Las obreras: Chicana Politics of Work and Family*, edited by Vicki L. Ruiz, 237–56. Aztlán Anthology Series, vol. 1. Los Angeles: UCLA Chicano Studies Research Center Publications, 2000.

———. "Introduction: A Woman of the Borderlands." In *Life along the Border*, by Jovita González, edited with an introduction by María Eugenia Cotera, 3–33. College Station: Texas A&M University Press, 2006.

———. *Native Speakers: Ella Deloria, Zora Neal Hurston, Jovita González, and the Poetics of Culture*. Austin: University of Texas Press, 2008.

Craib, Raymond B. "A Nationalist Metaphysics: State Fixations, National Maps, and the Geo-Historical Imagination in Nineteenth-Century Mexico." *Hispanic American Historical Review* 82, no. 1 (2002): 35–36.

Cutler, John Alba. *Ends of Assimilation: The Formation of Chicano*. New York: Oxford University Press, 2015.

Davis, William Heath. *Sixty Years in California*. San Francisco: A. J. Leary, 1889.

Debo, Angie. *Geronimo: The Man, His Time, His Place*. Norman: University of Oklahoma Press, 1976.

DeLyser, Dydia Y. *Ramona Memories: Tourism and the Shaping of Southern California*. Minneapolis: University of Minnesota Press, 2005.

Dussel, Enrique. "World-System and 'Trans'-Modernity." *Nepantla: Views from South* 3, no. 2 (2002): 221–44.

Dwinelle, John W. "Commemoration." In *Our Centennial Memoir, Founding of the Missions, San Francisco de Asís, in Its Hundredth Year, the Celebration of Its Foundation, Historical Reminiscences of the Missions of California*, edited by P. J. Thomas, 81–97. San Francisco: P. J. Thomas, 1877.

Eames, Ninetta. "Autumn Days in Ventura." *Overland Monthly* 14, no. 84 (Dec. 1889): 561–80.

Flint, Richard, and Shirley Cushing Flint, eds. *Documents of the Coronado Expedition, 1539–1542: "They Were Not Familiar with His Majesty, nor Did They Wish to Be His Subjects."* Albuquerque: University of New Mexico Press, 2012.

Flores, Richard. "Adina de Zavala and the Politics of Restoration." In *History and Legends of the Alamo and Other Missions in and around San Antonio*, by Adina de Zavala, edited and introduced by Richard Flores, v–lviii. Houston: Arte Público, 1996.

Gaonkar, Dilip Parameshwar. "On Alternative Modernities." *Public Culture* 11, no. 1 (1999): 1–18.

Garcia, Mario T. *Mexican Americans: Leadership, Ideology, and Identity, 1930–1960*. New Haven: Yale University Press, 1989.

Gates, Paul. "The California Land Act of 1851." *California Historical Quarterly* 50, no. 4 (Dec. 1971): 395–430.

Geronimo. *Geronimo, His Own Story: The Autobiography of a Great Patriot Warrior, As Told to S. M. Barrett*. New York: Meridian, 1906. Reprint, 1996.

Glasrud, Bruce A., and Michael N. Searles, eds. *Buffalo Soldiers in the West: A Black Soldiers Anthology*. College Station: Texas A&M University Press, 2007.

González, Deena J. *Refusing the Favor: The Spanish-Mexican of Santa Fé*. New York: Oxford University Press, 1999.

González, Jovita. "Un incidente feo." Jovita González Mireles Manuscripts and Works, circa 1925–1980. Benson Latin American Collection, University of Texas, Austin.

———. *Life along the Border*. Edited with an introduction by María Eugenia Cotera. College Station: Texas A&M University Press, 2006.

———. "¿Quien Somos?" Jovita González Mireles Manuscripts and Works, circa 1925–1980. Benson Latin American Collection, University of Texas, Austin.

———. "Shades of the Tenth Muse." In *Las obreras: Chicana Politics of Work and Family*. edited by Vicki L. Ruiz, 249–56. Aztlán Anthology Series, vol. 1. Los Angeles: University of California, Los Angeles, Chicano Studies Research Center Publications, 2000.

———. "Social Life in Cameron, Starr, and Zapata Counties." Master's thesis, University of Texas, 1930.

———. *The Woman Who Lost Her Soul and Other Stories*. Edited and with an introduction by Sergio Reyna. Houston: Arte Público, 2000.

González, Jovita, and Eve Raleigh. *Caballero: A Historical Novel*. College Station: Texas A&M University Press, 1996.

Gordon, Richard A. "Following Estevanico: The Influential Presence of an African Slave in Sixteenth-Century New World Historiography." *Colonial Latin American Review* 15, no. 2 (Dec. 2006): 183–206.

Greene, Roland. "Not Works but Networks: Colonial Worlds in Comparative Literature." In *Comparative Literature in an Age of Globalization*, edited by Haun Saussy, 212–23. Baltimore: Johns Hopkins University Press, 2006.

Griffiths, Beatrice. *American Me*. Boston: Houghton Mifflin, 1948.

Griswold del Castillo, Richard. *The Treaty of Guadalupe Hidalgo: A Legacy of Conflict*. Norman: University of Oklahoma Press, 1990.

Gruesz, Kirsten Silva. *Ambassadors of Culture: The Transamerican Origin of Latino Writing*. Princeton NJ: Princeton University Press, 2002.

Guerin-Gonzáles, Camile. *Mexican Workers and American Dreams: Immigration, Repatriation, and California Farm Labor, 1900–1939*. New Brunswick NJ: Rutgers University Press, 1994.

Gutiérrez, David. *Walls and Mirrors: Mexican Americans, Mexican Immigrants, and the Politics of Ethnicity*. Berkeley: University of California Press, 1995. Reprint, Chapel Hill: University of North Carolina Press, 2011.

Gutiérrez, José Ángel. *The Making of a Chicano Militant: Lessons from Crystal*. Madison: University of Wisconsin Press, 1998.

Hernández, Guillermo E. "Las caraterísticas cómicas del Pocho y del Pachuco: Sus antecedentes literarios y populares." *Nuevo Texto Crítico* 2, no. 3 (1989): 171–81.

Higuera, Prudencia. "Gold Hunters of California: Trading with Americans." *Century* 41, no. 2 (Dec. 1890): 192–93.

Hixson, Walter L. "'They Promised to Take Our Land and They Took It': Settler Colonialism in the American West." In *American Settler Colonialism: A History*, by Walter L. Hixson, 113–44. New York: Palgrave MacMillian, 2013.

Huizar-Hernández, Anita. "'The Real Geronimo Got Away': Eluding Expectations in *Geronimo: His Own Story; The Autobiography of a Great Patriot Warrior*." *Studies in American Indian Literatures* 29, no. 2 (Summer 2017): 49–70.

Hutchins, John M. "A Colorful Accompaniment of Women, Servants, Slaves, and Other Camp Followers." In *Coronado's Well-Equipped Army: The Spanish Invasion of the American Southwest*, by John M. Hutchins, 89–98. Yardley PA: Westhome, 2014.

Hutton, Paul Andrew. *The Apache Wars: The Hunt for Geronimo, the Apache Kid, and the Captive Boy Who Started the Longest War in American History*. New York: Broadway, 2016.

Jackson, Helen Hunt. *Ramona: A Story*. Introduction by Michael Dorris, afterword by Sherer Mathes. 1884. New York: Signet Classics, 2002.

Jacobsen, Joel. *Such Men as Billy the Kid: The Lincoln County War Reconsidered*. Lincoln: University of Nebraska Press, 1994.

Jaramillo, Cleofas. *The Genuine New Mexico Tasty Recipes / Potajes Sabrosos*. Santa Fe: Seton Village Press, 1939.

Joyce, James. *A Portrait of the Artist as a Young Man*. New York: B. W. Huebsch, 1916.

Kenner, Charles L. *Buffalo Soldiers and Officers of the Ninth Cavalry, 1867–1898: Black and White Together*. Norman: University of Oklahoma Press, 1999.

Kolodny, Annette. "Letting Go of Our Grand Obsessions: Notes toward a New Literary History of the American Frontiers." *American Literature* 64, no. 1 (March 1992): 1–18.

Kuhn, Berndt. *Chronicles of War: Apache and Yavapai Resistance in the Southwestern United States and Northern Mexico, 1821–1937*. Tucson: Arizona Historical Society, 2014.

Lazo, Rodrigo, and Jesse Alemán, eds. *The Latino Nineteenth Century*. New York: New York University Press, 2016.

Leal, Luis. "Octavio Paz and the Chicano." Special issue on "Chicano Literature." *Latin American Literary Review* 5, no. 10 (Spring 1977): 115–23.

Leckie, William H., and Shirley A. Leckie. *The Buffalo Soldiers: A Narrative of the Black Cavalry in the West*. Revised ed. Norman: University of Oklahoma Press, 2003.

LeMenager, Stephanie. *Manifest and Other Destinies: Territorial Fictions of the Nineteenth-Century United States*. Lincoln: University of Nebraska Press, 2004.

Limón, José Eduardo. "Border Literary Histories, Globalization, and Critical Regionalism." *American Literary History* 20, nos. 1–2 (Spring/Summer 2008): 160–82.

London, Charmian. Prologue to *The Book of Jack London*, 3–14. New York: The Century Company, 1921.

López, Marissa K. *Chicano Nations: The Hemispheric Origins of Mexican American Literature*. New York: New York University Press, 2011.

———. "Feeling Mexican: Ruiz de Burton's Sentimental Railroad Fiction." In *The Latino Nineteenth Century*, edited by Rodrigo Lazo and Jesse Alemán, 168–90. New York: New York University Press, 2016.

Lugones, María. "The Coloniality of Gender." *Worlds & Knowledges Otherwise: A Web Dossier* 2, dossier 2 (Spring 2008): 1–17.

Lyman, George D. "The First Native-Born Californian Physician: A Memoir of Dr. Platon Mariano Guadalupe Vallejo." *California Historical Society Quarterly* 4, no. 3 (Sept. 1925): 284–89.

Maldonado-Torres, Nelson. "On the Coloniality of Being: Contributions to the Development of a Concept." *Cultural Studies* 21, no. 2 (March–May 2007): 240–70.

Marez, Curtis. "The Rough Ride through Empire: 'Los Comanches' after 1898." In *Recovering the U.S. Hispanic Literary Heritage*, vol. 4, edited by José F. Aranda Jr. and Silvio Torres-Saillant, 31–49. Houston: Arte Público.

McGettigan, Francisca Vallejo. *Along the Highway of the King*. Oakland: Howell-North Press, 1943.

———. Scripts for KYA radio series "Padres, Gringos and Gold," 1936–1937. BANC MSS C-H 3, Bancroft Library, University of California.

McWilliams, Carey. *North from Mexico: The Spanish-Speaking People of the United States*. 1948. Philadelphia: J. B. Lippincott, 1949.

Mena, María Cristina. "The Gold Vanity Set." *The Collected Stories of María Cristina Mena*. Edited and with introduction by Amy Doherty, 1–11. Houston: Arte Público, 1997.

Menchaca, Martha. *Recovering History, Constructing Race: The Indian, Black, and White Roots of Mexican Americans*. Austin: University of Texas Press, 2001.

Mignolo, Walter D. "Afterword: Human Understanding and (Latin) American Interests—The Politics and Sensibilities of Geocultural Location." *Poetics Today* 16, no. 1 (Spring 1995): 171–214.

———. "Coloniality: The Darker Side of Modernity." In *Modernologies: Contemporary Artists Researching Modernity and Modernism Catalog of the Exhibit at the Museum of Modern Art, Barcelona, Spain*, edited by curator Sabine Breitwisser, 39–49. Barcelona: MACBA, 2009. Catalog of the exhibit Modernologia/Modernologies/Modernology.

———. "Coloniality at Large: The Western Hemisphere in the Colonial Horizon of Modernity." CR: *The New Centennial Review* 1, no. 2 (2001): 19–54.

———. "Colonial Situations, Geographical Discourses and Territorial Representations: Toward a Diatopical Understanding of Colonial Semiosis." *Dispositio* 14, nos. 36/38 (1989): 94.

———. "Introduction: On Gnosis and the Imaginary of the Modern/Colonial World System." In *Local History / Global Designs: Coloniality, Subaltern Knowledges, and Border Thinking*, by Walter D. Mignolo, 3–46. Princeton NJ: Princeton University Press, 2000.

———. "Preface." In *Local Histories / Global Design: Coloniality, Subaltern Knowledges, and Border Thinking*, by Walter D. Mignolo, ix. Princeton NJ: Princeton University Press, 2000.

Mireles, E. E., and Jovita G. Mireles. *El español elemental, primer libro*. Austin: W. S. Benson, 1949.

"Miscellany." *American Speech* 20 (1945): 235.

Montejano, David. *Anglos and Mexicans in the Making of Texas, 1836–1986*. Austin: University of Texas Press, 1997.

Moyna, María Irene. "Back at the Rancho: Language, Maintenance, and Shift among Spanish Speakers in Post-Annexation California (1848–1900)." *Revista internacional de lingüística iberoamericana* 7, no. 2 (2009): 165–84.

Murrah-Mandril, Erin. *In the Mean Time: Temporal Colonization and the Mexican American Literary Tradition*. Lincoln: University of Nebraska Press, 2020.

Nolan, Frederick W. *The Billy the Kid Reader*. Norman: University of Oklahoma Press, 2007.

O'Hara, Matthew D., and Andrew B. Fisher, eds. *Imperial Subjects: Race and Identity in Colonial Latin America*. Chapel Hill: Duke University Press, 2009.

Olguín, B. V. "Sangre mexicana / corazón americano: Identity, Ambiguity, and Critique in Mexican-American War Narratives." *American Literary History* 14, no. 1 (Spring 2002): 83–114.

Ornstein, Jacob. "The Archaic and the Modern in the Spanish of New Mexico." *Hispania* 34, no. 2 (May 1951): 137–42.

O'Shea, Elena Zamora. *El mesquite*. 1935. Reprinted as *El Mesquite: A Story of the Early Spanish Settlements between the Nueces and the Rio Grande*, edited by Leticia M. Garza Falcon, introduced by Andres Tijerina. College Station: Texas A&M University Press, 2000.

O'Sullivan, John L. "The Great Nation of Futurity." *United States Democratic Review* 6, no. 23 (1839): 426–30.

Otero, Miguel Antonio, Jr. *The Real Billy the Kid*. New York: R. R. Wilson, 1936.

———. *The Real Billy the Kid, with New Light into the Lincoln County War*, introduced and edited by John-Michael Rivera. Houston: Arte Público, 1998.

Padilla, Genaro. *My History, Not Yours: The Formation of Mexican American Autobiography*. Madison: University of Wisconsin Press, 1993.

Paredes, Américo. *Cantos de adolescencia, Song of Youth (1932–1937)*. Translated with an introduction and annotations by B. V. Olguín and Omar Vásquez Barbosa. Houston: Arte Público, 2007.

———. *George Washington Gómez: A Mexicotexan Novel*. Houston: Arte Público, 1990.

———. *A Texas-Mexican Cancionero: Folksongs of the Border*. Champaign: University of Illinois Press, 1976.

———. *"With His Pistol in His Hand": A Border Ballad and Its Hero*. Austin: University of Texas Press, 1958.

Paz, Octavio. *El laberinto de la soledad*. Mexico City: Cuadernos Americanos, 1950.

Pease, Donald E. "National Identities, Postmodern Artifacts, and Postnational Narratives." In *National Identities and Post-Americanist Narratives*, edited by Donald E. Pease, 1–13. Durham: Duke University Press, 1994.

Pierce, Jason E. "Marvelous, Maligned, and Misunderstood: The Strange History of the Mesquite Tree in Texas." *Southwestern Historical Quarterly* 117, no. 4 (April 2014): 346–70.

Pitt, Leonard. *The Decline of the Californios: A Short History of the Spanish-Speaking Californians, 1846–1890*. Berkeley: University of California Press, 1966.

Pratt, Mary Louise. "Arts of the Contact Zone." *Profession*, 1991: 33–40.

Quijano, Aníbal. "Coloniality and Modernity/Rationality." *Cultural Studies* 21, nos. 2–3 (2007): 168–78.

———. "Coloniality of Power, Eurocentrism, and Latin America." *Nepantla: Views from South* 1, no. 3 (2000): 533–80.

Ramirez, Catherine S. *The Women in the Zoot Suit: Gender, Nationalism, and the Cultural Politics of Memory*. Durham: Duke University Press, 2009.

Revere, Joseph Warren. *A Tour of Duty in California*. New York: C. S. Francis, 1849.

Rifkin, Mark. "Making Peoples into Populations: The Racial Limits of Tribal Sovereignty." In *Theorizing Native Studies*, edited by Audra Simpson and Andrea Smith, 149–87. Durham: Duke University Press. 2014.

Rivera, Díana Noreen. "Reconsidering Jovita González's Life, Letters, and Pre-1935 Folkloric Production: A Proto-Chicana's Conscious Revolt against Anglo Patriarchy via Linguistic Performance." *Chicana/Latina Studies* 10, no. 2 (Spring 2011): 46–91.

Rivera, Tomás. ... *Y no se lo tragó la tierra* (... *And the Earth Did Not Part*). Translated by Herminio Rios. Berkeley: Quinto Sol Press, 1971.

Robinson, Sherry. *Apache Voices: Their Stories of Survival as Told to Eve Ball*. Albuquerque: University of New Mexico Press, 2000.

Rodriguez, Maggie Rivas. "Ignacio E. Lozano: The Mexican Exiled Publisher Who Conquered San Antonio and Los Angeles." *American Journalism* 21, no. 1 (2004): 75–89.

Rodriguez, Marc Simon. "More than Whiteness: Comparative Perspectives on Mexican American Citizenship from Law and History." *La Raza Law Journal* 18 (2007): 79–86.

Rosaldo, Renato. "Imperialist Nostalgia." Special issue on "Memory and Counter-Memory," *Representations* 26 (Spring 1989): 107–22.

Rosales, F. Arturo. "'Fantasy Heritage' Reexamined: Race and Class in the Writings of the Bandini Family Authors and Other Californios, 1828–1965." In *Recovering the U.S. Hispanic Literary Heritage*, vol. 2, edited by Erlinda Gonzales-Berry and Chuck Tatum, 81–103. Houston: Arte Público, 1996.

Rosenus, Alan. *General Vallejo and the Advent of the Americans*. Berkeley: Heyday, 1999.

Roybal, Karen R. *Archives of Dispossession: Recovering the Testimonios of Mexican American Herederas, 1848–1960*. Chapel Hill: University of North Carolina Press, 2017.

———. "Hidden Histories: Gendered and Settler Colonial Landscapes in Northern California." *Chicana/Latina Studies* 18, no. 1 (Fall 2018): 154–87.

Ruiz, Reynaldo. *Hispanic Poetry in Los Angeles, 1850–1900, La poesia angelina*. Lewiston: Edwin Mellon, 2000.

Ruiz de Burton, María Amparo. *Conflicts of Interest: The Letters of María Amparo Ruiz de Burton*. Edited by Rosaura Sánchez and Beatrice Pita. Houston: Arte Público, 2001.

———. *The Squatter and the Don: A Novel Descriptive of Contemporary Occurrences in California*. Edited by Rosaura Sánchez and Beatrice Pita. 1885. Reprint, Houston: Arte Público, 1992.

———. *Who Would Have Thought It?* Edited by Rosaura Sánchez and Beatrice Pita. 1872. Reprint, Houston: Arte Público, 1995.

Sáenz, José de la Luz. *Los méxico-americanos y la gran guerra y su contingente en pro de la democracia, la humanidad y la justicia*. San Antonio: Artes Gráficas, 1933. Reprint, College Station: Texas A&M University Press, 2014.

Saldaña-Portillo, María Josefina. "'Wavering on the Horizon of Social Being': The Treaty of Guadalupe-Hidalgo and the Legacy of Its Racial Character in Americo Paredes's *George Washington Gómez*." *Radical History Review* 89 (Spring 2004): 135–64.

Salinas, Gregoria. "Igual que Hermanos." *San Antonio La Prensa*, January 30, 1944, 13 and 15. Readex, *Hispanic American Newspapers, 1808–1980*, https://infoweb-newsbank.

Sánchez, George. *Becoming Mexican American: Ethnicity, Culture, and Identity in Chicano Los Angeles, 1900–1945*. New York: Oxford University Press, 1993.

Sánchez, Rosaura. *Telling Identities: The Californio Testimonio*. Minneapolis: University of Minnesota Press, 1995.

Sánchez, Rosaura, and Beatrice Pita. "Across the Line: La Frontera." In *Conflicts of Interest: The Letters of María Amparo Ruiz de Burton*, edited by Rosaura Sánchez and Beatrice Pita, 105–7. Houston: Arte Público, 2001.

Seguín, Juan Nepomuceno. *A Revolution Remembered: The Memoirs and Selected Correspondence of Juan N. Seguín*, edited by Jesús F. de la Teja. Austin: Texas State Historical Association, 2002.

Shinn, Charles Howard. "Pioneer Spanish Families in California, with Special Reference to the Vallejos." *Century Magazine: A Popular Quarterly* 41, no. 3 (Jan. 1891): 377.

Sibrian, Amalia. "Gold Hunters of California: A Spanish Girl's Journey from Monterey to Los Angeles." *Century Magazine: A Popular Quarterly* 43, no. 3 (Jan. 1891): 469.

Silva, Grant. "'The Americas Seek Not Enlightenment but Liberation': On the Philosophical Significance of Liberation for Philosophy in the Americas." *The Pluralist* 13, no. 2 (Summer 2018): 1–21.

Simpson, Audra. *Mohawk Interruptus: Political Life across the Borders of Settler States.* Durham: Duke University Press, 2014.

———. "The Ruse of Consent and the Anatomy of 'Refusal': Cases from Indigenous North America and Australia." *Postcolonial Studies* 20, no. 1 (2017): 18–33.

Sleeter, Christine E. Foreword to *Subtractive Schooling: U.S.-Mexican Youth and the Politics of Caring*, by Angela Valenzuela, xvii–xviii. Albany: State University of New York Press, 1999.

Sommer, Doris. *Foundational Fictions: The National Romances of Latin America.* Berkeley: University of California Press, 1991.

Steinbeck, John. *The Harvest Gypsies: On the Road to the Grapes of Wrath.* With an introduction by Charles Wollenberg. Berkeley: Heyday, 2011.

Steward, T. G. *Buffalo Soldiers: The Colored Regulars in the United States Army.* Mineola NY: Dover, 2014.

St. John, Rachel. *Line in the Sand: A History of the Western U.S.-Mexico Border.* Princeton NJ: Princeton University Press, 2011.

Suárez, Mario. *Chicano Sketches: Short Stories.* Edited by Francisco A. Lomelí, Cecilia Cota-Robles Suárez, and Juan José Casillas-Nuñez. Tucson: University of Arizona Press, 2004.

Tafolla, Santiago. *A Life Crossing Borders: Memoir of a Mexican-American Confederate, Las memorias de un mexicoamericano en la Confederación.* Edited by Carmen Tafolla and Laura Tafolla, translated by Fidel L. Tafolla. Houston: Arte Público, 2010.

Tatum, Stephen. *Inventing Billy the Kid: Visions of the Outlaw in America, 1881–1981.* Tucson: University of Arizona Press, 1997.

Thomas, P. J., ed. *Our Centennial Memoir, Founding of the Missions, San Francisco de Asís, in Its Hundredth Year, the Celebration of Its Foundation, Historical Reminiscences of the Missions of California.* San Francisco: P. J. Thomas, 1877.

"Topics of the Time: Gold Hunters of California, the Making of California." *Century Magazine: A Popular Quarterly* 41, no. 1 (Nov. 1890): 151.

"Two Years before the Mast." *United States Magazine and Democratic Review* 8 (Oct. 1840): 318–35.

Utley, Robert M. *Geronimo.* New Haven CT: Yale University Press, 2012.

———. *High Noon in Lincoln: Violence on the Western Frontier.* Albuquerque: University of New Mexico Press, 1987.

Valdez, Elena V. "Chicana/o Literature and the Folkloric Difference." PhD dissertation, Rice University, 2019.

Valdez, Luis. "La Plebe." Introduction to *Aztlán: An Anthology of Mexican American Literature*, edited by Luis Valdez and Stan Steiner, xiii–xxxiv. New York: Vintage Books, 1972.

———. *Zoot Suit*. Los Angeles: Center Theatre Group, Mark Taper Forum, 1978.

Valenzuela, Angela. *Subtractive Schooling: U.S.-Mexican Youth and the Politics of Caring*. Albany: State University of New York Press, 1999.

Vallejo, Francisca. *See* McGettigan, Francisca Vallejo.

Vallejo, Guadalupe. "Ranch and Mission Days in Alta California." *Century Magazine: A Popular Quarterly* 41, no. 2 (Dec. 1890): 183.

Vallejo, Mariano Guadalupe. *Recuerdos históricos y personales tocante á la Alta California: Historia política del país, 1769–1849; Costumbres de los californios; Apuntes biográficos de personas notables*. 5 vols. BANC MSS CD 17–21. Bancroft Library, University of California, Berkeley.

Vallejo, Platón. "A Letter to William Heath Davis." In *Herencia: The Anthology of Hispanic Literature of the United States*, edited by Nicolás Kanellos, Kenya Dworkin y Méndez, José B. Fernández, Erlinda González-Berry, Agnes Lugo-Ortiz, and Charles Tatum, 100–102. New York: Oxford University Press, 2002.

———. *Memoir of the Vallejos: New Light on the History, before and after "the Gringo" Came, Based on Original Documents and the Recollections of Dr. Platón M. G. Vallejo*. Arranged for publication by James H. Wilkins of The Bulletin. The Bancroft Library, University of California, Berkeley, 1914.

Varon, Alberto. *Before Chicano: Citizenship and the Making of Mexican American Manhood, 1848–1959*. New York: New York University Press, 2018.

Venegas, Daniel. *Las aventuras de Don Chipote, o Cuando los pericos mamen*. 1928. Reprint, Houston: Arte Público, 1998.

Veracini, Lorenzo. *Settler Colonialism: A Theoretical Overview*. New York: Palgrave Macmillan, 2010.

Villarreal, José. *Pocho*. Garden City NY: Doubleday, 1959.

Vizcaino-Alemán, Melina. *Gender and Place in Chicana/o Literature: Critical Regionalism and the Mexican American Southwest*. New York: Palgrave Macmillan, 2017.

Wallis, Eileen V. "Introduction." In *Earning Power: Women and Work in Los Angeles, 1880–1930*, 1–10. Reno: University of Nevada Press, 2010.

———. "'Keeping Alive the Old Traditions': Spanish-Mexican Club Women in Southern California, 1880–1940." *Southern California Quarterly* 91, no. 2 (Summer 2009): 133–54.

Warren, Adelina (Nina) Otero. *Old Spain in Our Southwest*. New York: Harcourt, Brace, 1936.
Weber, David J. *The Spanish Frontier in North America*. New Haven CT: Yale University Press, 1992.
Williams, Raymond. *Marxism and Literature*. London: Oxford University Press, 1978.
Wilson, William E. "Author's Summary." *Modern Language Journal* 30, no. 6 (Oct. 1946): 345.
Winthrop, John. "A Model of Christian Charity" (1630). In *The Puritans in America: A Narrative Anthology*, edited and with an introduction by Alan Heimert and Andrew Delbanco, 81–92. Cambridge MA: Harvard University Press, 1985.
Wogan, Daniel. "Discussion." *Hispania* 34 (May 1951): 142.
Wolfe, Patrick. "Settler Colonialism and the Elimination of the Native." *Journal of Genocide Research* 8, no. 4 (2006): 387–409.
Ybarra, Priscilla. *Writing the Goodlife: Mexican American Literature and the Environment*. Tucson: University of Arizona Press, 2016.
Zamora, Emilio. "Fighting on Two Fronts: José de la Luz Saenz and the Language of the Mexican-American Civil Rights Movement." In *Recovering the U.S. Hispanic Literary Heritage*, vol. 4, edited by José F. Aranda Jr. and Silvio Torres-Saillant, 214–39. Houston: Arte Público.
Zavala, Adina Emilia de. *History and Legends of the Alamo and Other Missions in and around San Antonio*. San Antonio: Standard Printing Company, 1917.
———. *The Story of the Siege and Fall of the Alamo: A Resumé*. San Antonio, 1911.

INDEX

Ainslie, Jorge. See *Los Pochos* (Ainslie)
the Alamo, 6, 14, 22, 76, 152
Along the Highway of the King (Francisca Vallejo), 85, 104
Alta California. *See* California; Californios and Californianas
Altrocchi, Julia Cooley, 86, 87–88
Amendáriz, Pedro, 188, 189
American literary monolingualism, 193–94
American literary studies, 193–95, 231–32
anti-immigration literature, 206–7. See also *Los Pochos* (Ainslie)
Anzaldúa, Gloria, 168, 228
Arballo, María Feliciana, 91
arrivants, 115
Atherton, Gertrude, 85
"Autumn Days in Ventura" (Eames), 29–34
Las aventuras de Don Chipote (Venegas), 206–7

Bancroft, Hubert Howe, 32, 38–39, 54
Bandini, Helen Elliot, 38, 40–41
Bandini family archive, 82, 238n9
Barker, Eugence C., 171

Barr, Juliana, 120
Barrett, S. M., 120
barrios, 191
Bell, Avril, 6
Bhabha, Homi, 18
Billy the Kid, 113, 141, 142, 143, 146. See also *The Real Billy the Kid* (Otero)
biopolitics, 117
Blackwell, Maylei, 118
border gnosis, 176
Bradstreet, Anne, 158–59, 169. *See also* "Shades of the Tenth Muse" (González)
Byrd, Jodi, 115, 116, 117–18, 119, 121

Caballero (González), 179, 211
Cabeza de Baca, Fabiola, 205
California: Anglo statehood narratives, 81; Catholicism, 37, 45, 56, 57; *Century Magazine* article series, 35–36, 40, 47–50, 238n4; Del Valle land grant tourism, 29–30; fiesta time, 86; gold rush, 36, 70, 83–84; Graham Affair, 46; Mexican American experiences, 14;

California (cont.)
  political vulnerability, 78; popularity in print culture, 36–39; popular perceptions, 37–38; post-1848 changes, 32–33. See also San Francisco
Californio and Californiana nostalgia: of coloniality, 80, 82; exaggerations, 62; functions of, 26; gold rush impacts, 83–84; Mariano Guadalupe Vallejo, 53, 69; "Padres, Gringos, and Gold" radio show, 75, 101–2; Platón Vallejo, 62; "Ranch and Mission Days in Alta California," 42–43; settler, 78; uses, 80; Vallejo family generally, 77, 81; in writings generally, 82–83
Californio and Californiana writings: in *Century Magazine*, 35, 238n4; English, lack of, 50; indigenous labor, 131; lack of, 39–40; "Un tipo" (anonymous poem), 50–52, 200–201. See also Californio and Californiana nostalgia; "Ranch and Mission Days in Alta California" (Guadalupe Vallejo); Vallejo, Francisca; Vallejo, Mariano Guadalupe; Vallejo, Platón
Californios and Californianas: Anglo-American relations, 81; Catholicism, 59–60, 74, 90; *Century Magazine* contributors, 35, 40, 238n4; Chicanx studies perspectives, 82–83; class markers, 132; colonial difference production, 43; coloniality of power, 78; colonization resistance, 35; decline, 32–34, 38, 92; Del Valle family, 29–30, 32, 33; Edenic rhetoric, 62; gold rush impacts, 83; historiography, 39–41, 46–47, 54, 56–57; and indigenous peoples, 131–33; modernity of subtraction experiences, 34; patrimony, 65; racism toward, 37–38, 60–61; Spanish fantasy heritage, 74–75, 83; storytelling practices, 38–39; symbolic historical roles, 82–83; women's clubs, 74–75. See also Californio and Californiana nostalgia; Californio and Californiana writings; Ruiz de Burton, María Amparo; Vallejo family

Capitán Escandón, 134
Carrillo, Francisca Benicia, 90–92
Carrillo, Leo, 79, 104, 205
Carrillo, María Ygnacia López de, 91, 92
Carson, James Taylor, 135
Casis, Lilia, 181
Castañeda, Antonia, 81
Castañeda, Carlos, 156, 167
Catholicism: California, 37, 45, 56, 57; Californios and Californianas, 59–60, 74, 90; colonialism, 22, 56, 90, 111, 132–33; Jovita González, 150, 155, 156, 157, 159, 183
Century Magazine: Anglo-American exceptionalism, 35–36; Californiana contributors, 35, 40, 238n4; Californio history, 40; "Gold Hunters of California" series, 35–36; gold rush emphasis, 36; "A Spanish Girl's Journey from Monterey to Los Angeles," 47–50. See also "Ranch and Mission Days in Alta California" (Guadalupe Vallejo)
Cervantes, Lorna Dee, 104–5
Cervantes-Rodríguez, Ana Margarita, 196, 199
Chicana feminism in "Shades of the Tenth Muse," 158–59

Chicana/o language, 192
Chicana/o literature: language, 192–93; periods, 22–23; *Pocho*, 206, 208; presses enabling, 226
Chicana/o Movement, 17; blood memory, 105; colonialism critiques, 79–80; identity, 240n17; language, 195; perspectives on Otero, 79, 138; Spanish fantasy heritage perspectives, 79. *See also* Gutiérrez, José Ángel
chicana/o versus *Chicana/o* terms, 241n2
Chicanx literature, 195, 212
Chicanx studies: burdens of modernity and colonialism, 109; Californios and Californianas, 82–83; critical regionalism, 23; decolonization, 227–28; *Mexican* term, 152; Miguel Antonio Otero Jr., 138; Spanish language, 222–23. *See also* Chicana/o Movement; Recovering the U.S. Hispanic Literary Heritage project
Cisneros, Sandra, 212
Cohen, Matt, 54–55
colonial difference, 43, 109; barrios, 191; Californio and Californiana production, 43; coloniality of nostalgia, 76–84; cultural production, 15; discourses on Californios and Californianas, 43; Mexican Americans pre-1848, 20–21; racial loyalty, 118; "Ranch and Mission Days in Alta California," 43–44
colonialism: Catholicism, 22, 56, 90, 111, 132–33; competing enterprises, 19; historical treatments, 19–20; liberal ideals, 8; racial hierarchies, 188; racial hierarchy imposition, 188; semiotic field, 44–46

coloniality, 4–5, 8; of being, 115–16, 187; the Enlightenment, 9–10; of gender, 161–64; and modernity, 3–4, 21, 227; of nostalgia, 76–84; origins, 111; race, 5; across raced communities, 137–38. *See also* modernity of subtraction; racial loyalty
coloniality of power, 5, 8; "Autumn Days in Ventura," 31–32; biopolitics, 117; Californios and Californianas, 78; early Mexican American literature, 9; frontier Mexicans, 128; *George Washington Gómez*, 163; language, 196; *Mexican* term, 152; racial loyalty, 116; schools, 17. *See also* colonial difference; racial loyalty
colonial mimicry, 18
colonial semiosis, 80–81
Comer, Krista, 23
"Como el Nenufar" (Paredes), 223
conquistadores: Alonso de Ojeda, 107, 239n2; Capitán Escandón, 134; Francisco Vázquez de Coronado, 107–8, 111, 146, 239n2; and the requerimiento, 109
contact zones, 114–15, 135
Coronado, Francisco Vázquez de, 107–8, 111, 146, 239n2
Coronado, Raúl, 14
Cortez, Gregorio, 200, 231
Cotera, María, 154, 155; Jovita González, 170, 181; Jovita González's master's thesis, 171, 172–73; "Shades of the Tenth Muse" (González), 158–59, 167, 169
Craib, Raymond, 11–12
critical regionalism, 23–24, 154
Cruz, Sor Juana de la, 158–59, 169. *See also* "Shades of the Tenth Muse" (González)

Cuddy, Lucy, 87–88
cultural semiosis, 80–81, 135–36

Dana, Henry Richard, 36–37, 39
Davis, William Heath, 60
Debo, Angie, 137
decolonial imaginaries, 229
Del Valle family, 29–30, 32, 33
DeLyser, Dydia, 29, 32–33
D'Erzel, Catalina, 222
desegregation, 147–48
Dobie, J. Frank, 156, 178, 181
Dussel, Enrique, 11, 227, 229
Dwinelle, John W., 56

Eames, Ninetta, 29–34, 237n1
education, 16–17
English-Spanish asymmetry, 196, 199
Estrada, Genaro, 182

feminism and feminist critique, 90, 154–55, 158–59, 231
Flint, Richard, 108–9
Flint, Shirley Cushing, 108–9
folklore, 155
folk songs, 127–31
Fort Apache (Ford, film), 185–87; Apaches, 185–87; cinematography, 188–89, 190; coloniality of being, 187; language, 188, 189, 190; racial loyalty, 186, 187–90; screenplay, 241n1

Gaonkar, Dilip Parameshwar, 13
gender: coloniality of, 161–64; *George Washington Gómez*, 163–64; Mexican identity, 150–51; *Los Pochos*, 212, 215, 217, 222; Spanish fantasy heritage, 84. *See also* González, Jovita

geography, 25, 231–32
George Washington Gómez (Paredes), 161; bildungsroman structure, 211; colonial conflict, 168; coloniality of power, 163; gender, 163–64; Mexican Revolution, 207–8; modernity of subtraction, 162; World War I, 176–77
Geronimo, 112, 113, 120, 123. *See also* Geronimo's autobiography
Geronimo's autobiography, 27, 112; as contact zone, 114; cultural semiosis, 135–36; domesticity, 124; as homeland narrative, 119–26; Mexican massacre of family, 124–26; Mexico and Mexicans, 119–20, 121, 123–26; modernities, 135; motivation for telling, 136; place, 135–37; racial loyalties, 119; U.S. military, 126; warrior status, 123, 124
globalization and coloniality, 4–5
gold rush, 36, 70, 83–84
"The Gold Vanity Set" (Mena), 159
González, Henry B., 79
González, Jovita, 82; borderlands, 168–69, 170–71, 172–73, 175; *Caballero*, 179, 211; Catholicism, 150, 155, 156, 157, 159, 183; education, 170–72, 180–81, 182–83; as educator, 179–81, 182–83; gender interests and concerns, 155, 170, 171–72; "Un incidente feo," 149, 150, 180; influences, 223; "La Inmaculada del Tepeyac," 184; lack of connection to other writers, 233; life and career, 156, 167; marriage, 155, 158–60, 167, 169, 178–79; master's thesis in Texas history, 170–72; mentioned, 205; National Honorary Spanish Fraternity, 181; "The Philosopher of the Brush Country," 173–76,

177–78; pluralist politics, 154–55, 181; and *La Prensa* newspaper, 156–58, 178, 180, 181, 182, 183–84; public persona, 183–84; "¿Quiénes Somos?," 133–34; racism experiences, 150; regional Mexicanness, 27, 154; social connections and status, 156–58, 181; South Texas, 170–75; subject position, 27, 169–70, 172, 173, 180. *See also* "Shades of the Tenth Muse" (González)

goodlife writing, 65

Goyaałé. *See* Geronimo

Graham, Isaac, 46

Great Depression, 99

Greene, Roland, 114

Griffiths, Beatrice, 197, 198

Gutiérrez, José Ángel, 192

Hidalgo, Miguel, 11

The House on Mango Street (Cisneros), 212

Huizar-Hernández, Anita, 119

identity: barrios, 191; Chicana/o Movement, 240n17; communal, 65; and gender, 150–51; and language, 191; Mexican-American War impacts, 7–8; Mexican national, 11–12; national, 203–4; pachucos and pachucas, 203–5; place-based, 7–8, 136–37, 191, 232; pocho, 223; regional, 14; settler hybrids, 131; suppression of indigenous, 131

"Igual que hermanos" (Salinas), 224–25

"Un incidente feo" (González), 149, 150, 180

Inclán, Miguel, 188, 189

indigenous peoples: and Californios and Californianas, 131–33; crisscrossing colonization, 114; displacement, 112, 114, 115, 118, 171, 228, 232; Francisco Vázquez de Coronado's expedition, 107–8, 239n2; identity suppression, 131; labor, 131–32; Mexican-American War, 19; modernity, 7, 229; Mohawks, 115; in nationalist imaginaries, 25; persecution and subjugation, 123, 126; racial loyalty, 115; racism experiences, 49, 128, 131, 240n17; *The Real Billy the Kid*, 142; Recovering the U.S. Hispanic Literary Heritage project, 121–22; the requerimiento, 107–9, 239n2; and settler borders, 120; settler colonialism, 78, 115; and Spanish language, 121; in the West, 111–12; the Zuni, 107–8, 111, 112. *See also* Geronimo

"Los inditos" (folk song), 127–31

"La Inmaculada del Tepeyac" (González), 184

intercultural mimesis, 122–23

Jackson, Helen Hunt. *See Ramona* (Jackson)

Jacksonian politics, 36–37

Jones, William Carey, 97

Joyce, James, 161

kinship, 116–17

Kolodny, Annette, 194–95, 222

Labyrinth of Solitude (Paz), 18

language: American literary monolingualism, 193–94; American literary studies, 193–95; Chicana/o literature, 192–93; Chicana/o Movement, 195; Chicanx literature, 195; Chicanx studies, 222–23; coloniality of power,

language (*cont.*)
196; colonial power relations, 200;
English's impacts on Spanish, 52, 201;
English-Spanish asymmetry, 196, 199;
Fort Apache, 188, 189, 190; identity,
191; Mexican American literature,
192–93; Mexican Americans, 196;
mistranslations, 200; modernity of
subtraction, 200, 202; pachucos and
pachucas, 196, 197; "Padres, Gringos,
and Gold" radio show, 87; pocho,
197; *Los Pochos*, 210; "A Spanish Girl's
Journey from Monterey to Los Angeles," 47–49; Spanish newspapers, 52–
53; *The Squatter and the Don*, 52–53.
See also pochismo; Spanish language
Latinidad, 4, 5
The Latino Nineteenth Century (Lazo and
Alemán), 22
Latinx indigeneities, 119
Leal, Luis, 201–2
LeMenager, Stephanie, 19
La Leyenda Negra (the Black Legend), 37
liberation philosophy, 8, 10–11
Limón, José, 24
Lincoln County War, 112; African American soldiers, 113, 139, 140, 142, 144–46; Battle of Lincoln, 142–43; Billy the Kid, 113, 141, 142, 143; origins, 140–41; *The Real Billy the Kid*, 139, 142–44; Santa Fé Ring, 139–40, 142
Longfellow Institute, 193–94
Lopez, Floridalma Boj, 118
López, Marissa, 53–54, 71, 150
López de Santa Anna, Antonio, 12
Lozano, Igancio, 156, 181–82, 223
Lugones, María, 154, 155, 164, 229
Lutz, Amy, 196, 199

Lyman, George D., 67–68

Maldonado-Torres, Nelson, 115–16, 188, 229
Manifest Destiny: copying of Mexican vaqueros, 122; ideological underpinnings, 111; Mariano Guadalupe Vallejo's views on, 69–70; racial loyalties, 142; *The Real Billy the Kid*, 141–42; term origins, 110
Marez, Curtis, 122
McGettigan, Francisca Vallejo. *See* Vallejo, Francisca
McWilliams, Carey, 75, 79, 198
Mena, María Cristina, 159, 233
Menchaca, Martha, 113, 121, 126–27, 228
Mexican American literature, 1–2; coloniality, 228; colonial mimicry, 18; cultural-political contexts, 2, 4; early (pre-1848), 8–9, 20–21, 25, 228; excesses, 21–22; language, 192–93; modernity, 9, 25, 233; place, 25, 26, 230; regionality, 25; transmodernity, 24; women authors, 104–5
Mexican Americans: Americanization, 13–14, 16–17; archive, 5; California, 14; citizenship, 9, 101, 153; civic discrimination against, 153; contemporary sociopolitical status, 235; de-Mexicanization, 17–18; as historical figures, 178; history recovery, 121; identifying terms, 205; immigrants, 13; in-betweenness, 13–14, 202; Indianization, 126–35; indigenous heritage denials, 133–34; interwar period, 196; language, 196; Mexican-American War aftermath, 12–13; modernity of subtraction, 16–22, 34,

113, 129; modernity of subtraction experiences, 16–22, 34, 113, 129; and nation-state, 13–14; New Mexico, 14; official histories absences, 176, 177; pochos and pochas, 28, 206, 223; racialization as indigenous, 126–38; refugees, 13, 201, 205; regional identities, 14; social status, 2, 13; Texas, 14; women, 164; World War I, 176–77; World War II, 190, 225. *See also* Californios and Californianas; *Mexican* term; pachucos and pachucas; settler hybrids and hybridity

Mexican-American War, 3–4, 12; destabilization of Mexico, 123–24; identity impacts, 7–8; ideological underpinnings, 38; initial aftermath, 26; layered colonialism, 232–33; newly conquered peoples, 126–27; racial segregation following, 126–27, 133; territories fought over, 19; Treaty of Guadalupe Hidalgo, 4, 9, 11–12, 101, 153, 240n15

Mexican American writers, 21–22, 23, 193, 233–34. *See also individual authors*

Mexican identity contests, 150

Mexican Revolution, 4, 164, 201, 205

Mexican term, 151–54

Mexico: citizen disenfranchisement, 113, 126–27; citizenship, 123–24; colonizing enterprises, 19; 1824 Constitution, 11–12; independence, 11; national identity development, 11–12; Porfirio Díaz dictatorship, 13; Texas border violence, 127–28

Mignolo, Walter: border gnosis, 176; colonial difference, 2, 9, 14–15, 43, 109; colonialism, 10; colonialism as semiotic field, 44–46; colonial power, 135, 227; cultural semiosis, 80–81, 135–36; denials of coevalness, 135–36; modernity, 1, 3, 10, 229

migrant labor, 99–101, 205, 209

Mireles, Edmundo, 158, 159, 167, 172, 179, 181, 183

modernity: authenticity ideologies, 6–7; burdens, 1–2, 80, 90, 109; and colonialism, 134–35; and coloniality, 3–4, 21, 227; definitional attempts, 227; emancipatory ideologies, 227, 229; in-between peoples, 10–11; Mexican American literature, 9, 25, 233; new space/time, 15–16; in New World, 11; origins, 111; peripheries, 16; and place, 7, 14–15, 230; postwar era, 190; regional linkages, 122; settler hybrids, 134–35; subjugating functions, 9–10; subjugation of the other, 9–10; transmodernity, 11, 24. *See also* modernity of subtraction; racial loyalty

modernity of subtraction, 2; counterbalances, 18; critical regionalism, 24; education, 16–17; *George Washington Gómez*, 162; language, 200, 202; Mexican American experiences, 16–22, 34, 113, 129; Mexican American literature, 233; *Mexican* term, 151; place, 34, 71, 81; racial loyalty, 118; Vallejo family, 81

Native studies, 138, 228

New Mexico, 14, 122–23, 141–42. *See also* Geronimo; Lincoln County War

newspapers. See *La Prensa* newspaper; Spanish-language press

Ninth U.S. Cavalry, 113, 142–44, 146

nostalgia: coloniality, 76–84; critical limits, 129; divergent aspects, 77; imperialist, 69; Miguel Antonio Otero Jr., 82; for Old California, 62; public memories, 72; settler, 76–78; "A Spanish Girl's Journey from Monterey to Los Angeles," 49–50. *See also* Californio and Californiana nostalgia; Spanish fantasy heritage

Ojeda, Alonso de, 107, 239n2
oral culture, 155
Ornstein, Jacob, 197–98, 202
O'Sullivan, John L., 110–11
Otero, Miguel Antonio, Jr., 79, 82, 138, 146, 205. See also *The Real Billy the Kid* (Otero)
Others and Othering, 116, 117, 121–22, 188
Overland Monthly magazine, 29, 38, 40, 50

Pacheco, José Antonio Romualdo, Jr., 91
pachucos and pachucas: discrimination, 204; language, 196, 197; Mexican writings on, 202–5; national identity, 203–5; stereotypes, 196, 198, 201–2, 203; studies of, 197–98, 201. *See also* pochismo
Packman, Ana Bégué de, 104, 205
Padilla, Genaro, 82
"Padres, Gringos, and Gold" radio show (Francisca Vallejo), 71, 72–73, 85–86; American conquest rhetoric, 94; California's pastoral period, 94–96; Californio domesticity, 89–90; class privileges, 73–74; cultural project, 75; culture-based sovereignty, 95–96, 102; family grievances, 73; fiesta time, 86, 87; first broadcast, 86, 91–92; Guadalupe Vallejo (cousin), 89–90; historical contexts, 99; land dispossession, 92–94, 98; language, 87; Mariano Guadalupe Vallejo (grandfather), 88–89, 102–3, 104; matrilineal narratives, 90–92; Mexican heritage, 101; nostalgia, 75, 101–2; "La Paloma," 87; racial views, 74; sequoia imagery, 102–3; Spanish fantasy heritage, 75, 87, 96, 102; squatterism, 96–98, 100, 101; transcripts, 75, 86–87; vulnerability, 102–3

"La Paloma" (song), 87
Paredes, Américo: border conflicts, 128; "Como el Nenufar," 223; Greater Mexico thesis, 17–18, 205; "Los inditos" folk song, 127–31; lack of connection to other writers, 233; pocho identity, 223; regional memory, 129; South Texas, 175; *With His Pistol in His Hand*, 128, 134, 156, 171. See also *George Washington Gómez* (Paredes)
patrimony, 65–66, 72
Paz, Octavio, 18, 201
Pease, Donald, 233
Peña, Enrique de la, 206
Pérez, Emma, 228
"The Philosopher of the Brush Country" (González), 173–76, 177–78
Pico, Pío, 70, 89
Pita, Beatrice, 234
place, 230; Californio and Californiana nostalgia, 84, 96; contact zones, 114–15, 135; geography, 25, 231–32; Geronimo's autobiography, 135–36; identity, 7–8, 136–37, 191, 232; imperialist nostalgia, 69; language, 191; loss of land, 20; Mexican American literature, 25,

26, 230; in Mexican American versus mainstream culture, 232; modernity, 7, 14–15, 230; modernity of subtraction, 34, 71, 81; nostalgia, 71, 84, 96, 129; "The Philosopher of the Brush Country," 174; in Platón Vallejo's writings, 62; political imaginary, 230–31; processes changing, 26; reading modernity through, 18–19, 231. *See also* regionalism

pochismo, 197; acceptance of, 201; in English publishing, 225; evolution, 223–24; history, 198–99; Mexican attacks on, 198, 202–3; phrase lists, 203; studies of, 197, 202; women in the workforce, 224–25

Pocho (Villarreal), 206, 208

Los Pochos (Ainslie), 28, 206; Anglo treatment of immigrants and Mexican Americans, 216–18, 219–20; as anti-immigration, 206–7, 208–9, 212, 213–14, 221; audience, 207; *chicano* term, 216; class, 207, 209–10; critiques of Anglo values, 212–15; gender, 212, 215, 217, 222; historical contexts, 222; labor, 216–17; language, 210; marriage plots, 211–12, 215–16, 220–21; migrant labor, 209; nationalism, 216; pochos, 210–11, 218–21; race and racism, 218

pochos and pochas, 28, 206, 223. *See also* Paredes, Américo; pochismo; *Pocho* (Villarreal); *Los Pochos* (Ainslie)

"Poema para los californios muertos" (Cervantes), 104–5

postcolonialism, 116, 117–18

Pratt, Mary Louise, 114

La Prensa newspaper: Chicana/o literature, 226; Jovita González in, 156–58,
178, 180, 181, 182, 183–84; Lilia Casis, 181; Mexican immigrant life, 28, 222; pluralistic politics, 181–82; promotion of women writers, 156

publication events, 54–55

"¿Quiénes Somos?" (González), 133–34

Quijano, Aníbal: coloniality, 4, 5, 116, 154; horizon of liberation, 12; modernity, 9–10, 15–16, 229

race: hierarchies imposition, 188; Indianization of Mexicans, 126–38; segregation, 126–27, 133; Southwest and West politics, 129. *See also* racial loyalty; racism

raced communities, connections between, 147

raced histories, 5

racialized Others, 116, 117, 121–22

racial loyalty, 27, 116; colonial difference, 118; coloniality of power, 116; contact zones, 114; folk song examples, 127–31; *Fort Apache*, 186, 187–90; Geronimo's autobiography, 119; "Un incidente feo," 150; indigenous-settler coexistence, 115; kinship, 116–17; Manifest Destiny, 142; modernity of subtraction, 118; origins, 188; *The Real Billy the Kid*, 139–40, 144

racism: Californios and Californianas, 37–38, 60–61; indigenous peoples, 49, 128, 131, 240n17; Jovita González's experiences, 150; Mexican Americans generally, 13, 131, 150, 240n17; nonindigenous raced communities, 117; Platón Vallejo's experiences, 60–61; *Los Pochos*, 218; the West, 112

INDEX 265

radio programs. *See* "Padres, Gringos, and Gold" radio show (Francisca Vallejo)

Ramona (Jackson), 14; epigraph quotations, 29; historical contexts, 32–33; impact, 33; progressive politics, 84–85; real-world inspirations, 29–30; tourism inspired by, 29–31; travel writing on, 29–34

"Ranch and Mission Days in Alta California" (Guadalupe Vallejo), 40–41; Alta California settlers, 61; author interview following, 200; *Century Magazine* article, 131–33; citizenship rhetorics, 44–45; colonial difference, 43–44; colonial semiosis, 44–46; ideology, 42; nostalgia, 42–43; territorial representation, 46–47; tone, 41

Rancho Camulos, 29–34

La Raza Unida Party, 192

The Real Billy the Kid (Otero), 27, 113, 138; absence of indigenous peoples, 142; African American soldiers, 142, 144–45; as contact zone, 114; historical methods, 146–47; Kid's death, 147; Lincoln County War, 139, 142–44; Manifest Destiny, 141–42; raced narratives, 138–39, 144; racial loyalty, 139–40, 144; settler hybridity, 139

Recovering the U.S. Hispanic Literary Heritage project, 5, 8, 18; benefits, 22; goals, 80; historic wrongs, 117; indigenous Others, 121–22; nativos, 120–21; roles in U.S. Native studies, 138; Spanish language, 194; transatlantic geography, 25

Recuerdos históricos y personales (Mariano Guadalupe Vallejo), 53–54

regional identity, 14

regionalism: critical, 23–24, 154; early Mexican American literature, 25; environmental ideologies, 65; Mexican American writers, 23, 234; modernity, 122

regional memory, 129

"Remember me! When frozen, cold..." (Francisca Vallejo), 67

requerimiento, 107–9, 239n2

residual histories, 20

Revere, Joseph Warren, 89

Rifkin, Mark, 116–17

Rivera, Díana Noreen, 164, 169, 184

Rivera, John-Michael, 138–39, 140, 141

Rivera, Tomás, 212

Roosevelt, Theodore, 122

Rosaldo, Renato, 69, 77

Rosales, F. Arturo, 82–83, 199–200, 238n9

Rosenus, Alan, 46

Roybal, Karen R., 91, 92, 169–70

Ruiz de Burton, María Amparo, 32, 38, 45; advice to Platón Vallejo, 234–35; Californio oppression, 234–35; class privileges, 73; connections to other writers, 233; place, 231; regionalism, 234; *The Squatter and the Don*, 52–53, 61, 97, 121, 141, 211; *Who Would Have Thought It?*, 159

Saenz, José de la Luz, 177

Saint Teresa, 160

Saldaña-Portillo, María Josefina, 163

Salinas, Gregoria, 224–25

Sánchez, Rosaura, 82, 234

Sandoval, Chela, 228

San Francisco: fiesta time, 86; John Steinbeck's journalism, 99; Mariano Guadalupe Vallejo's history of, 53–60; women's social clubs, 74
Seguín, Juan Nepomuceno, 5–6
Serra, Fray Junípero, 133
settler colonialism: fundamental features, 116; indigenous peoples' acceptance of, 115; replacement function, 77; the requerimiento, 109–10; staged oppositions, 111; state recognition of indigenous peoples, 78; texts authorizing and naturalizing, 109–11. *See also* Manifest Destiny; racial loyalty; the West
settler hybrids and hybridity, 6–7; identity creation, 131; indigenous heritage denial, 133; Mexican American writers, 21–22; modernity, 134–35; processes creating, 119, 142; *The Real Billy the Kid*, 139
settler nostalgia, 76–78
"Shades of the Tenth Muse" (González), 154; and author's marriage, 155, 158–60, 167, 169; borders, 168–69; Chicana feminist readings, 158–59; closure, 167, 169; colonial conflict, 168; colonial power, 166; critical regionalism, 154; dialogues, 164–67, 169; folkloric qualities, 160; gender, 158–59, 166, 168, 169–70; historical contexts, 161, 167; rhetorical strategies, 184; South Texas folklore, 155; Woodhull's prayer, 167–68; writing of, 158
Sharp, John, 198, 202
Shell, Marc, 193–94
Shinn, Charles Howard, 35, 38–39

Sibrian, Amalia, 47–50, 52
Simpson, Audra, 78, 115, 116
Sleeter, Christine, 17
Sollors, Werner, 193–94
Sommer, Doris, 233
the Southwest, 145–46. *See also* Lincoln County War; New Mexico
sovereignty: European conceptions versus indigenous practices, 120; "Padres, Gringos, and Gold" radio show, 95–96, 102; patrimony, 72; settler entitlement, 78; Vallejo's Mission San Francisco history, 53
Spanish-American War, 122, 146
Spanish fantasy heritage: Californios and Californianas, 74–75, 83, 87, 96, 102; capitalist consumption, 76; Chicana/o Movement perspectives, 79; class, 84; examples, 74–75; gender, 84; in literature, 85; manifestations, 76; material reality, 105; progressive politics, 84; settler colonialism, 77–78
The Spanish Frontier of North America (Weber), 107–8
"A Spanish Girl's Journey from Monterey to Los Angeles" (Sibrian), 47–50
Spanish language: American history of, 195, 198–99; barrios, 191; on the border, 197–98; as colonizer and colonized, 195; *Fort Apache*, 188, 189, 190; linguistic and sociological interest in, 196; politics, 192, 200–201; as racial marker, 199; Recovering the U.S. Hispanic Literary Heritage project, 194; regulatory controls, 197. *See also* language; pochismo; Spanish-language press

Spanish-language press, 205; cultural importance, 223, 225–26; decline, 226; pochos, 28, 206, 223. See also *La Prensa* newspaper

The Squatter and the Don (Ruiz de Burton), 52–53, 61, 97, 121, 141, 211

squatters, 96–98, 99–100, 101

Steinbeck, John, 99–101

Suárez, Mario, 225

subtractive education, 16–17

Tafolla, Santiago, 199

territorial losses: indigenous peoples, 112, 114, 115, 118, 171, 228, 232; Mexican American experiences, 18–22. See also modernity of subtraction

Texas: the Alamo, 6, 14, 22, 76, 152; American and European settlers, 11; Anglo colonization, 231; border violence, 127–28; Mexican American experiences, 14; Mexican identity tensions, 150; *Mexican* term, 152; Revolution, 14; University of, 170, 181–82, 192; War of Independence, 12. See also González, Jovita; Paredes, Américo

Thomas, P. J., 55, 59

"Un tipo" (anonymous poem), 50–52, 200–201

transit figures of empire, 119

transmodernity, 11, 24

Treaty of Guadalupe Hidalgo, 4, 9, 11–12, 101, 153, 240n15

twice colonized places, 7

"The Twilight of the Dons" (Cuddy), 87–88

Two Years before the Mast (Dana), 36–37, 39

Ulica, Jorge, 202–3

University of Texas, 170, 181–82, 192

Urrieta, Luis, Jr., 118

U.S. military, 112–13, 123, 142–44, 146

Valdez, Elena V., 155

Valdez, Luis, 191, 223

Valenzuela, Angela, 16–17

Vallejo, Francisca, 66, 71; *Along the Highway of the King*, 85, 104; body of work, 104; life and career, 85; mother (Lily Poole Wiley), 92; name use, 91, 239n11; "Remember me! When frozen, cold . . . ," 67; "The Twilight of the Dons" contribution, 87; "The Violet to the Sequoia," 102–3. See also "Padres, Gringos, and Gold" radio show (Francisca Vallejo)

Vallejo, Guadalupe: English, 52; Francisca Vallejo's radio show, 89–90; and indigenous people, 131–33; newspaper interviews, 199–200; Spanish teaching, 199–200. See also "Ranch and Mission Days in Alta California" (Guadalupe Vallejo)

Vallejo, Mariano Guadalupe: access to power, 68–69; American annexation of California, 69–71, 88–89; Anglo America views, 32, 54–55, 68–69; Anglo settlers as pioneers, 89; Bear Flag Revolt, 200; Californio community concerns, 38; Chicana/o Movement perspectives on, 79; connections to other writers, 233; death, 40; family, 60; Francisca Vallejo's radio program, 88–89, 102–3, 104; historical writings, 39, 53–54; legacy, 60–61, 75; Manifest Destiny, 69–70; Mission San Francisco history, 53–60; modernity views, 71; nostalgia uses, 53, 69; *Recuerdos históricos y personales*, 53–54; and son Platón, 67; *The Squatter and the Don* inspiration, 97

Vallejo, Platón: advice from Ruiz de Burton, 234–35; Anglo settlers as pioneers, 89; Californios, 63–64; communal identity, 65; cultural project, 75; Edenic rhetoric, 62; education and career, 68, 235; exceptionalism, 61; and father Mariano, 67, 68, 69–70; gold rush, 70; letter to William Heath Davis, 60–63, 64–65; memoirs, 63–64, 66, 68, 95, 238n8; modernity, 63–65; nostalgia, 62; patrimony, 65–66; racism experienced, 60–61; regional environmental ideology, 65; tributes to, 67

Vallejo family: Californio history promotion, 80; coloniality of nostalgia, 81; cultural project, 74–75; exceptionalism, 72; family archive, 238n9; indigenous labor mentioned in writings, 131; mentioned, 205; modernity of subtraction, 81; nostalgia, 77, 81; Spanish fantasy heritage, 72; views on Californios, 77. *See also* Vallejo, Francisca; Vallejo, Guadalupe; Vallejo, Mariano Guadalupe; Vallejo, Platón

Varon, Alberto, 33, 76, 83–84

Vasconcelos, José, 205

Vasquez, Alfredo G., 203–5

Venegas, Daniel, 206–7, 233

Veracini, Lorenzo, 78

Villarreal, José, 206, 208

"The Violet to the Sequoia" (Francisca Vallejo), 102–3

Virgin of Guadalupe, 160

Vizcaíno-Alemán, Melina, 23

Wallis, Eileen, 74

Weber, David J., 107–8

the West, 111–13, 123. *See also Fort Apache* (Ford, film); Geronimo; Lincoln County War; Manifest Destiny; racial loyalty

Who Would Have Thought It? (Ruiz de Burton), 159

Wilkins, James H., 238n8

Williams, Raymond, 20

Wilson, William E., 197

Winthrop, John, 111

With His Pistol in His Hand (Paredes), 128, 134, 156, 171

Wogan, Daniel, 202

Wolfe, Patrick, 77, 115

women's social clubs, 74

World War I, 173, 176–77. *See also* "The Philosopher of the Brush Country" (González)

World War II, 190, 225

Ybarra, Priscilla, 65–66

Zamora, Emilio, 177

Zavala, Adina de, 76, 205

Zoot Suit (Valdez), 223

IN THE POSTWESTERN HORIZONS SERIES

The Places of Modernity in Early Mexican American Literature, 1848–1948
José F. Aranda Jr.

Dirty Wars: Landscape, Power, and Waste in Western American Literature
John Beck

Post-Westerns: Cinema, Region, West
Neil Campbell

The Rhizomatic West: Representing the American West in a Transnational, Global, Media Age
Neil Campbell

Weird Westerns: Race, Gender, Genre
Edited by Kerry Fine, Michael K. Johnson, Rebecca M. Lush, and Sara L. Spurgeon

Positive Pollutions and Cultural Toxins: Waste and Contamination in Contemporary U.S. Ethnic Literatures
John Blair Gamber

A Planetary Lens: The Photo-Poetics of Western Women's Writing
Audrey Goodman

Dirty Words in Deadwood*: Literature and the Postwestern*
Edited by Melody Graulich and Nicolas Witschi

True West: Authenticity and the American West
Edited by William R. Handley and Nathaniel Lewis

Teaching Western American Literature
Edited by Brady Harrison and Randi Lynn Tanglen

Manifest Destiny 2.0: Genre Trouble in Game Worlds
Sara Humphreys

We Who Work the West: Class, Labor, and Space in Western American Literature
Kiara Kharpertian
Edited by Carlo Rotella and Christopher P. Wilson

Captivating Westerns: The Middle East in the American West
Susan Kollin

Postwestern Cultures: Literature, Theory, Space
Edited by Susan Kollin

Westerns: A Women's History
Victoria Lamont

Manifest and Other Destinies:
Territorial Fictions of the Nineteenth-
Century United States
Stephanie LeMenager

Unsettling the Literary West:
Authenticity and Authorship
Nathaniel Lewis

Morta Las Vegas: CSI *and*
the Problem of the West
Nathaniel Lewis and Stephen Tatum

Late Westerns: The Persistence of a Genre
Lee Clark Mitchell

María Amparo Ruiz de Burton:
Critical and Pedagogical Perspectives
Edited by Amelia María de la Luz
Montes and Anne Elizabeth Goldman

In the Mean Time: Temporal
Colonization and the Mexican
American Literary Tradition
Erin Murrah-Mandril

To order or obtain more information on these or other
University of Nebraska Press titles, visit nebraskapress.unl.edu.

www.ingramcontent.com/pod-product-compliance
Lightning Source LLC
Chambersburg PA
CBHW022001220426
43663CB00007B/910